Learning Python for Data

Fundamental Python Skills for Starting with Data

Learning Python for Data

Fundamental Python Skills for Starting with Data

Matt Harrison

hairysun.com

COPYRIGHT © 2023

While every precaution has been taken in the preparation of this book, the publisher and author assumes no responsibility for errors or omissions, or for damages resulting from the use of the information contained herein.

Contents

1 Why Python?   **3**
- 1.1 Audience 4
- 1.2 Structure of the Book 5
- 1.3 Teams 6
- 1.4 Acknowledgments 6
- 1.5 Coding Conventions 7
- 1.6 Errata 8

2 Which Version of Python?   **9**
- 2.1 Python installation 9
- 2.2 Anaconda 10
- 2.3 Which Editor? 11
- 2.4 Summary 12
- 2.5 Exercises 12

3 The Interpreter   **13**
- 3.1 Compiled vs Interpreted 13
- 3.2 REPL 15
- 3.3 A REPL example 15
- 3.4 Summary 17
- 3.5 Exercises 17

4 Using Jupyter   **19**
- 4.1 Using a REPL in Jupyter 19
- 4.2 Using Notebook 20
- 4.3 Using Lab 20
- 4.4 Jupyter Modes 21
- 4.5 Common Commands 23
- 4.6 Line and Cell Magics 23
- 4.7 Summary 24
- 4.8 Exercises 24

5 Running Programs   **25**
- 5.1 Programs 25
- 5.2 Unixy embellishments 26

Contents

	5.3	Summary	28
	5.4	Exercises	28

6 Writing and Reading Data — 29
   6.1   Simple output 29
   6.2   Getting user input 30
   6.3   Summary 31
   6.4   Exercises 31

7 Variables and Objects — 33
   7.1   Cattle tags 33
   7.2   Mutation and State 36
   7.3   Python Variables are like Tags 36
   7.4   Reference Counting 37
   7.5   Rebinding variables 39
   7.6   Naming variables 41
   7.7   Additional Naming Considerations 41
   7.8   Summary 44
   7.9   Exercises 44

8 More about Objects — 45
   8.1   Identity 45
   8.2   Type 47
   8.3   Mutability 48
   8.4   Using Jupyter Notebook 49
   8.5   Summary 53
   8.6   Exercises 53

9 Numbers — 55
   9.1   Basics 55
   9.2   Addition 56
   9.3   Subtraction 57
   9.4   Multiplication 58
   9.5   Division 58
   9.6   Modulo 59
   9.7   Power 60
   9.8   Order of operations 61
   9.9   Other operations 61
   9.10 Summary 62
   9.11 Exercises 62

10 Numbers in NumPy — 63
   10.1 NumPy 63
   10.2 Installing NumPy 63
   10.3 Working with NumPy 64
   10.4 Addition with NumPy 64

    10.5 Subtraction, Multiplication, Division with NumPy 65
    10.6 Exponentiation and Modulo in NumPy 65
    10.7 Matrix Operations with NumPy 66
    10.8 Element-wise Multiplication 67
    10.9 Transpose of a Matrix 67
    10.10 Exploring Numerical Operations with NumPy 67
    10.11 NumPy's Handling of Special Numerical Values 68
    10.12 Summary 69
    10.13 Exercises 69

11 Strings   71
    11.1 Creating Strings 71
    11.2 Formatting Strings 74
    11.3 F-string Examples in Data Science 74
    11.4 Format String Syntax 76
    11.5 Debugging F-Strings 77
    11.6 String Methods 77
    11.7 Summary 78
    11.8 Exercises 78

12 Strings and Methods   79
    12.1 Methods 79
    12.2 Endswith 82
    12.3 Find 84
    12.4 Format 84
    12.5 Join 85
    12.6 Lower 85
    12.7 Startswith 86
    12.8 Strip 86
    12.9 Upper 87
    12.10 Other methods 87
    12.11 Summary 87
    12.12 Exercises 87

13 Strings in Pandas   89
    13.1 Installing Pandas 89
    13.2 Calling methods on a Pandas Series 89
    13.3 Endswith and Startswith 90
    13.4 Find 91
    13.5 Lower, Upper, and Capitalize 91
    13.6 Strip 91
    13.7 Join 92
    13.8 Summary 92
    13.9 Exercises 92

14 dir, help, and pdb   93

Contents

14.1	Dir	93
14.2	Tab Completion in Jupyter	94
14.3	Dunder Methods	95
14.4	Help	96
14.5	Documentation in Jupyter	96
14.6	Pdb	97
14.7	Summary	98
14.8	Exercises	98

15 Comments, Booleans, and None 101
15.1	Comments	101
15.2	Booleans	102
15.3	Truthiness in Pandas Series	106
15.4	None	107
15.5	np.nan	108
15.6	Summary	109
15.7	Exercises	109

16 Conditionals and Whitespace 111
16.1	Operations	111
16.2	Combining conditionals	112
16.3	If Statements	114
16.4	Else Statements	115
16.5	More Choices	115
16.6	Whitespace	116
16.7	Pandas Chains	116
16.8	Summary	117
16.9	Exercises	117

17 Containers: Lists, Tuples, and Sets 119
17.1	Lists	119
17.2	Sequence Indices	120
17.3	List Insertion	121
17.4	List Deletion	121
17.5	Sorting Lists	122
17.6	Useful List Hints	126
17.7	Tuples	127
17.8	Sets	130
17.9	Summary	132
17.10	Exercises	132

18 NumPy Sequences 135
18.1	NumPy Arrays	135
18.2	NumPy Array Operations	136
18.3	NumPy Array Shape	136
18.4	Statistical Methods	137

18.5 Manipulating Arrays with NumPy	138
18.6 Mathematical Methods	139
18.7 Summary	141
18.8 Exercises	141

19 Pandas Series — 143
19.1 Series	143
19.2 Series Indices	144
19.3 Series Insertion and Deletion	144
19.4 Sorting Series	145
19.5 Useful Series Hints	146
19.6 Summary	147
19.7 Exercises	147

20 Iteration — 149
20.1 The For Loop	149
20.2 Looping with an index	151
20.3 Breaking Out of a Loop	152
20.4 Skipping over Items in a Loop	153
20.5 The In Statement can be used for Membership	153
20.6 Removing Items from Lists During Iteration	154
20.7 Else Clauses	155
20.8 List Comprenhensionshs	156
20.9 Filtering with Comprehensions	157
20.10 While Loops	158
20.11 While Example	159
20.12 Assignment Expressions	161
20.13 Summary	162
20.14 Exercises	162

21 Dictionaries — 163
21.1 Overview	163
21.2 Dictionary Assignment	164
21.3 Retrieving Values from a Dictionary	166
21.4 The In Operator	166
21.5 Dictionary Shortcuts	167
21.6 Setdefault	167
21.7 Deleting Keys	169
21.8 Dictionary iteration	170
21.9 Merging Dictionaries	172
21.10 Dictionary Comprehensions	173
21.11 Dictionaries with Pandas	174
21.12 Dict Comprehensions with Pandas	175
21.13 Using the Assign Method with Column Names that Contain Spaces	176
21.14 Value Mapping	176

Contents

    21.15 Summary 177
    21.16 Exercises 177

22 Functions   179
    22.1 Black Boxes 179
    22.2 Invoking functions 182
    22.3 Scope 182
    22.4 Multiple Parameters 184
    22.5 Default Parameters 185
    22.6 Lambda Functions 187
    22.7 Examples of Lambda Functions 188
    22.8 Using Lambda Functions with Python Built-ins 188
    22.9 Using Functions with Pandas 189
    22.10 Using Rename with Functions 190
    22.11 Using Pipe with Functions 190
    22.12 Naming Conventions for Functions 191
    22.13 Summary 192
    22.14 Exercises 192

23 Indexing and Slicing   193
    23.1 Indexing 193
    23.2 Slicing Sub Lists 194
    23.3 Striding Slices 196
    23.4 Slicing in pandas 197
    23.5 Summary 198
    23.6 Exercises 198

24 File Input and Output   201
    24.1 Opening Files 201
    24.2 Reading Text Files 202
    24.3 Reading Binary Files 204
    24.4 Iteration with Files 204
    24.5 Writing Files 205
    24.6 Closing Files 206
    24.7 Designing Around Files 207
    24.8 CSV files in Pandas 208
    24.9 Summary 209
    24.10 Exercises 210

25 Unicode   211
    25.1 Background 211
    25.2 Basic steps in Python 213
    25.3 Encoding 214
    25.4 Decoding 216
    25.5 Unicode and Files 218
    25.6 Unicode in SQLite 219

Contents

25.7 Retrieving Unicode from SQLite Database 220
25.8 Non-ASCII Data and Pandas 220
25.9 Summary 221
25.10 Exercises 221

26 Classes 223
26.1 Objects 223
26.2 Planning for a Class 226
26.3 Defining a Class 227
26.4 Creating an Instance of a Class 231
26.5 Calling a Method on a Class 234
26.6 Examining an Instance 235
26.7 Private and Protected 236
26.8 A Simple Program Modeling Flow 237
26.9 Summary 238
26.10 Exercises 239

27 Classes for Data Science Work 241
27.1 The DataFrame Class 241
27.2 Examining the DataFrame 242
27.3 Calling a DataFrame Method 242
27.4 Using Classes with Scikit-learn 243
27.5 Calling a LogisticRegression Method 244
27.6 Summary 245
27.7 Exercises 245

28 Subclassing a Class 247
28.1 Parents and Children 247
28.2 Counting Stalls 250
28.3 super 251
28.4 Subclassing a Scikit-Learn Transformer 253
28.5 Summary 254
28.6 Exercises 254

29 DataClasses 257
29.1 What is a Dataclass? 257
29.2 How to Create a Dataclass 258
29.3 How to Use a Dataclass 259
29.4 Methods in Dataclasses 259
29.5 Summary 260
29.6 Excercises 260

30 Exceptions 261
30.1 Stack Traces 261
30.2 Look Before you Leap 263
30.3 Easier to Ask for Forgiveness 264

Contents

    30.4 Multiple exception cases 265
    30.5 Finally Clause 266
    30.6 Else Clause 268
    30.7 Raising Exceptions 269
    30.8 Wrapping Exceptions 270
    30.9 Defining your own Exceptions 272
    30.10 Summary 273
    30.11 Exercises 273

31 Importing Libraries   **275**
    31.1 Libraries 275
    31.2 Multiple ways to Import 275
    31.3 Conflicting import names 278
    31.4 Star Imports 280
    31.5 Nested Libraries 280
    31.6 Import Organization 281
    31.7 Summary 282
    31.8 Exercises 282

32 Packages and Modules   **283**
    32.1 Modules and Packages 283
    32.2 Importing Packages 283
    32.3 PYTHONPATH 284
    32.4 sys.path 285
    32.5 Summary 286
    32.6 Exercises 286

33 Regression with XGBoost   **289**
    33.1 Data for Regression 289
    33.2 EDA 292
    33.3 Line Plots 292
    33.4 Predict cfs in a week 293
    33.5 Creating a Dataset for Modelling 296
    33.6 Creating some Models 298
    33.7 Visualization 299
    33.8 Summary 301

34 A Complete Example   **303**
    34.1 cleanup.py 303
    34.2 What Does this Code Do? 307
    34.3 Common Layout 308
    34.4 Shebang 309
    34.5 Docstring 309
    34.6 Imports 310
    34.7 Metadata and Globals 310
    34.8 Logging 311

34.9	Other Globals	311
34.10	Implementation	312
34.11	Testing	312
34.12	if **name** == '**main**':	312
34.13	Summary	314
34.14	Exercises	314

35 Conclusion   315

Index   317

About the Author   325

    Also Available 326
    One More Thing... 326

Foreword

Forward: "Effective Python for Data Scientists"

Welcome to "Effective Python for Data Scientists"! In this comprehensive and insightful book, you are about to embark on an exciting journey into the world of Python programming, specifically tailored for data scientists. Whether you're a seasoned data analyst looking to expand your skill set or a beginner eager to dive into the realm of data science, this resource is your ultimate companion.

In "Effective Python for Data Scientists," you will discover a wealth of knowledge and practical techniques to harness the full power of Python in your data science endeavors. This book goes beyond just teaching you the syntax and basics of Python; it delves into the best practices, strategies, and tools that will make you a more efficient and effective data scientist.

Each chapter of this book is carefully crafted to provide you with actionable insights, real-world examples, and hands-on exercises that reinforce your understanding. From data manipulation and preprocessing to exploratory data analysis, visualization, and machine learning, you will learn how to leverage Python and its rich ecosystem of libraries to extract valuable insights from your data.

What sets "Effective Python for Data Scientists" apart is its focus on practicality and efficiency. You will find expert tips, tricks, and techniques that optimize your code, improve performance, and enhance reproducibility. Furthermore, this book explores the integration of popular libraries such as pandas, NumPy, Matplotlib, scikit-learn, and TensorFlow, empowering you to tackle complex data science tasks with ease.

Whether you aspire to become a data scientist, work with data in your field of expertise, or simply gain a deeper understanding of Python's role in data analysis, "Effective Python for Data Scientists" is designed to help you succeed. Embrace the challenge, immerse yourself in the world of Python, and unlock the vast potential that data science holds.

Get ready to embark on an enriching learning journey and equip yourself with the essential Python skills to excel in the data-driven era. May this book serve as your trusted guide as you navigate the exciting and ever-evolving landscape of data science. Let's dive in together, and may your path to becoming an effective data scientist be illuminated by the wisdom contained within these pages.

Chapter 1

Why Python?

The rise of Python is nothing short of meteoric, and its real-world impact is evident in many sectors. According to the 2021 Stack Overflow Developer Survey, Python ranked among the top three most popular programming languages. This isn't just a fleeting trend; universities around the globe are acknowledging its prominence. Prestigious institutions like MIT and Stanford have integrated Python as a foundational language in their computer science curriculums, solidifying its place in the academic sphere.

When it comes to compensation, Python developers have a significant edge. Per Glassdoor[1], a data engineer from Austin in 2023 makes 112K per year. A senior data engineer makes over 160K. This lucrative pull is not just limited to traditional software roles. With the ongoing data revolution, Python has positioned itself as the go-to language for data analytics and machine learning.

For over two decades, I've been at the forefront of Python development, not just as a developer but also as a data scientist. My journey has seen me work on natural language processing, reporting engines, failure analysis, loan default prediction, AI to model route planning, and predictive analyses that drive decision-making. I've engineered robust websites and backends, all while applying software engineering best practices.

My passion extended beyond coding and numbers. I've also worn the hat of an author, a speaker, and a mentor. I've taken to stages at international conferences, penned transformative books, and designed courses that have enlightened many. Over the past decade, I've dedicated my professional life to molding the next generation of Python and data professionals, teaching Python and data to thousands, from startups to Fortune 500 giants.

Yet, as I spent more time in the education space, a glaring gap emerged: a dearth of Python learning material tailored explicitly for learning Python with the intent of using it for the burgeoning field of data science. Recognizing this, I've crafted this book, carving out a path for those aspiring

---

[1]https://www.glassdoor.com/Salaries/austin-data-engineer-salary-SRCH_IL.0,6_IM60_KO7,20.htm

1. Why Python?

to use Python in the data realm. This isn't just a textbook; it's a mentorship. Every concept is taught for a purpose and tied to real-world scenarios. I don't want to waste your time, but I also know there are severe knowledge gaps in the data space. I want to fill those gaps and give you the skills you need to succeed.

The best time to learn Python was 20 years ago. The next best time is now. Let's get started.

1.1 Audience

This book is for technical students who want to learn Python, especially those interested in data science or data engineering. It's also for those who want to learn Python with a focus on best practices for real-world data applications. Many books teach Python, but few teach it with a data-centric approach. This book aims to fill that gap.

I don't want to waste your time going down rabbit holes that don't matter. I want to teach you the fundamentals of Python needed for data science and engineering, and I want to do it in a fun and engaging way. I want you to learn Python correctly so you can use it to solve real-world problems.

I've taught thousands of folks in training over the years and seen what they are doing and what skills they need. I've also seen what they don't need. I've distilled all of that knowledge into this book. I've also been able to draw upon my own experience as a data scientist and software engineer in this book. I've been doing this for over 20 years and learned a lot along the way. I want to share that knowledge with you.

The book might jump from built-in libraries to third-party libraries. I do this not to confuse you but to compare and contrast the built-in libraries with the third-party libraries. For example, if you are considering going into data, you will need to understand the difference between how Python represents numbers and how NumPy represents them. Following the introduction of lists, I expose you to parallel data structures in NumPy and Pandas. Data folks will need to understand more than just the built-in libraries.

This book will expose you to some of Python's most popular libraries used for data work. Namely, NumPy, Pandas, XGBoost, scikit-learn, and SQLite. However, this book is not a treatise on those subjects (I have written complete books on two of those subjects). I will give you the Python skills you will need to start working with these libraries and give you a quick introduction. If you put in the effort to work through this book, you will be able to understand the syntax for working effectively with those libraries.

As an educator, I like to provide echoes throughout my book. If you find yourself saying "that sounds familiar" or "he said that same thing over there," that's intentional. I want to reinforce the concepts. I repeat them because they tend to be concepts that folks ignore at first mention or don't fully grasp.

The outcome of this educational endeavor largely rests with you, the reader. Reading and comprehending this book would rank you as "highly proficient" on many online Python evaluations. However, theoretical knowledge is but one aspect of mastery. Practical application is pivotal. This book equips you with essential tools, but their utility is contingent upon your practice. Exercises are included with a chapter to aid in reinforcing concepts, and their completion is strongly recommended.

Furthermore, I advise you to integrate your newfound knowledge into personal projects. Continuous practice augments comprehension and skill. Please consider tagging or mentioning me if you share your projects on social networks. Observing the tangible achievements of learners is always rewarding, and I love to recognize and applaud such accomplishments.

1.2 Structure of the Book

This book offers a structured learning path through Python. Along the way, there might be rocks in the path. I don't necessarily want to prevent you from hitting them or stubbing your toe on them. I want you to be aware of them and know how to recover from them. I want to empower you to be productive. Sometimes, I seem to provide useless, mundane, or even trivial knowledge. I do so not to bother you but to prepare you for what you will encounter later. After using Python for over two decades and helping thousands on their journey, I have seen a few grains of sand, rocks, and even boulders that might present themselves. It doesn't do you any good to have a red carpet laid down for you during the book only to drop you off in a field of boulders when you are done. I want you to be prepared for the boulders. I want you to be able to navigate around them or over them. I want you to be able to get to your destination.

A focal point of our exploration is Python's object management mechanism - an elemental aspect often overlooked in many instructional materials, potentially due to its difference from other languages. We address it head-on, explaining the inherent performance characteristics of Python and demonstrating how external libraries bolster its efficiency, making it suitable for data science and engineering.

Our journey commences with Python's syntax, segueing into its built-in types and the manipulation of numerical and textual data. We then navigate through Python's container objects, such as lists, tuples, and dictionaries. Here, we will contrast Python's built-in types against renowned libraries like NumPy and Pandas, emphasizing the brevity and performance enhancements they offer.

Subsequently, the discourse shifts to control structures, loops, functions, and classes. As we unravel the significance of functions in encapsulating logic, we'll discuss classes, spotlighting their utility in crafting bespoke data types. Leveraging the scikit-learn library, we'll examine how to employ classes in machine learning model generation.

1. Why Python?

Our exploration then proceeds to Python's capabilities in file manipulation. This includes reading and writing files, both text and binary. We will show how to interact with CSV files via Pandas and databases with SQLite.

After an overview of exceptions and libraries, the text presents pragmatic Python applications with case studies, such as a predictive model for river flow patterns and a command-line utility for data science tasks.

It's imperative to note that while this publication centers around Python as a language and its indispensable features for the data domain, it doesn't serve as an exhaustive guide on data science or engineering. For those distinct areas, you should look for follow-up resources. This volume is purposefully tailored to furnish a robust understanding of Python, laying a solid foundation for further specialization in data science and engineering.

1.3 Teams

For teams embarking on the journey through this book, I commend your collaborative approach. Engaging collectively in the learning process fosters motivation and amplifies efficiency, as team members can leverage collective insights and expertise.

Throughout my professional tenure, I've had the privilege of collaborating with numerous teams, and one recurring catalyst for expedited learning has been structured training. To that end, I offer tailored training sessions that can be customized to align with your team's unique objectives. For inquiries, I'm reachable at matt@metasnake.com.

Beyond foundational training, I extend specialized support in Python and data analytics. Together, we'll navigate a bespoke learning trajectory, enabling you to adeptly handle, analyze, and transform data, or even engineer business-centric models. My offerings merge the benefits of training and consultancy, culminating in a session where you acquire new proficiencies and derive actionable solutions and code tailored to your specific data scenarios. The end product equips you with both knowledge and ready-to-run code.

1.4 Acknowledgments

Much thanks to my reviewers, who helped me make this book better: Stephen Adams, Al Krinker, Gregory P Amis, Naveenan Arjunan, Raj Arun, Bilal Assaad, Michael Aydinbas, Michael Aye, Adam Baker, Kevin Barry, Paul Barry, Mark Bickerton, Jason Brant, Jessica Brock, Mike Brough, Hugh Brown, Jhean Camargo, Luis Carlos, Jake Carter, Dean Chanter, Ryan Cheley, Rancy Chepchirchir, Francois Chesnay, Jason Chung, Darius Coste, Szymon Maciej Czop, Bilal D, Boris Dapaah, Zachary Day, Elias Durosinmi, Mikael Elhouar, Recep Erol, Kevin Fatyas, Joseph Fayese, Ralph Gross, Ankur Gupta, Thomas Halton, Joshua Hammond, Kevin Hanson, Mahmud Hasan, Wade Johnson, Paul Johnson, Ronnie Joshua, Karthik K, Peter Kaszt, Arvid Kingl, Andrii

Kruchko, Levente Kulcsár, Marvin Lomo, Robert Lucente, Ricky Macharm, Elijah Aaron Mogel, ashraf mohammad, Abdul Moied, Tiago Montes, Diego Morales, Claudio Moreno, Gul Muneer, soumen nayak, Dmitrii Nechaev, Andrew Nicholls, Ionut Oprea, Thomas Perilhou, Kai Prenger, Michael Purtell, Kushal K R, Mukul Ram, Mark Rimkus, Hamish Robertson, Ever Orlando Reyes Ruiz, Kenneth Savisaar, Andrew Sem, Jimmy Shen, Alcides Simao, Mugunthan Soundararajan, Burke Squires, Michael Sterling, Mary Anne Thygesen, Kanishka Tiwary, Tamás Ujhelyi, Neal Waterstreet, and John Zettler. I also want to thank my family for their support and encouragement. I couldn't have done this without you.

Also, a few personal thanks to friends and inspiration in the Python community who have helped me along the way or paved the way for my career. Guido van Rossum, Raymond Hettinger, David Beazley, JJ Behrens, Wesley Chun, Titus Brown, Grig Gheorghiu, Michael Kennedy, Brian Okken, Micheal Driscoll, Chad Harrington, Danny Roy Greenfeld, Audrey Roy Greenfeld, Ben Bangert, Noah Gift, Alfredo Deza, Calvin Hendryx-Parker, Travis Oliphant, Eric Snow, and many others. I am sure I am forgetting some people, but I am grateful for all of you.

1.5 Coding Conventions

Readers will encounter annotations of paramount significance designed to reinforce important concepts in this book. Such annotations will be formatted as:

> **Note**
> This represents a salient point warranting your attention.

The nature of these annotations may vary; they might serve as cautionary advisories, provide helpful insights, or introduce advanced topics that readers can approach at their discretion.

Python generally operates seamlessly across diverse platforms. However, occasionally, we need to use specific command-line instructions. For UNIX-based architectures, you might need to run commands from the Terminal. A $ prompt precedes these commands:

```
$ python3 -m pip install pandas
```

You would not type the $ prompt, but rather the command that follows it.
Conversely, Windows users should opt for either the Command Prompt or PowerShell, with commands introduced by the > prompt:

```
> python -m pip install pandas
```

Throughout the book, when showcasing Python execution, I often utilize the >>> prompt, denoting the Python interpreter's environment. It's crucial

1. Why Python?

to note that this prompt is illustrative and not intended for you to type if you are following along. For instance, to show the output of the `print()` function:

```
>>> print("Hello World")
Hello World
```

In such scenarios, if you were following along, your coding input would merely be `print("Hello World")`, with the subsequent output rendered as `Hello World`.

On certain occasions, I'll present code without any preceding prompt. This typically pertains to extended scripts or instances where the immediate output isn't the focal point.

1.6 Errata

I'm not perfect, and I make mistakes. If you find any errors in this book, please report them to me at the GitHub repository.

Chapter 2

Which Version of Python?

This book will focus on modern Python. The commonly supported versions are version 3.7 and above. Python 3.12 is the latest version as of this book. Note that some scientific libraries may take some time to support the latest version. Running the prior version of Python would be a safe bet when a new version is released (i.e., using 3.11 when 3.12 is new).

Minor version updates and differences will be noted as new features are discussed. In general, the code from this book should "just work" in Python 3.

2.1 Python installation

Python 3 is not installed on most platforms. Some Linux distributions ship with it, but Windows and Mac users must install it.

For Windows folks, go to the download area of the Python website[1] and find a link that says "Python 3.10 Windows Installer". This will link to a .msi file that will install Python on your Windows machine. Download the file, open it by double-clicking it, and follow the instructions to finish the installation.

> **Note**
>
> On the Windows installer, there is an option labeled "Add Python to PATH". Please make sure it is checked. That way, when you run python from the command prompt, it will know where to find the Python executable. Otherwise, you can go to System Properties (click WIN+Pause or run environ from the start menu), Advanced system settings, and click on the Environment Variables button. There, you can update the PATH variable by adding the following:
>
> C:\Program Files\Python 3.11;C:\Program Files\Python 3.11\Scripts

---

[1] https://www.python.org/downloads

2. Which Version of Python?

If you have UAC (User Account Control) enabled on Windows, then the path is:

```
C:\Users\<username>\AppData\Local\Programs\Python\Python311
```

Likewise, Mac users should download the Mac installer from the Python website.

Mac users might also want to look into the Homebrew version[1]. If you are familiar with Homebrew, run the command `brew install python3`, and you should be good to go. You can specify a specific version of Python by running `brew install python@3.11`.

Once you have python installed you will want to create a virtual environment. This will allow you to install packages without affecting the system Python installation. To create a virtual environment, run the following command (on Unix or Windows):

```
python -m venv py311
```

This will create a new directory called py311 with a copy of the Python executable and the standard library. To activate the environment, run the following command:

```
$ source py311/bin/activate
```

On Windows, the command is:

```
> py311\Scripts\activate.bat
```

You will need to install the following packages to follow along with this book. This command also works on all platforms after activating the virtual environment:

```
pip install numpy pandas matplotlib scikit-learn jupyter
```

2.2 Anaconda

Another option is to use the Anaconda distribution. This runs on Windows, Mac, and Linux and provides many pre-built binaries for scientific calculations. Traditionally, these libraries have been annoying to install as they wrap libraries written in C and Fortran that require some setup for compiling.

To install anaconda, go to the download page[2] and select the appropriate installer. The installer will be a large file, so it may take some time to download. Once downloaded, run the installer.

---

[1]https://brew.org
[2]https://www.anaconda.com/download

2.3. Which Editor?

Once you have installed Anaconda, you can run the following command to create a new environment:

```
conda create -n py311 python=3.11
```

This will create a new environment called py311 with Python 3.11 installed. You can activate the environment by running:

```
conda activate py311
```

To follow along with this book you will need to install the following packages:

```
conda install numpy pandas matplotlib seaborn scikit-learn jupyter
```

2.3 Which Editor?

In addition to installing Python, you will need a tool to write and execute your code. A popular tool among data scientists and researchers is Jupyter Notebook.

Jupyter Notebook is an open-source web application that allows you to create and share documents that contain live code, equations, visualizations, and narrative text. It supports multiple programming languages, including Python, R, and Julia.

Learning to use the features of Jupyter Notebook can make coding and data analysis easier. Jupyter Notebook allows you to write, test, and execute code in a single environment, and it has many built-in features for data visualization and exploration. Google Colab is a cloud-based version of Jupyter Notebook that allows you to run your code on Google's servers. If you are familiar with Jupyter Notebook, you will find Colab easy to use. Simarlarly, Azure Notebooks is a cloud-based version of Jupyter Notebook that allows you to run your code on Microsoft's servers.

Some popular alternatives to Jupyter Notebook include Spyder, PyCharm, and VS Code with the Python extension. However, Jupyter Notebook remains popular among data scientists and researchers due to its ease of use and interactive features.

For data engineers writing Python code, the powerful features of VS Code or PyCharm are compelling. I recommend that folks interested in data learn Jupyter as it is a common tool and move on to other editors or IDEs if they need more powerful features.

I use Jupyter for research and prototyping and an IDE VS Code for production code. I will cover both in this book. Data engineers will likely use both. Jupyter for the initial data exploration and prototyping and an IDE for building, testing, and deploying production code. Note that VS Code has a Jupyter extension that allows you to run Jupyter notebooks from within VS Code. Many folks will stay in VS Code running notebooks and switch to the editor when they need to write production code.

2. Which Version of Python?

Because many hold editors very close to their hearts, I will not recommend a particular editor. I do recommend that you become familiar with Jupyter. I will cover Jupyter in this book. We will also write Python code, but it will not be specific to an editor.

A later chapter will get you started with Jupyter.

2.4 Summary

Python 3 is the current version of Python. Unless you work on legacy code, you should favor using this version. You can find the latest version on the Python website.

Most modern editors contain some support for Python. There are various levels of features that editors and IDEs provide. If you are getting started programming, give Jupyter a try. It is a great place to start.

2.5 Exercises

1. Install Python 3 on your computer. Make sure you can start Python.
2. If you are used to a particular editor, investigate its support for Python. For example, does it:

    - Do syntax highlighting of Python code?
    - Easily run Python code?
    - Provide a debugger for stepping through your Python code?

Chapter 3

The Interpreter

Among programming languages Python, is known for its simplicity and developer efficiency. It falls under the *interpreted* or *scripting languages* category of programming languages. In this chapter, we'll unravel the mechanisms of Python's interpreter, contrasting it with compiled languages, exploring the performance trade-offs, and emphasizing its optimal use cases.

3.1 Compiled vs Interpreted

Python is commonly classified as an *interpreted* language. Another term used to describe an interpreted language is *scripting* language. To run a computer program on the CPU, the program must be in a format that the CPU understands, namely *machine code*. Interpreted languages do not *compile* directly to machine code. Instead, there is a layer above, an *interpreter* that performs this function.

There are pros and cons to this approach. As you can imagine, on-the-fly translating can be time-consuming. Interpreted code, like Python programs, tends to run slow. They might be 10–100 times slower than compiled languages like C. On the flip side, writing code in Python optimizes for developer time. It is not uncommon for a Python program to be 2–10 times shorter than its C equivalent. Also, a compilation step can be time-consuming and distracting during development and debugging.

Many developers and companies are willing to accept this trade-off. Smaller programs (read fewer lines of code) take less time to write and are easier to debug. Programmers can be expensive—if you can throw hardware at a problem, it can be cheaper than hiring more programmers. Debugging ten lines of code is more manageable than debugging 100 lines of code. Studies [1] have shown that the number of bugs found in code is proportional to the number of lines of code. Hence, if a language permits you to write fewer lines of code to achieve a given task, you will likely have fewer bugs.

---

[1] https://bit.ly/48wdn2r

3. The Interpreter

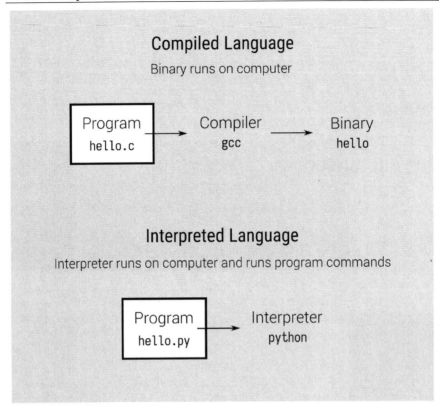

Figure 3.1: Difference between a compiled language and an interpreted language. A compiler runs to create an executable. An interpreter is an executable that loads code and runs it on top of itself.

While interpreted code tends to run slower than compiled languages, the performance gap is often deemed acceptable in data science workflows.

Writing code in C or C++ can create very fast code. However, the time spent writing and debugging the code can be significant. And C and C++ are notorious for being difficult to debug. Python's ecosystem offers numerous optimized libraries, such as NumPy and pandas, that efficiently handle numerical operations, mitigating the execution speed difference in many data science scenarios. Additionally, advancements in just-in-time (JIT) compilation techniques, exemplified by tools like Numba, provide opportunities to optimize critical code sections for improved performance when necessary.

3.2 REPL

Python has an *interactive interpreter* or *REPL* (Read Evaluate Print Loop). This is a loop that waits until there is input to read in, then evaluates it (interprets it), and prints out the result. When you run the python3 executable by itself, you launch the interactive interpreter in Python. Other environments, such as the editor that comes with Python, IDLE, also embed an interactive interpreter.

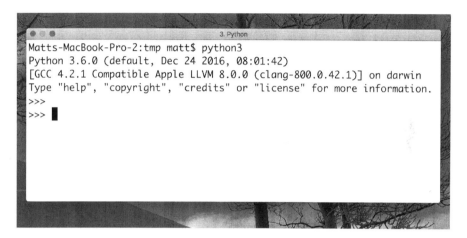

Figure 3.2: To launch the REPL, type python3 in the prompt and it will start a Python session

> **Note**
>
> This book generally starts Python 3 with the python3 executable. On Windows, the executable is named python. If you are on Windows, replace python3 with python. On Unix systems, you shouldn't have to change anything.
>
> When you start the interpreter, it will print out the version of Python, some information about the build, and some hints to type. Finally, the interpreter will give you a prompt, >>>.
>
> Another option is to start Jupyter Notebook, by typing jupyter notebook. Be aware that Jupyter does not show a prompt in the cell.

3.3 A REPL example

Below is an example of why the Read, Evaluate, Print Loop was given this name. If you typed python3 from the command line, you will see >>> (on Jupyter you will just have a code cell).

Type 2 + 2 like shown below and hit enter:

3. The Interpreter

```
$ python3
>>> 2 + 2
4
>>>
```

In the above example, `python3` was typed, which opened the interpreter. The first `>>>` could be thought of as the *read* portion. Python is waiting for input. 2 + 2 is typed in, read, and *evaluated*. The result of that expression—4—is *printed*. The second `>>>` illustrates the *loop* because the interpreter is waiting for more input.

The REPL, by default, prints the result of an expression to standard out (unless the result is `None`, which will be explained in a later chapter). This behavior is inconsistent with normal Python programs, where the `print` function must be explicitly invoked. But it saves a few keystrokes when in the REPL.

> **Note**
>
> The `>>>` prompt is only used on the first line of each input. If the statement typed into the REPL takes more than one line, the ... prompt follows:
>
> ```
> >>> sum([1, 2, 3, 4, 5,
> ...     6, 7])
> ```
>
> These prompts are defined in the sys module:
>
> ```
> >>> import sys
> >>> sys.ps1
> '>>> '
> >>> sys.ps2
> '... '
> ```
>
> A later chapter will explain what modules are. For now, know that there are variables that define what the prompts look like.

The REPL ends up being quite handy. You can use the interactive interpreter to write small functions, test out code samples, or even function as a calculator. Perhaps more interesting is to go the other way. Run your Python code in the REPL. Your code will run, but you will have access to the REPL to inspect the state of your code. (You will see how to do this in IDLE soon). / The `>>>` is a *prompt*. That is where you type your program. Type `print("hello world")` after the `>>>` and hit the enter key. Ensure there are no spaces or tabs before the word `print`. You should see this:

```
>>> print("hello world")
hello world
```

If you see this, congratulations, you are writing Python. Consider yourself inducted into the world of programming. You have just run a program—"hello world". Hello world is the canonical program that most people write when encountering a new language. To exit the REPL from the terminal, type `quit()`. Unix users may also type Ctrl-D.

> **Note**
>
> Programming requires precision. If you were not careful in typing exactly `print("hello world")` you might have seen something like this:
>
> ```
> >>> print("hello world
>   File "<stdin>", line 1
>     print("hello world
>                       ^
> SyntaxError: EOL while scanning string literal
> ```
>
> Computers are logical, and if your logic does not make sense, the computer can warn you, perform irrationally (or at least what appears so to you), or stop working. Do not take it personally, but remember that languages have rules, and any code you write has to follow those rules. In the previous example, the rule that states if you want to print text on the screen, you need to start and end the text with quotes was violated. A missing quote on the end of the line consequently confused Python.

3.4 Summary

As Python is an interpreted language, it provides a REPL. This allows you to explore the features of Python interactively. You don't need to write, compile, and run code. You can launch a REPL and start trying out code.

I find that developers who are new to Python tend to see the REPL as a novelty. They are timid about using it. Don't fear the REPL. Give it a try. It can make the development process easy and quick.

There are other REPLs for Python. One popular one is Jupyter, which presents a web-based REPL. We will explore that in the next chapter.

3.5 Exercises

1. Open the Python 3 REPL and run "hello world". Review the chapter to see what this one line program looks like.
2. Open the REPL IDLE and run "hello world".

3. The Interpreter

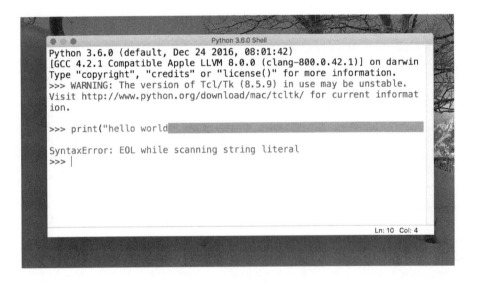

Figure 3.3: IDLE will try to highlight where the error occurred. The highlight following world is supposed to indicate where the syntax error occurred. It is normally a salmon color.

Chapter 4

Using Jupyter

A common tool for engineers, scientists, and data people is Jupyter [1]. Jupyter is an open-source web application that allows you to create and share documents containing live code. It is an excellent platform for using a Python REPL. Jupyter also allows you to work with various programming languages, in addition to Python, including R and Julia.

4.1 Using a REPL in Jupyter

Jupyter can be incredibly useful for data analysis and exploration. You can input code snippets to test their functionality or to experiment with a data set quickly. Because the results of each command are displayed immediately, you can quickly iterate through your analysis until you find the desired output. Additionally, using a REPL from Jupyter makes documenting your progress and thought process more manageable as you work through an analysis, as you can intersperse text and code cells.

Jupyter is a generic term for a notebook interface. The original tool was called Jupyter Notebook (actually, it was called iPython Notebook and was renamed Jupyter to emphasize that it works with the Julia, Python, and R languages). An updated version called Jupyter Lab was introduced later.

Jupyter Notebook and Jupyter Lab are open-source web applications that allow you to create and share live documents containing code, equations, visualizations, and narrative text. However, there are some significant differences between the two.

Jupyter Notebook is the classic Jupyter application that has been around longer. It has a simpler user interface.

JupyterLab is the newer version of Jupyter and is designed to be more versatile and extensible. It offers a more feature-rich and customizable interface that can be extended to fit your specific needs. For example, with JupyterLab, you can drag and drop the tabs to customize your workspace according to your workflow.

---

[1] https://jupyter.org/

4. Using Jupyter

Both Notebook and Lab have code cells; from this book's point of view, you can use either tool to follow along.

4.2 Using Notebook

To install Jupyter Notebook, run the command:

`pip install notebook`

You can launch the Jupyter Notebook with the command:

`jupyter notebook`

As of version 7, when Jupyter Notebook launches, it launches you into a stripped down version of the Lab interface. To access the old Notebook interface, you can go to the View -> "Open in NbClassic" menu item.

I talk about Lab and Notebook because there are still many services that use the classic notebook interface rather than the lab interface. However, many of the commands are the same in both lab and notebook.

To create a new notebook, click on the "New" button and select "Notebook". You should see a new notebook window pop up. This window is both an editor and a Python REPL.

Type your code into the first cell of the notebook. Since you are doing the hello world example, type:

`print("hello world")`

To run the code, click on the "Run" button or press the "Control" and "Enter" keys together. Jupyter Notebook will immediately evaluate your code and display the output below the cell.

This might seem trivial, but the notebook now has the state of your code. You only printed to the screen in this case, so there is little state. In future examples, you will see how you can use Jupyter to quickly try out code, see the results, and inspect the output of a program.

4.3 Using Lab

To install JupyterLab, run the command:

`pip install jupyterlab`

You can launch the tool with the command:

`jupyter lab`

4.4. Jupyter Modes

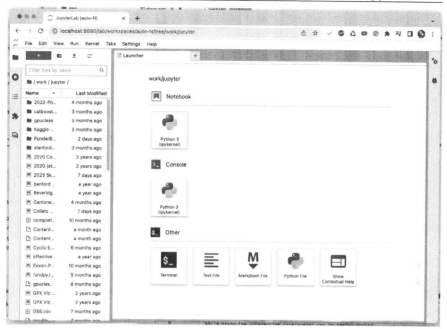

Figure 4.1: Landing page after starting JupyterLab.

When JupyterLab launches, you will see the dashboard where you can navigate to your files and create new notebooks. To create a new notebook, click on the "Notebook" button in the "Launcher" pane or the + button above the file navigator. You should see a new notebook window pop up. This window is both an editor and a Python REPL.

Type your code into the first cell of the notebook. Since you are doing the hello world example, type:

```
print("hello world")
```

To run the code, click on the "Run" button or press the "Control" and "Enter" keys together. Jupyter Notebook will immediately evaluate your code and display the output below the cell.

4.4 Jupyter Modes

In both Lab and Notebook, there are two modes: Edit mode and Command mode.

Edit mode is where you can edit the contents of a cell. In Jupyter Notebook, this mode is denoted by a green box around the current cell. In JupyterLab, you will see a cursor in the cell, and the background color of the cell will change from grey to white.

21

4. Using Jupyter

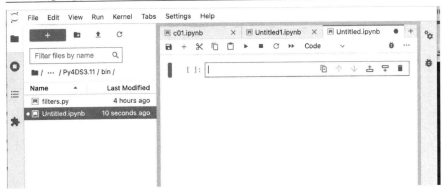

Figure 4.2: Jupyter Lab has been launched and a new notebook window has been created.

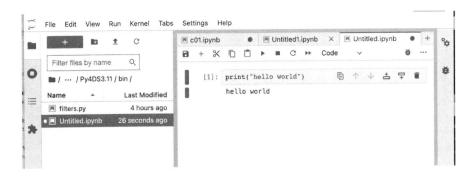

Figure 4.3: Code typed into the notebook and executed.

When in edit mode, you can type into the cell and edit the contents of the cell. You can also use keyboard shortcuts within edit mode, such as *Ctrl + Enter* to run the cell or *Ctrl + Shift + -* to split the cell at the current cursor position.

To enable edit mode, you can type Enter when a cell is highlighted or double-click on the content of the cell. To exit edit mode and go back to command mode, you can execute the cell (*Ctrl + Enter*) or hit Escape.

Command mode, on the other hand, is where you can perform various actions on the notebook without editing its contents. This mode is indicated by a blue box around the current cell. In command mode, you can navigate between cells using the arrow keys, delete cells by pressing 'dd' (the d key twice), create new cells using the 'a' or 'b' keys, and more.

The main difference between these two modes is that edit mode is focused on editing the contents of a cell, while command mode is focused on managing the notebook's structure and organization. Knowing how to navigate between these modes and use their respective actions effectively is key to working efficiently in Jupyter.

4.5 Common Commands

Here is a brief description of some of the keyboard shortcuts that are useful commands in command mode in Jupyter:

- h - Show keyboard shortcuts.
- a - Inserts a new cell **a**bove the current cell.
- b - Inserts a new cell **b**elow the current cell.
- x - Cuts the current cell.
- c - Copies the current cell.
- v - Pastes the cell that was cut or copied.
- dd - Deletes the current cell. (You need to hit d twice.)
- m - Changes the current cell to a markdown cell.
- y - Changes the current cell to a code cell.
- ii - Interrupts the kernel running in the current notebook session.
- 00 - Restarts the kernel running in the current notebook session.
- Ctrl-Enter - Runs the current cell.
- Enter - Go into edit mode.

These commands can save a lot of time when you're working within Jupyter notebooks. You can quickly create new cells, change cell types, delete cells, and interrupt or restart the kernel using keyboard shortcuts. This can help you focus more on coding and data analysis and less on navigating the notebook interface.

4.6 Line and Cell Magics

Jupyter has a concept of *magics* that are special commands that you can run in a cell. These commands are prefixed with a % or %% and are called *line magics* and *cell magics*, respectively. Line magics are commands that are run on a single line, while cell magics are commands that are run on the entire cell.

For example, the %timeit line magic can be used to time how long it takes to run a line of code. You can use it like this:

```
%timeit x = range(10000)
```

This command will run the range(10000) command some number of times and time how long it takes to run.

A line magic only works on a single line of code. A cell magic, on the other hand, works on the entire cell. Here is an example of using the %%timeit cell magic:

4. Using Jupyter

```
%%timeit
x = range(10000)
total = 0
for i in x:
    total += i
mean = total / len(x)
```

This command runs the whole cell multiple times and returns the average time it took to run the cell.

There are many other line and cell magics that you can use in Jupyter. You can see a list of them by running the %lsmagic command in a cell. This will print out a list of all the magics that are available in your notebook.

Some of the most useful magics are:

- %matplotlib inline - This line magic will display matplotlib plots inline in the notebook. (This is the default behavior in JupyterLab and not needed there.)
- %timeit - This line magic will time how long it takes to run a line of code.
- %%timeit - This cell magic will time how long it takes to run a cell of code.
- %debug - This line magic will start the interactive debugger.
- %pdb - This line magic will enable the interactive debugger.
- %%html - This cell magic will render the cell as HTML.
- %%javascript - This cell magic will run the contents of the cell as JavaScript code.
- %%writefile - This cell magic will write the contents of the cell to a file.

4.7 Summary

In this chapter, you learned how to install and use Jupyter Notebook and JupyterLab. You learned how to create a new notebook, run code, and navigate between cells. You also learned about the difference between edit mode and command mode and how to use keyboard shortcuts to perform actions in each mode.

4.8 Exercises

1. What is the difference between Jupyter Notebook and JupyterLab?
2. How do you create and run a new code cell in Jupyter?
3. How do you change a cell's type from code to markdown?
4. How can you save your work in a Jupyter Notebook?
5. What happens when you interrupt the kernel running in a Jupyter notebook?
6. How do you restart the kernel running in a Jupyter notebook?

Chapter 5

Running Programs

Transitioning from the interactivity the REPL to executing standalone programs is a fundamental progression for every budding Pythonista. The chapter shows the procedures and nuances of running your Python scripts outside the REPL environment.

We'll venture into how to execute Python files, familiarize ourselves with Unix-specific conventions, and understand the significance of various terminal commands associated with running scripts. By the end of this chapter, you will be equipped to run Python from Jupyter and a terminal.

5.1 Programs

While the interactive interpreter can be useful during development, you (and others) will want to deploy your program and *run* it outside of the REPL. In Python, this is easy as well. To run a Python program named hello.py, open a terminal, go to the directory containing that program, and type:

```
$ python3 hello.py
```

> **Note**
>
> When running a command from the command line, this book will precede the command with a $. This will distinguish it from interpreter contents (>>> or ...) and file contents (nothing preceding the content).
>
> One common mistake that I find that folks make is they type the above into a REPL. This will not work because the REPL processes Python code. This is not Python code. It is a command to tell the terminal to run the python3 executable.

5. Running Programs

> **Note**
>
> The previous command, `python3 hello.py`, will probably fail unless you have a file named `hello.py`.

In the previous chapter, you used the REPL to run "hello world". How does one run the same program standalone? Create a file named `hello.py` using your favorite text editor.

In your `hello.py` file type:

```
print("hello world")
```

Please save the file, go to its directory, and *execute* the file (here *execute* and *run* have the same meaning, i.e. type `python3` before the file name, and let the Python interpreter evaluate the code for you.)

> **Note**
>
> Typing `python3` standalone launches the interpreter. Typing `python3 some_file.py` executes that file.

If you were successful at running `hello.py`, it would print out `hello world`.

5.2 Unixy embellishments

On Unix platforms (Linux and OS X, among others), files such as `hello.py` are often called *scripts*. A script is a program, but the term is often used to distinguish native code from interpreted code. In this case, scripts are interpreted code, whereas the output from the compilation step of a language that compiles to machine code (such as C) is *native code*.

> **Note**
>
> It is not uncommon to hear about shell scripts, Perl scripts, Python scripts, etc. What is the difference between a Python script and a Python program? Nothing, really, it is only semantics. A Python "script" usually refers to a Python program run from the command line, whereas a Python program is any program written in Python (which range from small 1-liners to fancy GUI applications to "enterprise" class services). Jupyter would be an example of a "program".

Unix environments provide a handy way to make your script executable on its own. By putting a *hash bang* or *shebang* (#!) on the first line of the file, followed by the path to the interpreter, and by changing the *executable bit* on the file, you can create a file that can run itself.

To have the script execute with the Python interpreter found in the environment, update your `hello.py` file to:

5.2. Unixy embellishments

```
#!/usr/bin/env python3
print("hello world")
```

> **Note**
>
> This new first line tells the shell that executes the file to run the rest of the file with the #!/usr/bin/env python3 executable. (Shell scripts usually start with #!/bin/bash or #!/bin/sh.) Save hello.py with the new initial line.
>
> #!/usr/bin/env is a handy way to indicate that the first python3 executable found on your PATH environment variable should be used. Because the python3 executable is located in different places on different platforms, this solution turns out to be cross-platform. Note that Windows ignores this line. Unless you are absolutely certain that you want to run a specific Python version, you should probably use #!/usr/bin/env.
>
> Using hardcoded hashbangs such as:
>
> - #!/bin/python3
> - #!/usr/bin/python3.3
>
> might work fine on your machine, but it could lead to problems when you try to share your code and others do not have python3 where you specified it. If you require a specific version of Python, it is common to specify that in the README file.

Now you need to make the file executable. Open a terminal, cd to the directory containing hello.py and make the file executable by typing:

```
$ chmod +x hello.py
```

This sets the *executable bit* on the file. The Unix environment has different permissions (set by flipping a corresponding bit) for reading, writing, and executing a file. If the executable bit is set, the Unix environment will look at the first line and execute it accordingly, when the file is run.

> **Note**
>
> If you are interested in knowing what the chmod command does, use the man (manual) command to find out by typing:
>
> ```
> $ man chmod
> ```

Now you can execute the file by typing its name in the terminal and hitting enter. Type:

```
$ ./hello.py
```

5. Running Programs

And your program (or script) should run. Note the ./ included before the name of the program. Normally when you type a command into the terminal, the environment looks for an executable in the PATH (an environment variable that defines directories where executables reside). Unless . (or the parent directory of hello.py) is in your PATH variable you need to include ./ before the name (or the full path to the executable). Otherwise, you will get a message like this:

```
$ hello.py
bash: hello.py command not found
```

Yes, all that work just to avoid typing python3 hello.py. Why? The main reason is that you want your program to be named hello (without the trailing .py). And perhaps you want the program on your PATH so you can run it at any time. By making a file executable, and adding a hashbang, you can create a file that looks like an ordinary executable. The file will not require a .py extension, nor will it need to be explicitly executed with the python3 command.

5.3 Summary

In this chapter, you learned how to run Python programs from the command-line. You also learned how to make a Python program executable on its own. You learned about the hashbang, and how to set the executable bit on a file. Finally, we can use the chmod command to make a file executable on Unix platforms.

5.4 Exercises

1. Create a file hello.py with the code from this chapter in it.

2. Run hello.py from a terminal.

3. If you have an editor that you prefer, run hello.py from it.

4. If you are on a Unix platform, create a file called hello. Add the hello world code to it, and make the appropriate adjustments such that you can run the code by typing:

   ./hello

Chapter 6

Writing and Reading Data

In every programmer's journey, transitioning from creating simple calculations to building interactive applications that communicate with users is an exhilarating phase. The chapter bridges this transition, introducing you to the methods and tools in Python that allow for interactive dialogue between the user and the program.

Within this chapter, we'll explore the foundational functions of Python: print for presenting data and input for collecting it.

6.1 Simple output

The easiest way to provide the user with output is to use the print function, which writes to *standard out*. "Standard out," commonly abbreviated as stdout, originates from UNIX operating systems and refers to the default stream where the operating system outputs data for command-line programs. When you are in a terminal, standard out is printed on the terminal:

```
>>> print('Hello there')
Hello there
```

> **Note**
>
> This book will show content as if it were typed into the REPL with a prompt, >>>. If you want to follow along in Jupyter, type in the content following the prompt into a cell and then execute the cell.
>
> In Jupyter, standard output is written to the output area below a cell.

If you want to print out multiple items, you can provide them separated by commas. Python will insert a space between them. You can put strings and numbers in a print function:

```
>>> print('I am', 10, 'years old')
I am 10 years old
```

6. Writing and Reading Data

```
[18]: print('Hello There')
      Hello There
```

Figure 6.1: Running content from Jupyter.

The *Strings* chapter will look at strings in detail. It will discuss how to format them to get output to look a certain way.

6.2 Getting user input

The built-in input function will read text from a terminal. This function accepts text, which it prints out as a prompt to the screen and waits until the user types something on *standard in* and hits enter. "Standard input," often abbreviated as stdin, also originates from UNIX operating systems and refers to the default stream from which the operating system reads input data for command-line programs. In a terminal, standard input can be read from what you type in:

```
>>> name = input('Enter your name:')
```

If you typed the above into the interpreter (the spaces around the = are not required, but convention suggests that you type them to make your code more readable), it might look like your computer is frozen. In reality, Python waits for you to type in some input and hit enter. After you type something in and press enter, the variable name will hold the value you typed. Type the name Matt and press the enter key. If you print name, it will print the value you just typed:

```
>>> print(name)
Matt
```

The value entered into the terminal when input is called is always a *string*. If you tried to perform math operations on it, it might not give you the answer you want:

```
>>> value = input('Enter a number:')
3

>>> other = input('Enter another:')
4
```

If you try to add value and other right now, you concatenate them (or join them together) because they are strings:

30

```
>>> type(value)
<class 'str'>
>>> value + other
'34'
```

If you want to add these strings as if they were numbers, you need to change them from a string into a number type. To convert a string to another type like an integer (a whole number) or float (a decimal number), you will need to use the `int` and `float` constructors respectively.

If you want to add `value` and `other` numerically, you have to convert them to numbers using `int`:

```
>>> int(value) + int(other)
7
```

A future chapter will talk more about strings and number types.

6.3 Summary

Python gives you two functions that make it easy to print data to the screen and read input from the user. These functions are `print` and `input`. Remember that you will always get a string back when you call the `input` function.

6.4 Exercises

1. Create some Python code that will prompt you to enter your name. Print out `Hello` and then the name.
2. Create a program to ask a user how old they are. Print out some text telling them how old they will be next year.

Chapter 7

Variables and Objects

Variables and objects are the heroes of Python programming. Variables allow us to label, and reference objects. Objects allow us to store information.

In this chapter, we'll explore how Python variables function as labels that we can attach to objects.

We'll also touch upon Python's memory management and its garbage collection system. By the end, you'll understand the crucial role variables and objects play in Python.

7.1 Cattle tags

My grandfather owned a cattle ranch, so bear with me as I channel a rustic analogy - I promise it won't be too haywire. If you've ever run a ranch, you know how crucial a savvy foreman is. Their job? Keeping an eagle eye on your cattle - essentially safeguarding your valuable assets.

Enter: cattle tags. These snazzy little tags aren't just for show – they're for identifying and tracking each unique cow.

Now, switching gears from the ranch to the digital realm - in programming, you're essentially wrangling data instead of cattle. Your program has chunks of valuable information you wish to corral. This trove of data forms the state. For example, if your data wrangling involves tracking human details, you'd be keen on noting down specifics like age, address, and name.

Just like how ranchers tag their cattle to keep track of them, programmers create variables to keep track of data. Look at the example again:

```
>>> status = "off"
```

What's happening here? You're instructing Python to create a *string* with the contents of off. But wait, there's more! You're also spawning a variable named status to attach to that string. Now, whenever you're curious about this mysterious value, all you've got to do is whisper (or, well, type):

```
>>> print(status)
off
```

7. Variables and Objects

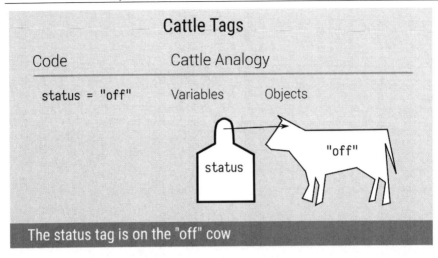

Figure 7.1: Comparing Python objects to cows and variables to cattle tags. The variable is attached to an object and used to identify it.

It is possible to create *state* and lose it to the ether if you neglect to put it in a variable. It is somewhat useless to create objects that you would not use, but again it is possible. Suppose you want to keep track of the bulb's wattage. If you write:

```
>>> "120 watt"
'120 watt'
```

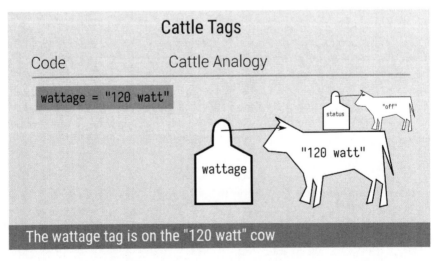

Figure 7.2: We can create as many variables as we want.

7.1. Cattle tags

There's a gotcha. While Python does create a string, there's a slight hiccup. You see, this bit was typed out in REPL, which means it prints out the object's result. Neat, right? Well, hold onto your horses because here's the twist: we forgot to attach a variable to the object. Yikes! Now, that string is like a wild cow, no one knows how to access it or who it belongs to. Without a variable to store the object, you can't use it.

If this were information that you really needed in your program, a better approach would be to give it a variable, like the following:

```
>>> wattage = "120 watt"
```

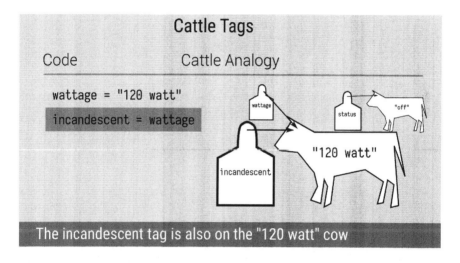

Figure 7.3: If we assign a variable to another variable, it does not make a new object. It attaches that variable to the object that the other variable was attached to. An object can have multiple variables pointing to it. However, a variable cannot point to multiple objects. This is similar to a cow tag. You could have a cow that has multiple tags on it. But you wouldn't have a tag that was attached to two (or more) cows at the same time. However, we could tag the tag off of one cow and put it on another.

Later on, in your program, you can summon wattage anytime you need it. You can print it out, and you can even assign another variable to it or assign wattage to another new value (say if your incandescent bulb broke and you replaced it with an LED bulb):

```
>>> incandescent = wattage
>>> wattage = "25 watt"
>>> print(incandescent, wattage)
120 watt 25 watt
```

Similar to herding cattle, managing state is a core aspect of programming. And variables? They are the trusty ear tags that allow you to access and manage state.

7. Variables and Objects

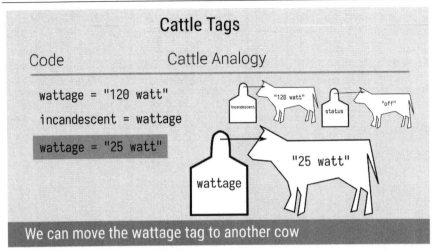

Figure 7.4: We can also move a tag to a new cow. Existing tags are not moved when this happens.

7.2 Mutation and State

In addition to state, we also need to deal with *mutation*. State deals with a digital representation of a model. For example, if you want to model a light bulb, you may want to store its current status—is it on or off? Other possibly interesting states you could store include the type of bulb (CFL or incandescent), wattage, size, dimmable, etc.

Mutation deals with changing the state to a new or different state. For the light bulb example, it could be helpful to have a power switch that toggles the state and changes it from off to on.

How is this related to variables? Remember that in Python, everything is an object. We generally will use a variable to access the state. In objects that are mutable, we can get the object and then update the state as needed.

Once you have objects that hold state and are mutable, you have opened a world of possibilities. You can model almost anything you want if you can determine what state it needs and what actions or mutations need to apply to it.

7.3 Python Variables are like Tags

Variables are the building blocks of keeping track of the state. You might think of a variable as a label or cattle tag. Important information is tagged with a variable name. To continue the light bulb example, suppose that you want to remember the state of your light bulb. Having that data is only useful if you have access to it. To access it and keep track of its state, you must have a *variable* to tag that data. Here the state of the bulb is stored in a variable named status:

```
>>> status = "off"
```

Let's deep dive into what is going on here. Starting from the right, the word "off" is surrounded by quotes. This is a *string literal*, or a built-in datatype for which Python has a special syntax. The quotes tell Python that this object is a *string*. So Python will create a string object. A string stores textual data—in this case, the letters off.

This object has a few properties of interest. First, it has an *id*. You can think of the id as where Python stores this object in memory. It also has a *type*, in this case, a string. Finally, it has a *value*. Here the value is 'off' because it is a string.

In many programming languages, the = sign is the *assignment operator*. Do not be afraid of these technical terms. They are more benign than they appear. The assignment operator connects or binds together a variable name and its object. It indicates that the name on the left of it is a variable that will point to the object on the right. In this case, the variable name is status.

To drive the point home, let's reread the code from the left this time. status is a variable that is assigned to the object that Python created for us. This object has a type, string, and holds the value of "off".

7.4 Reference Counting

When Python creates a variable, it tells the object to increase its *reference count*. When objects have variables or other objects pointing to them, they have a positive reference count. When variables go away (for example, when you exit a function, variables created in that function will go away), the reference count goes down. When this count goes down to zero, the Python interpreter assumes no one cares about the object anymore, and *garbage collects* it. This means it removes it from its memory, so your program doesn't get out of control and use all the memory of your computer.

> **Note**
>
> If you want to inspect the reference count of an object, you can call sys.getrefcount on it:
>
> ```
> >>> import sys
> >>> names = []
> >>> sys.getrefcount(names)
> 2
> ```
>
> Do note that as this count may seem high, the documentation for this function states:

7. Variables and Objects

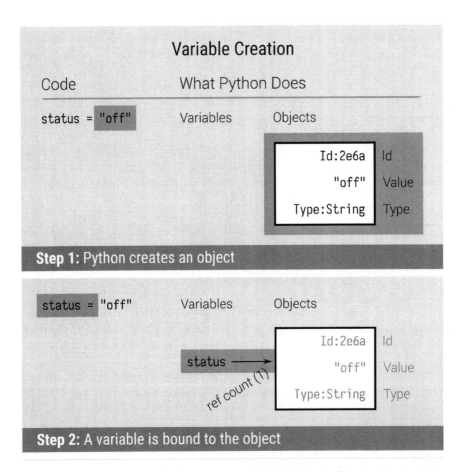

Figure 7.5: Two steps of an assignment to a literal. First, Python creates an object. The object has a value - "off", a type - string, and an id (the location of the object in memory). After the object is created, Python looks for any variable named status. If it exists, Python updates what object the variable is pointing to, otherwise, Python creates the variable and points it to the object.

38

7.5. Rebinding variables

> Return the reference count of object. The count returned is generally one higher than you might expect, because it includes the (temporary) reference as an argument to getrefcount().
>
> Even though Python gives you this ability, typically, you don't worry about the reference count and let Python handle cleaning up objects for us.

Garbage collection is a feature of Python, and typically, Python does this for you automatically, without any prompting from a user. In some languages, you must manually tell the program to allocate and deallocate memory.

7.5 Rebinding variables

Like cow tags, variables tend to stay with an object for a while, but they are transferable. Python lets you easily change the variable:

```
>>> num = 400
>>> num = '400'   # now num is a string
```

In the above example, num was initially pointing to an integer, but then was told to point to a string. This is different from other languages, where you must declare the type of a variable and cannot change it. Python is a *dynamically typed* language, meaning that the type of a variable is determined at runtime. Having said that, I would recommend that you do not change the type of a variable. It can lead to confusion and bugs in your code.

> **Note**
>
> The variable does not care about the type. In Python, the type is attached to the object.
>
> There is no limit to how often you can change a variable. But you should be careful not to change a variable if you still need access to the old data. Once you remove all variables from an object, you are essentially telling Python to destroy (*garbage collect* is the proper geeky term) the object when it has the chance to free up any internal memory it occupies.

> **Note**
>
> This is a case where Python allows you to do something, but you probably don't want to do it in real life. Just because you can rebind a variable to a different type doesn't mean you should. Changing the type of a variable is confusing to you when you read your code later. It

7. Variables and Objects

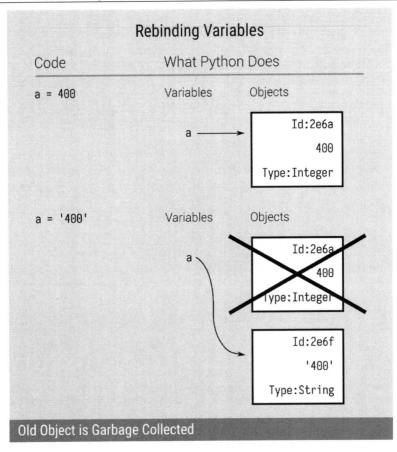

Figure 7.6: This illustrates rebinding variables. Variables can be rebound to any type. Python makes no effort to prevent this or complain. When an object no longer has any variable pointing to it, it is cleaned up by Python or garbage collected.

is also confusing to others who are using your code. Don't use the same variable to point to different types.

This is a point of confusion for those who are new to Python. They sometimes reuse the same variable throughout their code because they mistakenly believe it will save memory. As you have seen, this is not the case. The variable itself is very lightweight. The object is what uses memory. Reusing a variable name will not make your code run faster, but it will confuse those who have to read the code later. Now they have to track in their mind what the type of the variable is because the programmer keeps switching it.

40

7.6 Naming variables

Python is somewhat particular about naming variables. It has conventions that most Python programmers follow. Some of these are enforced, some are not. One that the interpreter enforces is *a variable should not have the name of a keyword*. The word break is a keyword and hence cannot be used as a variable. You will get a SyntaxError if you try to use it as a variable. Even though this code looks perfectly legal, Python will complain:

```
>>> break = 'foo'
  File "<stdin>", line 1
    break = 'foo'
        ^
SyntaxError: invalid syntax
```

If you find yourself with a SyntaxError that looks like normal Python code, check that the variable name is not a keyword.

Keywords are reserved for use in Python language constructs, so it confuses Python if you try to make them variables.

The module keyword has a kwlist attribute, which is a list containing all the current keywords for Python:

```
>>> import keyword
>>> print(keyword.kwlist)
['False', 'None', 'True', 'and', 'as', 'assert',
'break', 'class', 'continue', 'def', 'del', 'elif',
'else', 'except', 'finally', 'for', 'from', 'global',
'if', 'import', 'in', 'is', 'lambda', 'nonlocal',
'not', 'or', 'pass', 'raise', 'return', 'try',
'while', 'with', 'yield']
```

Another method for examining keywords in the REPL is to run help(). This puts you in a help utility in the REPL, from which you can type commands (that aren't Python). Then type keywords and hit enter. You can type any of the keywords, and Python will give you some documentation and related help topics. To exit the help utility, hit enter by itself.

7.7 Additional Naming Considerations

In addition to the aforementioned rule about not naming variables after keywords, there are a few best practices encouraged by the Python community. The rules are simple—variables should:

- be lowercase
- use an underscore to separate words
- not start with digits
- not override a *built-in* function

7. Variables and Objects

Here are examples of variable names, both good and bad:

```
>>> good = 4
>>> a_longer_variable = 6

>>> bAd = 5   # bad - capital letters

>>> # this style is frowned upon
>>> badLongerVariable = 7


>>> # bad - starts with a number
>>> 3rd_bad_variable = 8
  File "<stdin>", line 1
    3rd_bad_variable = 8
      ^
SyntaxError: invalid syntax

>>> # bad - keyword
>>> for = 4
  File "<stdin>", line 1
    for = 4
        ^
SyntaxError: invalid syntax

>>> # bad - built-in function
>>> compile = 5
```

> **Note**
>
> Rules and conventions for naming in Python come from a document named "PEP 8 – Style Guide for Python Code"[a]. PEP stands for Python Enhancement Proposal, which is a community process for documenting a feature, enhancement, or best practice for Python. PEP documents are found on the Python website.
>
> ---
> [a]https://peps.python.org/pep-0008/

> **Note**
>
> Although Python will not allow keywords as variable names, it will allow you to use a *built-in* name as a variable. Built-ins are functions (such as `len` and `print`), classes (such as `int` or `IndexError`), or variables (such as `__name__`) that Python automatically preloads for you, so you get

7.7. Additional Naming Considerations

easy access to them. Unlike keywords, Python will let you use a built-in as a variable name without so much as a peep. However, you should refrain from doing this, it is a bad practice.

Using a built-in name as a variable name *shadows* the built-in. The new variable name prevents you from getting access to the original built-in. Doing so essentially takes the built-in variable and co-opts it for your use. As a result, access to the original built-in may only be obtained through the __builtins__ module. But it is much better not to shadow it in the first place.

Here is a list of Python's *built-ins* that you should avoid using as variables:

```
>>> dir(__builtins__)
['ArithmeticError', 'AssertionError',
'AttributeError', 'BaseException',
'BlockingIOError', 'BrokenPipeError',
'BufferError', 'BytesWarning', 'ChildProcessError',
'ConnectionAbortedError', 'ConnectionError',
'ConnectionRefusedError', 'ConnectionResetError',
'DeprecationWarning', 'EOFError', 'Ellipsis',
'EnvironmentError', 'Exception', 'False',
'FileExistsError', 'FileNotFoundError',
'FloatingPointError', 'FutureWarning',
'GeneratorExit', 'IOError', 'ImportError',
'ImportWarning', 'IndentationError', 'IndexError',
'InterruptedError', 'IsADirectoryError',
'KeyError', 'KeyboardInterrupt', 'LookupError',
'MemoryError', 'NameError', 'None',
'NotADirectoryError', 'NotImplemented',
'NotImplementedError', 'OSError', 'OverflowError',
'PendingDeprecationWarning', 'PermissionError',
'ProcessLookupError', 'RecursionError',
'ReferenceError', 'ResourceWarning',
'RuntimeError', 'RuntimeWarning',
'StopAsyncIteration', 'StopIteration',
'SyntaxError', 'SyntaxWarning', 'SystemError',
'SystemExit', 'TabError', 'TimeoutError', 'True',
'TypeError', 'UnboundLocalError',
'UnicodeDecodeError', 'UnicodeEncodeError',
'UnicodeError', 'UnicodeTranslateError',
'UnicodeWarning', 'UserWarning', 'ValueError',
'Warning', 'ZeroDivisionError', '_',
'__build_class__', '__debug__', '__doc__',
'__import__', '__loader__', '__name__',
'__package__', '__spec__', 'abs', 'all', 'any',
'ascii', 'bin', 'bool', 'bytearray', 'bytes',
'callable', 'chr', 'classmethod', 'compile',
```

7. Variables and Objects

```
'complex', 'copyright', 'credits', 'delattr',
'dict', 'dir', 'divmod', 'enumerate', 'eval',
'exec', 'exit', 'filter', 'float', 'format',
'frozenset', 'getattr', 'globals', 'hasattr',
'hash', 'help', 'hex', 'id', 'input', 'int',
'isinstance', 'issubclass', 'iter', 'len',
'license', 'list', 'locals', 'map', 'max',
'memoryview', 'min', 'next', 'object', 'oct',
'open', 'ord', 'pow', 'print', 'property', 'quit',
'range', 'repr', 'reversed', 'round', 'set',
'setattr', 'slice', 'sorted', 'staticmethod',
'str', 'sum', 'super', 'tuple', 'type', 'vars',
'zip']
```

> **Note**
>
> Here are a few built-ins that would be tempting variable names otherwise: dict, id, list, min, max, open, range, str, sum, and type.

7.8 Summary

In Python, everything is an object. Objects hold state, which is also called the value. To keep track of objects, you use variables. Python variables are like cattle tags, they are attached to the object and have a name. But the object has the important data, the value, and the type of data.

This chapter also discussed the rebinding of variables. Python allows you to do this, but you should be careful not to change the type of the variable, as that can be confusing to readers of the said code. Finally, the chapter discussed naming conventions for Python variables.

7.9 Exercises

1. Create a variable, pi, that points to an approximation for the value of π. Create a variable, r, for the radius of a circle that has a value of 10. Calculate the area of the circle (π times the radius squared). You can do multiplication with *, and you can square numbers using **. For example, 3**2 is 9.

2. Create a variable, b, that points to the base of a rectangle with a value of 10. Create a variable, h, that points to the height of a rectangle with a value of 2. Calculate the perimeter. Change the base to 6 and calculate the perimeter again.

Chapter 8

More about Objects

This chapter will dive into objects a little bit more. You will cover three crucial properties of objects:

- identity
- type
- value

8.1 Identity

Identity at its lowest level refers to an object's location in the computer's memory. Python has a built-in function called `id` that tells you the identity of an object:

```
>>> name = "Matt"
>>> id(name)
140310794682416
```

When you type this, the identity of the string "Matt" will appear as `140310794682416` (which refers to a location in the RAM of your computer). This will generally vary from computer to computer and for each time you start the shell, but the `id` of an object is consistent across the lifetime of a program.

A single cow can have two tags on its ears, and it is also possible for two variables to refer to the same object. If you want another variable—`first`—to also refer to the same object referred to by `name`, you could do the following:

```
>>> first = name
```

This tells Python to give the `first` variable the same id as `name`. Running `id` on either of the two variables will return the same id:

```
>>> id(first)
140310794682416
```

8. More about Objects

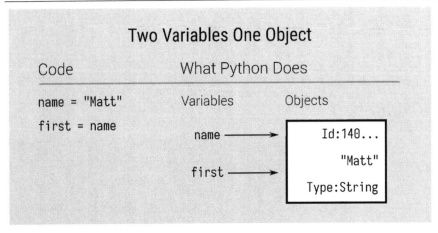

Figure 8.1: This illustrates what happens when you bind a variable to an existing variable. They both point to the same object. Note that this does not copy the variable! Also, note that the object has a value, "Matt", a type, and an id.

```
>>> id(name)
140310794682416
```

What is the identity used for? Not much. When you program in Python, you typically are not concerned with low-level details such as where the object lives in the computer's memory (or RAM). But identity is used to illustrate when objects are created and if they are mutable. It is also used indirectly for doing *identity checks* with is.

The is operator checks for identity equality and validates whether or not two variables point to the same object:

```
>>> first is name
True
```

If you print either first or name at the REPL, it will print the same value because they are both pointing to the exact same object:

```
>>> print(first)
Matt
>>> print(name)
Matt
```

If I had a cattle tag, I could take it off of one cow and attach it to another. Just like a cattle tag, you can take a variable and point it to a new object. I can make name point to a new object. You will see that the identity of name has changed. But first is still the same:

8.2. Type

```
>>> name = 'Fred'
>>> id(name)
140310794682434
>>> id(first)
140310794682416
```

8.2 Type

Another property of an object is its *type*. Common types are *strings, integers, floats,* and *booleans*. There are many other kinds of types, and you can create your own as well. The type of an object defines what data and operations it supports. Python allows you to easily view the type of an object with the built-in function, type:

```
>>> type(name)
<class 'str'>
```

The type function tells you that the variable name points to a string (str). The table below shows the types of various objects in Python.

Object	Type
String	str
Integer	int
Floating point	float
Boolean	bool
List	list
Dictionary	dict
Tuple	tuple
Function	function
User-defined class (subclass object)	type
Instance of class (subclass of class)	class
Built-in function	builtin_function_or_method
type	type

Due to *duck-typing*, the type function is not used too frequently. Rather than check if an object is of a specific type that provides an operation, normally you try and do that operation.

Sometimes, you have data and need to convert it to another type. This is common when reading data from standard in. Typically it would come in as a string, and you might want to change it into a number. Python provides built-in classes, str, int, float, list, dict, and tuple that convert (or coerce) to the appropriate type if needed:

```
>>> str(0)
'0'
```

47

8. More about Objects

```
>>> tuple([1,2])
(1, 2)
>>> list('abc')
['a', 'b', 'c']
```

> **Note**
>
> Duck typing comes from a saying used in the 18th century to refer to a mechanical duck. Much like the Turing Test, the saying went:
>
> > If it looks like a duck, walks like a duck and quacks like a duck, then it's a duck
>
> But I prefer the scene in *Monty Python and the Holy Grail*, where a lady is determined to be a witch because she weighs as much as a duck. (If this is confusing, go watch the movie, I find it enjoyable). The idea is that because she had characteristics (her weight) that were the same as a duck, she could be considered a witch.
>
> Python takes a similar approach. If you want to use a plus operation, you don't check whether the object is a number or string (or another type that supports addition). You just do the plus operation. If the operation fails, that's ok. It is an indication that you are not providing the correct type.

If you are familiar with object-oriented programming, duck typing eases the requirement for subclassing. Rather than inheriting multiple classes to take advantage of behaviors they provide, you need to implement the protocols (usually by defining a method or two). For example, to create a class that adds, you need to implement a .__add__ method. Any class can define that method and respond to the plus operation.

8.3 Mutability

Another interesting property of an object is its *mutability*. Many objects are *mutable* while others are *immutable*. Mutable objects can change their value in place. In other words, you can alter their state, but their identity stays the same. Objects that are immutable do not allow you to change their value. Instead, you can change their variable reference to a new object, but this will change the identity of the variable as well.

In Python, dictionaries and lists are mutable types. Strings, tuples, integers, and floats are immutable types. Here is an example demonstrating that the identity of a variable holding an integer will change if you change the value. First, you will assign an integer to the variable age and inspect the id:

```
>>> age = 1000
>>> id(age)
140310794682416
```

Notice that if you change the value of the integer, it will have a different id:

```
>>> age = age + 1
>>> id(age)
140310793921824
```

Here is an example of changing a list. You will start with an empty list, and examine the id. Note that even after you add an item to the list, the identity of the list is unchanged. It has the same id because it is mutable.

First, you will create a list and look at the id:

```
>>> names = []
>>> id(name)
140310794682432
```

Now, put a string inside the list. There are a few things to note. The return value of the .append method didn't show anything (i.e., it is not returning a new list). But if you inspect the names variable, you will see that the new name is in there. Also, the id of the list is still the same. You have mutated the list:

```
>>> names.append("Fred")
>>> names
['Fred']
>>> id(name)
140310794682432
```

Mutable objects should not be used for keys in dictionaries and can present problems when used as default parameters for functions.

8.4 Using Jupyter Notebook

At this point, it would be good to try this out in Jupyter (or your favorite editor with REPL integration). Because Jupyter comes with a REPL, you could type in the previous code and inspect it from there. To try it, open a new notebook and type the following code into a code cell:

```
name = "Matt"
first = name
age = 1000
print(id(age))
age = age + 1
print(id(age))
```

8. More about Objects

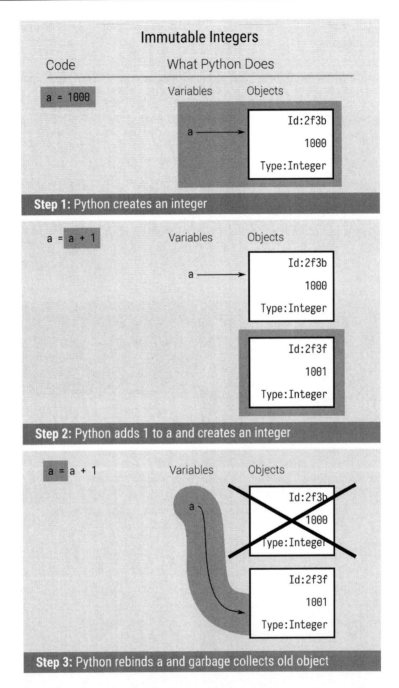

Figure 8.2: This illustrates that when you try to change an integer, you will necessarily create a new integer. Integers are immutable, and you can't change their value.

8.4. Using Jupyter Notebook

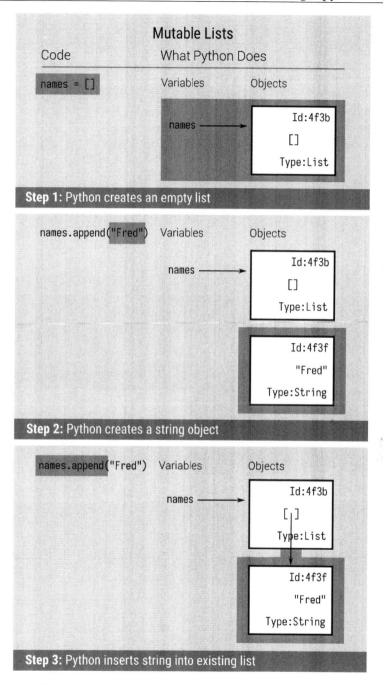

Figure 8.3: This illustrates that when you append an object to a list, you change the value of the list. The list is mutated. You can add and remove items from it, but the id of the list stays the same.

8. More about Objects

```
names = []
print(id(names))
names.append("Fred")
print(id(names))
```

Then, run the cell by clicking on the "Run" button or pressing the "Control" and "Enter" keys together. You should see four numbers printed out in the output area of the cell. The first two should be different, illustrating that an integer is immutable. The last two numbers are the same. They are the same because even though the list, names, was mutated, the id is still the same. This by itself is nothing particularly novel.

The interesting part is that if you type dir() in the next cell, it will show you the variables. You will see that the global variables from the previous cell are now available.

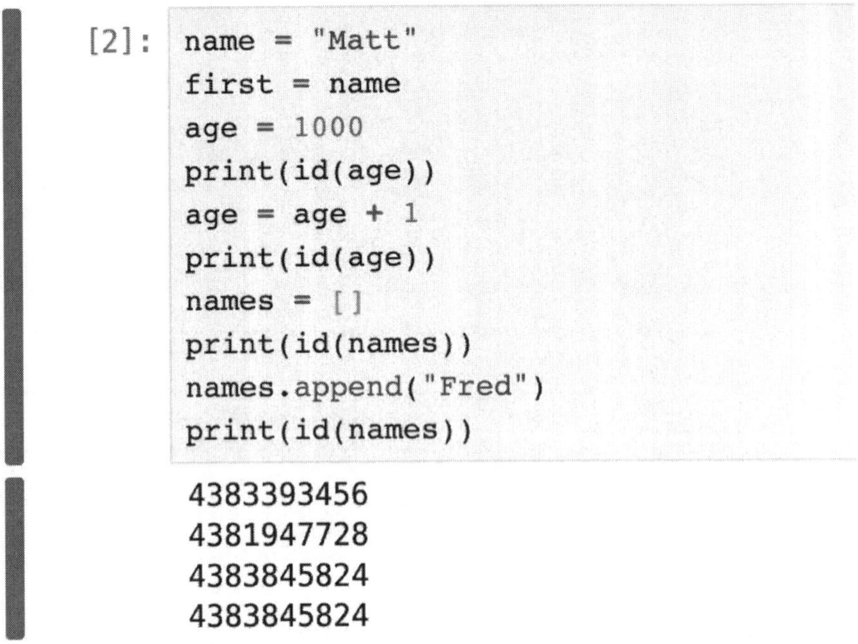

```
[2]: name = "Matt"
     first = name
     age = 1000
     print(id(age))
     age = age + 1
     print(id(age))
     names = []
     print(id(names))
     names.append("Fred")
     print(id(names))
```

```
4383393456
4381947728
4383845824
4383845824
```

Figure 8.4: This illustrates running code and then inspecting it from the REPL in Jupyter Notebook. If you do not use Jupyter Notebook, figure out how to do this from your editor.

You can access all the global variables from the REPL in Jupyter Notebook. You can inspect name or names. You can call functions or methods like names.append("George").

The ability to inspect what just ran allows you to try things out and check the results quickly. It is not uncommon for experienced Python developers to write code in the REPL, paste it into a cell, re-run the cell, write more code in the REPL, and continue writing code this way.

8.5 Summary

In Python, everything is an object. Objects have three properties:

- A Type - Indicates what the class is for the object.
- A Value - The data that the object holds. When you test if an object is equal to another object (with ==), you are checking against the value.
- An Id - A unique id for the object. In the Python version found at www.python.org, this is essentially the location in the object's memory, which will be a unique value. When you check whether two objects have the same identity (with is), you check whether the id is the same.

You also examined how mutable objects, such as lists, can change their value, while immutable objects, like numbers or strings, cannot be changed.

8.6 Exercises

1. Create a variable that points to a floating point number. Examine the id, type, and value of that number. Update the variable by adding 20 to it. Re-examine the id, type, and value. Did the id change? Did the value change?
2. Create a variable pointing to an empty list. Examine the id, type, and value of the list. Append the number 300 to the list. Re-examine the id, type, and value. Did the id change? Did the value change?

Chapter 9

Numbers

In this chapter, we will explore the numerical capabilities of Python, focusing on integers and floating points—two fundamental data types. While integers represent whole numbers (like 5 or -2000), floating points approximate real numbers with decimals (such as 0.5 or -1000.234).

Beyond basic arithmetic, we'll explore operations like division, power, modulo, and also the order of operations. It's worth noting that due to Python's object-oriented nature, even numbers are objects.

9.1 Basics

Integers in Python are objects with the class `int`:

```
>>> type(1)
<class 'int'>
```

Floating point numbers are of class `float`:

```
>>> type(2.0)
<class 'float'>
```

Python's floats are represented internally using a binary representation (per the IEEE 754 standard for floating point numbers). Floats have a certain amount of precision, and rounding errors are possible. In fact, one should expect rounding errors. (If you need more accuracy, the `decimal` module provides a more precise albeit slower implementation).

As a quick example of precision, examine what happens when you perform this apparently simple subtraction operation:

```
>>> print(1.01 - .99)
0.020000000000000018
```

One might expect this to be exactly 0.02. However, there is some precision error due to how computers store decimal values in binary approximations.

9. Numbers

The value one-third has infinite precision in the decimal world. Similarly, the value .1 has infinite precision in a binary world. Since computer memories have finite memory, there is a limit to how much precision can be stored. This is why you see the rounding error above.

9.2 Addition

The Python REPL can be used as a simple calculator. If you want to add two integers, type in the expression:

```
>>> 2 + 6
8
```

> **Note**
>
> The math example above did not bind the result to a variable. For a simple calculation, printing out the result to the terminal may be sufficient. If you need the result after the fact, the Python interpreter stores the last result in a variable named _:
>
> ```
> >>> 2 + 6
> 8
> >>> result = _
> >>> result
> 8
> ```

Note that adding two integers together results in an integer.
Likewise, you can also add two floats together:

```
>>> .4+.01
0.41000000000000003
```

This example illustrates once again that care is needed when using floating point numbers, as you can lose precision (the real result would be 0.41).

What happens when you add an integer and a float?

```
>>> 6 + .2
6.2
```

Python decided you need floating-point arithmetic because you are adding an integer and a float. In this case, Python converts or *coerces*, 6 to a float behind the scenes before adding it to .2. Python has given you the answer back as a float.

> **Note**
>
> Coercion generally does the right thing if you have an operation involving two numerics. For operations involving an integer and a float, the integer is coerced to a float.

> **Note**
>
> Coercion between strings and numerics does not occur with most mathematical operations. Two exceptions are the modulus (string formatting) operator and the multiplication operator.

When you use % with a string on the left side (the *left operand*) and any object (including numbers) on the right side (the *right operand*), Python performs the formatting operator:

```
>>> print('num: %s' % 2)
num: 2
```

If the left operand is a string and you use the multiplication operator, *, Python performs repetition:

```
>>> 'Python!' * 2
'Python!Python!'
>>> '4' * 2
'44'
```

> **Note**
>
> Explicit conversion can be done with the int and float built-in classes. (Although these look like functions, they are really classes):
>
> ```
> >>> int(2.3)
> 2
> >>> float(3)
> 3.0
> ```

9.3 Subtraction

Subtraction is similar to addition. Subtraction of two integers or two floats returns an integer or a float, respectively. For mixed numeric types, the operands are coerced before performing subtraction:

```
>>> 2 - 6
-4
>>> .25 - 0.2
```

9. Numbers

```
0.04999999999999999
>>> 6 - .2
5.8
```

9.4 Multiplication

In many programming languages, the * (asterisk) is used for multiplication. You can probably guess what is going to happen when you multiply two integers:

```
>>> 6 * 2
12
```

If you have been following carefully, you will also know what happens when you multiply two floats:

```
>>> .25 * 12.0
3.0
```

And if you mix the types of the product, you end up with a float as a result:

```
>>> 4 * .3
1.2
```

Note that the float result in these examples appears correct, though you should be careful, due to floating point precision issues, not to assume that you would always be so lucky.

9.5 Division

In Python (like many languages), the / (slash) symbol is used for division:

```
>>> 3 / 4
0.75
```

What if you want the result as an integer? You can use the // operator if you want that behavior. What integer does Python use? The *floor* of the real result—take the answer and round down:

```
>>> 3 // 4
0
```

9.6 Modulo

The *modulo* operator (%) calculates the modulus. This is the same as the remainder of a division operation when the operators are positive. This is useful for determining whether a number is odd or even (or whether you have iterated over 1000 items):

```
# the remainder of 4 divided by 3
>>> 4 % 3
1
>>> 3 % 2   # odd if 1 is result
1
>>> 4 % 2   # even if 0 is result
0
```

Note

Be careful with the modulo operator and negative numbers. Modulo can behave differently, depending on which operand is negative. It makes sense that if you are counting down, the modulo should cycle at some interval:

```
>>> 3 % 3
0
>>> 2 % 3
2
>>> 1 % 3
1
>>> 0 % 3
0
```

What should -1 % 3 be? Since you are counting down, it should cycle over to 2 again:

```
>>> -1 % 3
2
```

But when you switch the sign of the denominator, the behavior becomes weird:

```
>>> -1 % -3
-1
```

Python guarantees that the sign of the modulo result is the same as the denominator (or zero). To further confuse you:

9. Numbers

```
>>> 1 % -3
-2
```

The reasoning is this. For a numerator n and a denominator d, Python makes sure the relationship n = (n//d) * d + (n%d) is always satisfied.

The takeaway here is that you probably do not want to do modulo with negative numbers on the denominator unless you are sure that is what you need.

9.7 Power

Python also gives you the *power* operator by using ** (double asterisks). If you wanted to square 4 (4 is the base, 2 is the exponent), the following code will do it:

```
>>> 4 ** 2
16
```

Exponential growth tends to let numbers get large pretty quickly. Consider raising 10 to the 100th power:

```
>>> 10 ** 100
10000000000000000000000000000000000000000
0000000000000000000000000000000000000000
00000000000000000000000000
```

Remember how numbers are objects in Python. Python wants to optimize the storage of numbers. For example, storing a 64 bit integer value is efficient. But what if you need to store a 65 bit integer? (Or anything larger than 64 bits?) Python can automatically change the size of the number inside the object so it can store a *long* integer. You don't have to worry about this. The only downside is that it takes more memory to store it.

Python takes care of this for you automatically. You do not need to worry about it. But it is good to know that it is happening. In other languages you are exposed to overflow errors when you try to store a number that is too large for the type you are using.

An analogy might be a scale. You might want a small scale if you are always weighing small amounts. If you deal in sand, you will probably want to put the sand in a bag to make it easier to handle. You will have a bunch of small bags that you will use. But if you occasionally need to weigh larger items that do not fit on the small scale, you need to pull out a bigger scale and a bigger bag. Using the bigger bag and scale for many of the smaller items would be a waste.

Similarly, Python tries to optimize storage space for integers toward smaller sizes. When Python does not have enough memory (a small bag) to fit larger integers in, it *coerces* the integer into a *long integer*. This is actually desirable because, in some environments, you run into an *overflow error* here, where the program dies (or Pac-Man refuses to go over level 255—since it stored the level counter in an 8-bit number).

9.8 Order of operations

When you are performing math, you do not apply all the operations from left to right. You do the multiplication and division before the addition and subtraction. Computers work the same way. If you want to perform addition (or subtraction) first, use parentheses to indicate the order of operations:

```
>>> 4 + 2 * 3
10
>>> (4 + 2) * 3
18
```

As illustrated in the example, anything in parentheses is evaluated first.

If you are not sure what order the operations are performed in, use PEMDAS as a mnemonic. It stands for *parentheses, exponents, multiplication, division, addition, subtraction*. This is the order of operations that Python uses.

9.9 Other operations

The help section from the REPL is pretty useful. There is a topic called NUMBERMETHODS that explains how all of the number operations work. When you start implemented your own classes and want them to respond to the same operations as numbers, you can implement these methods to make your class behave like a number.

```
>>> help()
help> NUMBERMETHODS
Emulating numeric types
***********************

The following methods can be defined to emulate numeric objects.
Methods corresponding to operations that are not supported by the
particular kind of number implemented (e.g., bitwise operations for
non-integral numbers) should be left undefined.

object.__add__(self, other)
object.__sub__(self, other)
object.__mul__(self, other)
object.__matmul__(self, other)
   ...
```

9. Numbers

9.10 Summary

Python has built-in support for basic mathematical operations. Addition, subtraction, multiplication, and division are all included. Also, the power and modulus operations are available. If you need to control which order the operations occur, wrap parentheses around the procedure that you want to happen first.

If you need a simple calculator, rather than opening a calculator application, give Python a try. It should be more than capable for most tasks.

9.11 Exercises

1. This week, you slept for 6.2, 7, 8, 5, 6.5, 7.1, and 8.5 hours. Calculate the average number of hours slept.

2. Is 297 divisible by 3?

3. What is 2 raised to the tenth power?

4. Wikipedia defines leap years as:

   > Every year that is exactly divisible by four is a leap year, except for years that are exactly divisible by 100, but these centurial years are leap years if they are exactly divisible by 400. For example, the years 1700, 1800, and 1900 are not leap years, but the years 1600 and 2000 are.
   >
   > —https://en.wikipedia.org/wiki/Leap_year

   Write Python code to determine if 1800, 1900, 1903, 2000, and 2002 are leap years.

Chapter 10

Numbers in NumPy

This chapter introduces numerical computing in Python using NumPy, a powerful library that revolutionizes how we work with numbers in Python. NumPy, a cornerstone of data science in Python, offers highly efficient arrays and an assortment of mathematical functions to operate on these arrays. With its C and Fortran underpinnings, NumPy takes Python's numerical capabilities to new heights.

10.1 NumPy

NumPy, short for "Numerical Python" is much faster for working with numbers. The core of NumPy's speed advantage over pure Python comes from using optimized C and Fortran code under the hood. Python's high-level interpretation can result in slow processing when performing mathematical operations, particularly on large data sets or arrays. However, NumPy bypasses this bottleneck by using pre-compiled C and Fortran routines, delivering a vastly improved performance.

Beyond using pre-compiled routines, NumPy also benefits from its efficient memory layout. In Python, data types like lists are general-purpose and can hold different types of objects. The flexibility comes with overhead and doesn't allow for efficient memory usage. NumPy, on the other hand, uses contiguous blocks of memory. It ensures that each item in an array is of the same type, drastically reducing the memory footprint and leading to better cache coherence and overall speed. By making these significant improvements in the way numerical computations are performed and how memory is managed, NumPy has become a staple tool in the data science and machine learning community.

10.2 Installing NumPy

NumPy is not included with Python, and you will need to install it.
You can use the following command to install NumPy:

10. Numbers in NumPy

```
pip install numpy
```

10.3 Working with NumPy

Unlike pure Python, NumPy provides specialized numeric types, such as numpy.int_ for integers and numpy.float64 for floating point numbers. This specialization provides significant speed benefits when processing large amounts of numerical data. However, it also presents opportunities for overflow errors.

Here's how we determine the type of numbers in NumPy:

```
>>> import numpy as np
```

```
>>> np.array([1]).dtype
dtype('int64')
```

```
>>> np.array([2.0]).dtype
dtype('float64')
```

Here's an example of overflow in NumPy and how it differs from Python:

```
>>> np.array([2**63], dtype=np.int64)
Traceback (most recent call last):
  File "<stdin>", line 1, in <module>
OverflowError: Python int too large to convert to C long
```

```
>>> 2**63
9223372036854775808
```

As with Python, there is a level of precision in NumPy numbers, especially for floating point numbers due to the binary representation. One should anticipate rounding errors.

Consider the following example:

```
>>> np.array([1.01]) - np.array([.99])
array([0.0200000000000000018])
```

Here, you might expect the result to be exactly 0.02. However, due to the binary approximations, there's some precision error.

10.4 Addition with NumPy

NumPy arrays can be utilized to perform mathematical operations similar to how Python does. If you want to add two integers, you can do:

```
>>> np.array([2]) + np.array([6])
array([8])
```

10.5. Subtraction, Multiplication, Division with NumPy

Adding two floating point numbers can result in precision loss:

```
>>> np.array([.4]) + np.array([.01])
array([0.41000000000000003])
```

Adding an integer and a float in NumPpy also results in coercion, just like Python:

```
>>> np.array([6]) + np.array([.2])
array([6.2])
```

The integer is coerced to a float before the operation takes place.
Explicit conversion can be done with the `numpy.int_` and `numpy.float64` functions:

```
>>> np.array([2.3], dtype=np.int_)
array([2])
>>> np.array([3], dtype=np.float64)
array([3.0])
```

10.5 Subtraction, Multiplication, Division with NumPy

Performing arithmetic operations like subtraction, multiplication, and division with NumPy arrays is efficient. For instance, when you want to subtract one array from another, you can use the following syntax:
We can subtract values:

```
>>> np.array([2]) - np.array([1])
array([1])
```

We can also multiply them:

```
>>> np.array([2]) * np.array([3])
array([6])
```

And for division, the approach remains consistent:

```
>>> np.array([2]) / np.array([1])
array([2.])
```

10.6 Exponentiation and Modulo in NumPy

Many mathematical operations with NumPy, including both exponentiation and modulo, can be accomplished using dedicated functions or the familiar Python operators. Each approach comes with its advantages, depending on the situation.
For exponentiation, we can use the `np.power` function or the `**` operator:

10. Numbers in NumPy

```
>>> np.power(np.array([2]), np.array([3]))
array([8])
>>> np.array([2]) ** np.array([3])
array([8])
```

Similarly, for modulo operations, we have the np.mod function and the % operator:

```
>>> np.mod(np.array([10]), np.array([3]))
array([1])
>>> np.array([10]) % np.array([3])
array([1])
```

So, why choose one over the other?

1. Readability and Consistency: If you're transitioning from standard Python, using the ** and % operators feels more natural and maintains consistency in your code. This is especially true if your project switches between standard Python and NumPy operations.

2. Flexibility with Parameters: Functions like np.power and np.mod allow additional parameters in some contexts, which can provide more control over the operation.

10.7 Matrix Operations with NumPy

While NumPy is adept at handling individual values, its true strength emerges when manipulating matrices or data arrays. Beyond basic arithmetic, NumPy offers comprehensive tools for matrix operations. One of the primary advantages of using NumPy is its ability to efficiently process and compute arrays or matrices of data.

```
>>> a = np.array([[1, 2], [3, 4]])
>>> b = np.array([[5, 6], [7, 8]])
```

Mathematical operations on these arrays are straightforward:

```
>>> a + 2
array([[3, 4],
       [5, 6]])
>>> a * 10
array([[10, 20],
       [30, 40]])
>>> a / 5
array([[0.2, 0.4],
       [0.6, 0.8]])
>>> a ** 3
array([[ 1,  8],
       [27, 64]])
```

10.8 Element-wise Multiplication

Matrix multiplication can be done using the numpy.dot function or the @ operator:

```
>>> np.dot(a, b)
array([[19, 22],
       [43, 50]])

>>> a @ b
array([[19, 22],
       [43, 50]])
```

10.8 Element-wise Multiplication

For multiplying matrices element-by-element, the * operator is employed:

```
>>> a * b
array([[ 5, 12],
       [21, 32]])
```

10.9 Transpose of a Matrix

To transpose a matrix, you can use the .transpose method or access the .T attribute directly:

```
>>> np.transpose(a)
array([[1, 3],
       [2, 4]])

>>> a.T
array([[1, 3],
       [2, 4]])
```

10.10 Exploring Numerical Operations with NumPy

NumPy has many functions and methods designed specifically for numerical analyses, making it a powerful tool for data scientists, researchers, and programmers. Some of the commonly employed methods include .sum, .mean, .median, and .std, which respectively facilitate the computation of the summation, mean value, median value, and standard deviation of a set of numbers.

Consider the following array as an example:

```
>>> arr = np.array([1, 2, 3, 4, 5])
```

To determine the total sum of all elements in the array:

10. Numbers in NumPy

```
>>> np.sum(arr)
15
```

For computing the average value of the elements:

```
>>> np.mean(arr)
3.0
```

To ascertain the median or the middle value:

```
>>> np.median(arr)
3.0
```

Lastly, to evaluate the standard deviation, which gives insight into the spread of data values:

```
>>> np.std(arr)
1.4142135623730951
```

These functions provide a quick and efficient way to perform various essential numerical operations, making data analysis tasks more streamlined with NumPy.

10.11 NumPy's Handling of Special Numerical Values

NumPy, being a comprehensive library for numerical computations, incorporates mechanisms to represent and manage specific unique floating point values that emerge in computations. While distinct from ordinary numbers, these values are crucial for indicating specific mathematical situations.

For instance, np.inf symbolizes positive infinity, a value larger than any number. Its counterpart, -np.inf, signifies negative infinity, a value smaller than any number. Another special value, np.nan, stands for "Not a Number", typically used to denote indeterminate or undefined results.

Let's see how these special values behave in various operations:

```
>>> np.inf + 1
inf

>>> -np.inf - 1
-inf

>>> np.nan + 1
nan
```

> **Note**
>
> It's important to recognize that the operations involving np.inf, -np.inf, and np.nan conform to the IEEE 754 standard governing floating point

arithmetic. This standard dictates how computers handle arithmetic operations involving these special values, ensuring consistent results across different platforms and systems.

10.12 Summary

In this chapter, we explored NumPy, a powerful Python library known for its high performance and convenient features. We looked into NumPy's specialized number types, mathematical operations, matrix manipulation, and advanced numerical functionalities.

With its ability to handle extensive data sets quickly and efficiently, NumPy is a cornerstone in scientific computing with Python. It is much faster at math than using Python integer and float objects, as demonstrated in previous chapters.

10.13 Exercises

1. Create a NumPy array with integers from 1 to 10.
2. Perform element-wise multiplication on two NumPy arrays of your choice.
3. Calculate the dot product of two 2x2 NumPy matrices.
4. Convert a floating-point NumPy array to an integer array.
5. Compute the mean, median, and standard deviation of a NumPy array.
6. Subtract the mean of a NumPy array from each element (mean normalization).

Chapter 11

Strings

This chapter explores Python strings, from the basics of string manipulation to the elegant modernity of f-strings. We'll also explore some of the most helpful string methods, providing tools to quickly transform, analyze, and operate on string data.

11.1 Creating Strings

Strings are immutable objects that hold character data. A string could hold a single character, a word, a line of words, a paragraph, multiple paragraphs, or even zero characters.

Python denotes strings by wrapping them with ' (single quotes), " (double quotes), """ (triple-doubles) or '''''' (triple singles). Here are some examples:

```
>>> character = 'a'
>>> name = 'Matt'
>>> with_quote = "I ain't gonna"
>>> longer = """This string has
... multiple lines
... in it"""
>>> latin = '''Lorum ipsum
... dolor'''
>>> escaped = 'I ain\'t gonna'
>>> zero_chars = ''
>>> unicode_snake = "I love \N{SNAKE}"
```

Notice that the strings always start and end with the same quote style. As the with_quote example illustrates, you can put single quotes inside a double-quoted string—and vice versa. Furthermore, if you need to include the same type of quote within your string, you can *escape* the quote by preceding it with a \ (backslash). When you print out an escaped character, the backslash is ignored.

11. Strings

> **Note**
>
> Attentive readers may wonder how to include a backslash in a string. To include a backslash in a normal string, you must escape the backslash with ... you guessed it, another backslash:
>
> ```
> >>> backslash = '\\'
> >>> print(backslash)
> \
> ```

> **Note**
>
> Here are the common ways to escape characters in Python:
>
> | Escape Sequence | Output |
> | --- | --- |
> | \\ | Backslash |
> | \' | Single quote |
> | \" | Double quote |
> | \b | ASCII Backspace |
> | \n | Newline |
> | \t | Tab |
> | \u12af | Unicode 16 bit |
> | \U12af89bc | Unicode 32 bit |
> | \N{SNAKE} | Unicode character |
> | \o84 | Octal character |
> | \xFF | Hex character |

> **Note**
>
> If you do not want to use an escape sequence, you can use a *raw* string by preceding the string with an r. Raw strings are typically used in two places. They are used in *regular expressions*, where the backslash is also used as an escape character. You can use regular expressions to match characters (such as phone numbers, names, etc.) from text. The re module in the Python standard library provides support for regular expressions. Raw strings are also used in Windows paths where the backslash is a delimiter.

Raw strings interpret the character content literally (i.e., there is no escaping). The following illustrates the difference between raw and normal strings:

```
>>> slash_t = r'\tText \\'
>>> print(slash_t)
\tText \\
```

11.1. Creating Strings

```
>>> normal = '\tText \\'
>>> print(normal)
    Text \
```

Python also has a triple quoting mechanism for defining strings. Triple quotes are useful for creating strings containing paragraphs or multiple lines. Triple-quoted strings are also commonly used in *docstrings*. Docstrings will be discussed in the chapter on functions. Below is an example of a multi-line triple-quoted string:

```
>>> paragraph = """Lorem ipsum dolor
... sit amet, consectetur adipisicing
... elit, sed do eiusmod tempor incididunt
... ut labore et dolore magna aliqua. Ut
... enimad minim veniam, quis nostrud
... exercitation ullamco laboris nisi ut
... aliquip ex ea commodo consequat. Duis
... aute irure dolor in reprehenderit in
... voluptate velit esse cillum dolore eu
... fugiat nulla pariatur. Excepteur sint
... occaecat cupidatat non proident, sunt
... in culpa qui officia deserunt mollit
... anim id est laborum."""
```

A nice benefit of using triple-quoted strings is that you can embed single and double quotes inside it without escaping them:

```
>>> """This string has double " and single
... quotes ' inside of it"""
'This string has double " and single\nquotes \' inside of it'
```

Unless the embedded quotes butt up to the end of the string (using the same quote style but triple-quoted), then you will need to escape the final quote:

```
>>> """"He said, "Hello""""
Traceback (most recent call last):
  File "<stdin>", line 1
    """"He said, "Hello""""
                        ^
SyntaxError: EOL while scanning string literal


>>> """"He said, "Hello\""""   # Escape the ending quote
'He said, "Hello"'
```

73

11. Strings

11.2 Formatting Strings

Storing strings in variables is nice, but being able to compose strings of other strings and manipulate them is also necessary. One way to achieve this is to use string formatting.

In Python 3.6 and above, the preferred way to format strings is to use f-strings. Below, you tell Python to replace {} (a placeholder) with the contents of name or the string Matt:

```
>>> name = 'Matt'
>>> print(f'Hello {name}')
Hello Matt
```

Another useful property of formatting is that you can also format non-string objects, such as numbers:

```
>>> print(f'I:{1} R:{2.5} S:{"foo"}')
I:1 R:2.5 S:foo
```

11.3 F-string Examples in Data Science

When presenting data analysis results, formatting can be crucial in readability and presentation. F-strings in Python provide a versatile tool for this.

Suppose you're analyzing a song's popularity and want to display the artist's name prominently, centered within a banner. Here's how you might format that:

```
>>> artist = 'The Beatles'
>>> f"Artist of the Month: {artist:*^20}"
'Artist of the Month: ****The Beatles*****'
```

In this example, we use an f-string in Python to format the name of a band, 'The Beatles', as the "Artist of the Month". The band's name is centered within a 20-character wide string, and any extra spaces around the band's name are filled with asterisks.

In A/B testing scenarios, you'll often want to present a metric's percentage improvement or regression. Consider that the new webpage design improves the conversion rate by 8.3%. You can format this tidily with f-strings:

```
>>> improvement = 8.3/100
>>> f"Improvement: {improvement:=+7.2%}"
'Improvement: + 8.30%'
```

In the provided f-string, the variable improvement, which has a value of 0.083 or 8.3%, is formatted. The = places any padding after the sign, ensuring that the positive + sign (added by the + option) remains adjacent to the percentage. A total width of 7 characters, including the sign, number, and padding, is specified by the number 7. The .2 ensures two decimal places, while the % symbol converts the decimal value into a percentage. Thus, 0.083 is neatly formatted as '+ 8.30%'.

Let's say you are analyzing internet traffic data and have recorded each data packet's size in bytes. After some analysis, you find out the largest packet size recorded. For debugging or low-level data inspections, representing this value in both binary and hexadecimal can be crucial:

```
>>> largest_packet_size = 1720
>>> f"Binary Size: {largest_packet_size:b}"
'Binary Size: 11010111000'

>>> f"Hex Size: {largest_packet_size:x}"
'Hex Size: 6b8'
```

The first f-string converts the number into its binary representation, resulting in 'Binary Size: 11010111000'. The second f-string converts the same number into its hexadecimal representation, producing 'Hex Size: 6b8'.

By leveraging f-strings, we can ensure their results are accurate, neatly formatted, and easily understood.

> **Note**
>
> A great resource for formatting is the built-in help documentation available in the REPL. Type:
>
> ```
> >>> help()
> ```
>
> Which puts you in the help mode and gives you a help> prompt. Then type:
>
> ```
> help> FORMATTING
> ```
>
> You can scroll through here and find many examples. A bare return from the help> prompt will return you to the normal prompt.
>
> Another resource is found at https://pyformat.info/. This website contains many formatting examples with both .format and the older % operator.
>
> There is also an entry in help for strings, located under STRINGS.

11. Strings

11.4 Format String Syntax

There is a whole language for formatting strings. If you insert a colon following the field name, you can provide further formatting information. The format is below. Anything in square brackets is optional:

`:[[fill]align][sign][#][0][width][grouping][.precision][type]`

The following table lists the string formatting fields and their meaning.

Field	Meaning
fill	Character used to fill in align (default is space)
align	Alight output < (left align), > (right align), ^ (center align), or = (put padding after sign)
sign	For numbers + (show sign on both positive and negative numbers, - (default, only on negative), or *space* (leading space for positive, sign on negative)
#	Prefix integers. 0b (binary), 0o (octal), or 0x (hex)
0	Enable zero padding
width	Minimum field width
grouping	Number separator , (use comma for thousands separator), _ (Use underscore for thousands separator)
.precision	For floats (digits after period (floats), for non-numerics (max length)
type	Number type or s (string format default) see Integer and Float charts

The tables below list the various options you have for formatting integer and floating point numbers.

Integer Types	Meaning
b	binary
c	character - convert to Unicode character
d	decimal (default)
n	decimal with locale-specific separators
o	octal
x	hex (lower-case)
X	hex (upper-case)

Float Types	Meaning
e/E	Exponent. Lower/upper-case e

Float Types	Meaning
f	Fixed point
g/G	General. Fixed with exponent for large and small numbers (g default)
n	g with locale-specific separators
%	Percentage (multiplied by 100)

11.5 Debugging F-Strings

In Python 3.8, a specifier was introduced to aid in debugging variables with f-strings. By adding an equal sign, =, the f-string will include the code inside the f-string:

```
>>> name = "matt"
>>> f'{name=}'
"name='matt'"

>>> f'My name is {name.capitalize()=}'
"My name is name.capitalize()='Matt'"

>>> f'Square root of two: {2**.5=:5.3f}'
'Square root of two: 2**.5=1.414'
```

11.6 String Methods

There are a bunch of other string methods. I encourage you to explore them from the REPL (the next chapter will show you how to do this).

For example, Python 3.9 added the .removeprefix and .removesuffix methods. These convenience methods make it easy to remove the extension from a filename. Instead of having to slice out the filename (we cover slicing in a later chapter) like this:

```
>>> fname = 'resume.pdf'
>>> if fname.endswith('.pdf'):
...     trimmed = fname[:len(fname)-4]

>>> trimmed
'resume'
```

You can use the .removesuffix method:

```
>>> fname.removesuffix('.pdf')
'resume'
```

The string methods are provided to make it easy to perform common string operations.

11. Strings

11.7 Summary

In this chapter, strings were introduced. Strings can be defined with various delimiters. Unlike other languages, which may distinguish between a string defined with " and one defined with ', Python makes no distinction. Triple-quoted strings, however, may span multiple lines.

We also looked at the .format method and gave examples of formatting strings. Finally, the chapter introduced a new feature in Python 3.6, f-strings.

11.8 Exercises

1. Create a variable, name, pointing to your name. Create another variable, age, holding an integer value for your age. Print out a string formatted with both values. If your name was Fred and your age was 23, it would print:

   Fred is 23

2. Create a variable, paragraph, that has the following content:

   > "Python is a great language!", said Fred. "I don't ever remember having this much fun before."

3. Go to https://unicode.org and find the symbol omega in the Greek character code chart. Create a string that holds the omega character, using both the Unicode code point (\u form) and Unicode name (\N form). The code point is the hex number in the chart, the name is the bolded capital name following the code point. For example, the theta character has the code point of 03f4 and a name of GREEK CAPITAL THETA SYMBOL.

4. Make a variable, item, that points to a string, "car". Make a variable, cost, that points to 13499.99. Print out a line that has item in a left-justified area of 10 characters and cost in a right-justified area of 10 characters with 2 decimal places and commas in the thousands place. It should look like this (without the quotes):

   'car   13,499.99'

Chapter 12

Strings and Methods

This chapter focuses on strings and their associated methods. As we explore, remember Python's object-oriented nature: everything is an object, and objects often have methods associated with them.

12.1 Methods

Strings objects have methods that allow you to perform actions on the string. For example, you can capitalize a string, check if it ends with a certain character, or replace a substring with another string. Because strings are immutable, these methods do not mutate or change the existing string object but rather return a new string or a new result.

Jargon alert! *Methods* are functions that are called on an instance of a type. What does this mean? The string type allows you to *call* a method (another term for "call" is *invoke*) by placing a . (period) and the method name directly after the variable name holding the data (or the data itself), followed by parentheses with arguments inside of them.

> **Note**
>
> In this book, I place a period in front of methods. This is meant to remind you that you must have an object before the method. I will mention the .capitalize method rather than saying capitalize. The invocation looks like this on the text object:
>
> text.capitalize()
>
> This is in contrast to a function, like help, which you invoke by itself (there is no object or period before it):
>
> help()

Here is an example of calling the .capitalize method on a variable pointing to a string and a string literal. Note that this does not change the

12. Strings and Methods

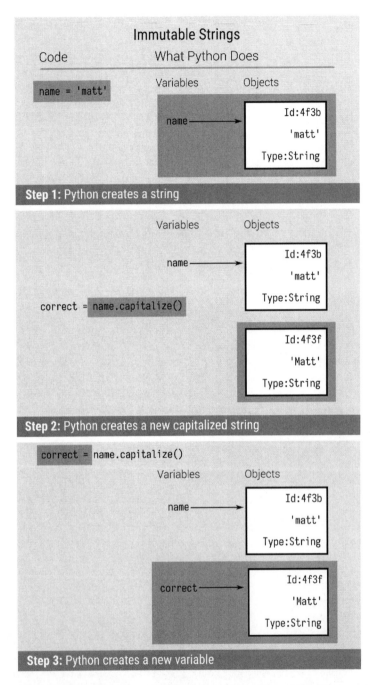

Figure 12.1: Illustration of calling a method on a string. The method does not change the string because it is immutable. Rather, the method returns a new string.

12.1. Methods

object on which it is called. Because a string is immutable, the result of the method is a new object with the capitalized value:

```
>>> name = 'matt'
>>> # invoked on variable
>>> correct = name.capitalize()
>>> print(correct)
Matt
```

Note that name does not change:

```
>>> print(name)
matt
```

Note the .capitalize method does not have to be called on a variable. You can invoke the method directly on a string literal:

```
>>> print('fred'.capitalize())
Fred
```

In Python, methods and functions are *first-class objects*. As was previously mentioned, everything is an object. If the parentheses are left off, Python will not throw an error. It will only show a reference to a method, which is an object:

```
>>> print('fred'.capitalize)
<built-in method capitalize of str object at
0x7ff648617508>
```

Having first-class objects enables more advanced features like *closures* and *decorators* (these are discussed in my intermediate Python book).

> **Note**
>
> Do integers and floats have methods? Yes, again, everything in Python is an object and objects have methods. This is easy to verify by invoking dir on an integer (or a variable holding an integer):
>
> ```
> >>> dir(4)
> ['__abs__', '__add__', '__and__',
>  '__class__',
>  ...
>  '__subclasshook__', '__truediv__',
>  '__trunc__', '__xor__', 'conjugate',
>  'denominator', 'imag', 'numerator',
>  'real']
> ```

12. Strings and Methods

Invoking a method on a number is somewhat tricky due to the use of the . to denote calling a method. Because . is common in floats, it would confuse Python if . were also used to call methods on numbers.

For example, the .conjugate method returns the complex conjugate of an integer. But if you try to invoke it on an integer, you will get an error:

```
>>> 5.conjugate()
Traceback (most recent call last):
  ...
    5.conjugate()
     ^
SyntaxError: invalid decimal literal
```

One solution to this is to wrap the number with parentheses:

```
>>> (5).conjugate()
5
```

Another option would be to assign a variable to 5 and invoke the method on the variable:

```
>>> five = 5
>>> five.conjugate()
5
```

However, in practice, it is fairly rare to call methods on numbers.

Here are a few string methods commonly used or found in the wild. Feel free to explore others using dir and help (or the online documentation).

12.2 Endswith

You might want to check the extension if you have a variable holding a filename. This is easy with .endswith:

```
>>> xl = 'Oct2000.xls'
>>> xl.endswith('.xls')
True
>>> xl.endswith('.xlsx')
False
```

> **Note**
>
> Notice that you had to pass in a *parameter* (or *argument*), 'xls', into the method. Methods have a *signature,* which is a funky way of saying that they need to be called with the correct number (and type) of parameters.

12.2. Endswith

For the .endswith method, it makes sense that if you want to know if a string ends with another string you have to tell Python which ending you want to check for. This is done by passing the end string to the method.

Note

Again, it is usually easy to find out this sort of information via help. The documentation should tell you what parameters are required as well as any optional parameters. Here is the help for endswith:

```
>>> help(xl.endswith)
Help on built-in function endswith:
endswith(...)
    S.endswith(suffix[, start[, end]]) -> bool
    Return True if S ends with the specified
    suffix, False otherwise. With optional
    start, test S beginning at that position.
    With optional end, stop comparing S at
    that position. suffix can also be a
    tuple of strings to try.
```

Notice the line:

```
S.endswith(suffix[, start[, end]]) -> bool
```

The S represents the string (or *instance*) you are invoking the method on, in this case, the xl variable. .endswith is the method name. Between the parentheses, (and), are the parameters. suffix is a *required* parameter, the .endswith method will complain if you do not provide it:

```
>>> xl.endswith()
Traceback (most recent call last):
  File "<stdin>", line 1, in <module>
TypeError: endswith() takes at least 1 argument
(0 given)
```

The parameters between the square brackets [and] are *optional* parameters. In this case, start and end allow you to only check a portion of the string. If you wanted to check if the characters starting at 0 and ending at 3 end with Oct you could do the following:

```
>>> xl.endswith('Oct', 0, 3)
True
```

Strings also have a .startswith method, so the correct way to check if a string starts with 'Oct' is:

12. Strings and Methods

```
>>> xl.startswith('Oct')
True
```

12.3 Find

The .find method allows you to find substrings inside other strings. It returns the *index* (offset starting at 0) of the matched substring. If no substring is found it returns -1:

```
>>> word = 'grateful'
>>> # 0 is g, 1 is r, 2 is a
>>> word.find('ate')
2
>>> word.find('great')
-1
```

12.4 Format

format allows for the easy creation of new strings by combining existing variables. The chapter on strings discussed this method:

```
>>> print('name: {}, age: {}'.format('Matt', 10))
name: Matt, age: 10
```

> **Note**
>
> Sometimes, you need to place code across multiple lines. If you have opened a left parenthesis, (, you can also place the arguments on multiple lines without a \:
>
> ```
> >>> print("word".find('ord'))
> 1
>
> >>> print("word"
> ...       .find('ord'))
> 1
> ```
>
> To help make the code more readable, indent the continued lines. Note that indenting with four spaces serves to indicate to anyone reading the code that the second line is a continuation of a previous statement:
>
> ```
> >>> print("word".\
> ...     find('ord'))
> 1
> >>> print("word".find(
> ```

12.5. Join

```
...     'ord'))
1
```

Why spread code that could reside in a single line across multiple lines? Where this comes into play in most code is dealing with code standards that expect lines to be less than 80 characters in length. If a method takes multiple arguments, it may be hard to follow the 80 character limit. (Note that Python itself does not care about line length, but readers of your code might). It is not uncommon to see a separate line for each argument to a method:

```
>>> print('{} {} {} {} {}'.format(
...     'hello',
...     'to',
...     'you',
...     'and',
...     'you'
... ))
hello to you and you
```

12.5 Join

Imagine you are working with a database and you want to select specific columns from a table. You might have the column names in a list, and you want to generate a SQL SELECT statement:

```
>>> columns = ["name", "age", "gender", "salary"]
>>> query = f"SELECT {', '.join(columns)} FROM employees;"
```

When you print the query, it will look like:

```
>>> print(query)
SELECT name, age, gender, salary FROM employees;
```

Using the .join method, you can efficiently generate strings that fit their specific needs, whether for database operations, file handling, or other data manipulations.

> **Note**
>
> For most Python interpreters, using .join is faster than repeated concatenation using the + operator. The above idiom is common.

12.6 Lower

The .lower method returns a copy of the string converted to lowercase. This is often useful for validating if the input matches a string. For example, some programs capitalize file extensions, while others do not. If you wanted to know if a file name had TXT or txt as an extension, you could do the following:

```
>>> fname = 'readme.txt'
>>> fname.endswith('txt') or fname.endswith('TXT')
True
```

A more Pythonic version would read:

```
>>> fname.lower().endswith('txt')
True
```

12.7 Startswith

Imagine you are working with dataset identifiers, where each dataset has an ID starting with a specific prefix indicating its category. For instance:

- "SALES_00123"
- "INV_45678"
- "EXP_78901"

You receive a dataset ID and want to determine its category:

```
>>> dataset_id = "SALES_00123"

>>> dataset_id.startswith("SALES_")
True

>>> dataset_id.startswith("INV_")
False
```

This simple check lets you quickly discern the category of the dataset from its ID.

12.8 Strip

It's common to work with data that may not be clean or standardized. For instance, when pulling data from external files or APIs, there might be extra spaces added inadvertently.

Imagine you are processing product IDs from an external source:

```
>>> product_id = "   PRD12345   "
>>> product_id.strip()
'PRD12345'
```

This ensures that even if the incoming data has unexpected spaces, you can easily clean it up for further processing.

For only leading or trailing whitespaces:

```
>>> product_id.lstrip()
'PRD12345   '
>>> product_id.rstrip()
'   PRD12345'
```

12.9 Upper

Sometimes, data might come in a mix of cases. For uniformity, especially in identifiers, you might need to convert them to uppercase.

Imagine dealing with country codes that should be in uppercase, but an entry comes in lowercase:

```
>>> country_code = "us"
>>> country_code.upper()
'US'
```

This helps ensure that all country codes are consistent and can be used as keys or identifiers without discrepancies.

12.10 Other methods

There are other string methods, but they are used less often. Feel free to explore them by reading the documentation and trying them out. The appendix provides a list of them.

> **Note**
>
> The STRINGMETHODS entry in the help section from the REPL contains documentation for all of the string methods, as well as some examples.

12.11 Summary

This chapter talked about methods. Methods are always called by putting an object and a period before the method name. You also looked at some of the more common methods of strings. One thing to remember is that a string is immutable. If you want to change a string's value, you must create a new string.

12.12 Exercises

1. Create a string, school, with the name of your elementary school. Examine the methods that are available on that string. Use the help function to view their documentation.
2. Create a string, country, with the value 'usa'. Create a new string, correct_country, that has the value in uppercase by using a string method.

12. Strings and Methods

3. Create a string, `filename`, with the value `'hello.py'`. Check and see if the filename ends with `'.java'`. Find the index location of `'py'`. See if it starts with `'world'`.
4. Open a REPL. Enter the help documentation and scan through the `STRINGMETHODS` entry.

Chapter 13

Strings in Pandas

In the previous chapter, you learned about strings and their methods in Python. Now, we will apply that knowledge in the context of pandas. Pandas is a popular data manipulation library in Python that provides high-level data structures and a wide variety of tools for analysis. Pandas allows you to manipulate tabular data like a spreadsheet or a database.

Unlike NumPy, which doesn't have strong support for arrays of strings, the Pandas library has support for strings. With Pandas 2.0 it has optimized many of these operations so you can apply them to a column of string values at once.

The cool thing about the Pandas string manipulation methods is that they are based on the Python string methods. If you know the Python methods, many will apply to Pandas.

13.1   Installing Pandas

The Pandas library is not included with Python. You will need to install it. You should also install the pyarrow library to take advantage of the optimizations in Pandas 2.

```
pip install pandas pyarrow
```

13.2   Calling methods on a Pandas Series

Since we are particularly focusing on strings, it's important to know that pandas provides a set of string functions that make it easy to operate on string data. These functions can be accessed using .str accessor in pandas Series objects.

Let's look into how we can use these functions to manipulate strings in pandas.

In pandas, you can perform string operations on Series and Indexes like on native Python strings.

Here is an example:

13. Strings in Pandas

```
>>> import pandas as pd
```

```
>>> names = pd.Series(['matt', 'fred', 'jack'], dtype='string[pyarrow]')
```

```
>>> names.str.capitalize()
0    Matt
1    Fred
2    Jack
dtype: string
```

As you can see, the `.str.capitalize` method returns a new Series with the capitalized names. The original Series does not change:

```
>>> names
0    matt
1    fred
2    jack
dtype: string
```

In pandas, calling a method directly on a Series (or a DataFrame) works like calling the method on a string literal in Python.

Pandas provides a variety of string methods, and here are a few commonly used ones:

13.3 Endswith and Startswith

To check if the strings in a Series end with a certain pattern, you can use the `.str.endswith` method. Similarly, to check if they start with a certain pattern, use the `.str.startswith` method:

```
>>> filenames = pd.Series(['report.xls', 'data.xlsx', 'summary.csv'])
>>> filenames.str.endswith('.xls')
0     True
1    False
2    False
dtype: bool
```

```
>>> filenames.str.startswith('data')
0    False
1     True
2    False
dtype: bool
```

13.4 Find

The .str.find method works in pandas like in Python. It finds substrings inside the strings in a Series. In this case, it returns a series with the index values for each entry:

```
>>> sentences = pd.Series(['grateful for everything', 'great day'])
>>> sentences.str.find('ate')
0    2
1   -1
dtype: int64
```

13.5 Lower, Upper, and Capitalize

These methods convert the strings in a Series to lowercase, uppercase, or capitalize them, respectively:

```
>>> items = pd.Series(['ItemA', 'ItemB', 'ItemC'],
...       dtype='string[pyarrow]')
>>> items
0    ItemA
1    ItemB
2    ItemC
dtype: string

>>> items.str.lower()
0    itema
1    itemb
2    itemc
dtype: string

>>> items.str.upper()
0    ITEMA
1    ITEMB
2    ITEMC
dtype: string

>>> items.str.capitalize()
0    Itema
1    Itemb
2    Itemc
dtype: string
```

13.6 Strip

The .str.strip() method removes leading and trailing whitespaces from the strings in a Series:

13. Strings in Pandas

```
>>> messy_names = pd.Series(['   Alice   ', '   Bob   ', '   Eve   '],
...          dtype='string[pyarrow]')
>>> messy_names.str.strip()
0    Alice
1    Bob
2    Eve
dtype: string
```

13.7 Join

If you have a series with lists of strings in it, this method returns a new series with a delimiter inserted between the strings:

```
>>> letters = pd.Series([['a', 'b', 'c'], ['d', 'e', 'f'], ['g', 'h', 'i']])
>>> letters.str.join('-')
0    a-b-c
1    d-e-f
2    g-h-i
dtype: object
```

13.8 Summary

In this chapter, we explored how to use string methods in Pandas, a data manipulation and analysis library in Python. The power of Pandas comes from its ability to apply operations across collections of data, and we saw this in action with the .str accessor, which allows us to apply string methods to the entire Series at once. We covered a variety of string methods, including .capitalize, .endswith, .startswith, .find, .lower, .upper, and .strip.

13.9 Exercises

1. Given the Series s = pd.Series(['Python', 'java', 'C++', 'javascript', 'R']), transform all the strings to uppercase.

2. Now, use a suitable string method to check which of these strings end with the letter 'n'.

3. Given the Series s = pd.Series([' python ', ' java ']), remove leading and trailing white spaces from each string.

4. Given the Series s = pd.Series(['apple.jpg', 'banana.png', 'cherry.gif', 'dates.jpeg']), identify the filenames that end with '.jpg' or '.jpeg'.

Chapter 14

dir, help, and pdb

In this chapter, we'll explore three of Python's invaluable utilities: `dir`, `help`, and the `pdb` library. Python's "batteries-included" philosophy offers developers a plethora of tools, with `dir` revealing an object's attributes and methods, `help` elucidating their functionalities, and `pdb` assisting in debugging.

14.1 Dir

We have only touched the surface of strings, but we need to take a break to discuss two important functions and one library that come with Python. The first function is `dir`, which illustrates how powerful and useful the REPL is. The `dir` function returns the attributes of an object. If we had a Python interpreter open and wanted to know what the attributes of a string are, we can do the following:

```
>>> dir('Matt')
['__add__', '__class__', '__contains__',
'__delattr__', '__dir__', '__doc__', '__eq__',
'__format__', '__ge__', '__getattribute__',
'__getitem__', '__getnewargs__', '__gt__',
'__hash__', '__init__', '__iter__', '__le__',
'__len__', '__lt__', '__mod__', '__mul__', '__ne__',
'__new__', '__reduce__', '__reduce_ex__', '__repr__',
'__rmod__', '__rmul__', '__setattr__', '__sizeof__',
'__str__', '__subclasshook__', 'capitalize',
'casefold', 'center', 'count', 'encode', 'endswith',
'expandtabs', 'find', 'format', 'format_map',
'index', 'isalnum', 'isalpha', 'isdecimal',
'isdigit', 'isidentifier', 'islower', 'isnumeric',
'isprintable', 'isspace', 'istitle', 'isupper',
'join', 'ljust', 'lower', 'lstrip', 'maketrans',
'partition', 'replace', 'rfind', 'rindex', 'rjust',
```

14. dir, help, and pdb

```
'rpartition', 'rsplit', 'rstrip', 'split',
'splitlines', 'startswith', 'strip', 'swapcase',
'title', 'translate', 'upper', 'zfill']
```

dir lists all the attributes of the object passed into it. Since you passed in the string 'Matt' to dir, the function displays the attributes of a string. This handy feature of Python illustrates its "batteries included" philosophy. Python gives you an easy mechanism to discover the attributes of any object. Other languages might require special websites, documentation, or IDEs to access similar functionality. But in Python, because you have the REPL, you can get this information quickly and easily.

The attribute list is in alphabetical order, and you can normally ignore the first couple of attributes starting with __. Later on, you will see attributes such as capitalize (which is a *method* that capitalizes a string), format (which, as was illustrated previously, allows for the formatting of strings), or lower (which is a *method* used to ensure the string is lowercase). These attributes happen to be *methods*, which are functions that are attached to objects. To call or *invoke* a function, you place a period after the object, then the method name, then parentheses.

The three methods are invoked below:

```
>>> 'matt'.capitalize()
'Matt'
>>> 'Hi {}'.format('there')
'Hi there'
>>> 'YIKES'.lower()
'yikes'
```

14.2 Tab Completion in Jupyter

In addition to its other powerful features, Jupyter Notebook also offers a convenient tool-*tab completion*. As the name suggests, it's a feature that allows you to autocomplete your code and reduce the amount of typing, thereby speeding up your programming work. Tab completion can be used for completing variable names, function names, or paths to files and directories, among other things.

To use tab completion in Jupyter Notebook, start typing the name of the object you're interested in. When you hit the Tab key, a dropdown list will appear, showing all the potential matches, including functions, variables, or classes that start with the typed letters. If there's only one possible match, Jupyter will complete it for you directly. Not only does this save you keystrokes, but it can also help prevent typos and bugs in your code.

Like the dir function in Python, tab completion can also reveal the methods and attributes of an object. After typing the name of an object followed by a dot (.), hit the 'Tab' key to see a dropdown list of the methods and attributes that belong to this object. You can scroll through the list and select the one you need, significantly reducing the chances of error.

14.3 Dunder Methods

You might be wondering what all the attributes starting with __ are. People call them *special methods, magic methods,* or *dunder* methods since they start (and end) with double underscores (Double UNDERscores). "Dunder add" is one way to say __add__, "the add magic method" is another. Special methods determine what happens under the covers when operations are performed on an object. For example, when you use the + or % operator on a string, the .__add__ or .__mod__ method is invoked respectively.

Beginner Pythonistas can usually ignore dunder methods. When you start implementing your own classes and want them to react to operations such as + or %, you can define them.

::: {.note} ::: {.admonition-title} Note :::

In the help() documentation is an entry, SPECIALMETHODS, that describes these methods.

Another place where these are described is on the Python website. Go to Documentation, Language Reference, Data Model. It is tucked away in there.

Here is an example of using a dunger method. The __add__ method is invoked when the + operator is used on a string. The following illustrates this. A string object has a __add__ method. Python calls this method when the + operator is used on a string:

```
>>> 'Matt' + ' ' + 'Harrison'
'Matt Harrison'

>>> 'Matt'.__add__(' ').__add__('Harrison')
'Matt Harrison'
```

Later on, we will talk about how to define your own classes and how to define your own methods. You might want to come back and revisit this example after reading that chapter. But here is an example of a class, Add10, that defines its own __add__ method. When you add any object to an Add10 object, it adds 10 to the object:

```
>>> class Add10:
...     def __init__(self, num):
...         self.num = num
...     def __add__(self, other):
...         # ignore the other object and just add 10
...         return self.num + 10
...
>>> Add10(5) + 42
15
```

14. dir, help, and pdb

14.4 Help

`help` is another built-in function that is useful in combination with the REPL. The book previously mentioned invoking `help()`, without any arguments, to bring up help documentation.

The `help` function also provides documentation for a method, module, class, or function if you pass them in as an argument. For example, if you are curious about what the attribute `upper` on a string does, the following gives you the documentation:

```
>>> help('some string'.upper)
upper() method of builtins.str instance
    Return a copy of the string converted to uppercase.
```

The `help` function, combined with the REPL, allows you to read up on documentation without having to go to a browser, or even have internet access. If you were stranded on a desert island, you should be able to learn Python, provided you have a computer with Python installed and a power source.

14.5 Documentation in Jupyter

Jupyter Notebook provides several other helpful features for accessing information about Python objects and functions: the ?, ??, and Shift-Tab commands. These commands can significantly enhance your understanding of Python objects, and facilitate smoother, more efficient coding in Jupyter Notebooks.

The ? command can be appended to the end of any Python object or function to access its docstring, the documentation string that provides a brief summary of what the object or function does. This is especially useful when working with libraries or functions you are not familiar with.

For example, if you want to learn more about the `range` function, you can type `range?` in a Jupyter cell and run it. This will bring up a window at the bottom of the screen showing the docstring for `range`.

> **Note**
>
> ? and ?? are specific to Jupyter. These commands will not work in a normal REPL.

You can use the ?? command for more detailed information. This command shows the source code and the documentation of the function or method, if available. This can be particularly useful when you want to understand how a function is implemented.

Finally, the Shift-Tab shortcut is a quick way to get information about a function while typing it. If you press Shift-Tab while your cursor is inside the parentheses of a function call, a tooltip will appear showing the function's

14.6. Pdb

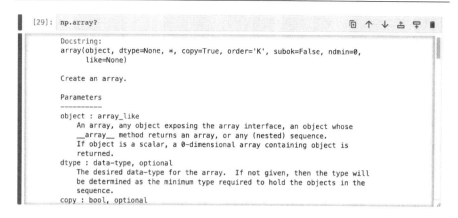

Figure 14.1: Using the ? operator to inspect the documentation in Jupyter.

signature (i.e., the arguments it takes) and a brief part of its docstring. If you press Shift-Tab twice in a row, the tooltip will be expanded to show more of the docstring. If you press Shift-Tab four times, the docstring will be expanded in a pager at the bottom of the screen. This is incredibly helpful for understanding a function's arguments and how to use it without navigating away from your current location in the notebook.

14.6 Pdb

Python also includes a debugger to step through code. It is found in a module named pdb. This library is modeled after the gdb library for C. To drop into the debugger at any point in a Python program, insert the code:

import pdb; pdb.set_trace()

These are two statements here, but I typically type them in a single line separated by a semicolon—that way I can easily remove them with a single keystroke from my editor when I am done debugging. This is also about the only place I use a semicolon in Python code (two statements in a single line).

When this line is executed, it will present a (pdb) prompt, similar to the REPL. Code can be evaluated at this prompt, and you can inspect objects and variables. Also, breakpoints can be set for further inspection.

Below is a table listing useful pdb commands:

Command	Purpose
h, help	List the commands available
n, next	Execute the next line
c, cont, continue	Continue execution until a breakpoint is hit

14. dir, help, and pdb

Command	Purpose
w, where, bt	Print a stack trace showing where execution is
u, up	Pop up a level in the stack
d, down	Push down a level in the stack
l, list	List source code around current line

Python 3.7 introduced the breakpoint function in the built-in namespace. It allows you to use:

breakpoint()

instead of:

import pdb; pdb.set_trace()

> **Note**
>
> In *Programming Pearls*, Jon Bentley states:
>
> > When I have to debug a little algorithm deep inside a big program, I sometimes use debugging tools... though, *print* statements are usually faster to implement and more effective than sophisticated debuggers.
>
> I've heard Guido van Rossum, the creator of Python, voice the same opinion: he prefers *print debugging*. Print debugging is easy, simply insert print functions to provide clarity as to what is going on. This is often sufficient to figure out a problem. Make sure to remove these debug statements or change them to logging statements before releasing the code. If more exploration is required, you can always use the pdb module.

14.7 Summary

Python provides many tools to make your life easier. If you learn to use the REPL, you can take advantage of them. The dir function will help you see what the attributes of an object are. Then, you can use the help function to inspect those attributes for documentation.

This chapter also introduced the pdb module. This module allows you to step through code, which can be useful for debugging.

14.8 Exercises

1. Open a REPL, and create a variable, name, with your name in it. List the attributes of the string. Print out the help documentation for the .find and .title methods.

2. Open a REPL, and create a variable, age, with your age in it. List the attributes of the integer. Print out the help documentation for the .numerator method.

Chapter 15

Comments, Booleans, and None

This chapter will introduce comments, booleans, and None. Comments have the potential to make your code more readable. The boolean and None types are widespread throughout Python code.

15.1 Comments

Comments are not a type per se because Python ignores them. Comments serve as reminders to the programmer. There are various takes on comments, their purpose, and their utility. There is a continuum from those who are against any and all comments to those who comment on almost every line of code, as well as those who are in between. If you contribute to a project, try to be consistent with their commenting scheme. A basic rule of thumb is that a comment should explain the *why* rather than the *how* (code alone should be sufficient for the how).

To create a comment in Python, start a line with a #. Anything that follows the hash is ignored:

```
>>> # This line is ignored by Python
```

You can also comment at the end of a line:

```
>>> num = 3.14   # PI
```

> **Note**
>
> A rogue use of comments is to disable code during editing temporarily. If your editor supports this, it is sometimes easier to comment out code rather than remove it altogether. However, the best practice is to remove commented-out code before sharing the code with others.
>
> Other languages support multi-line comments, but Python does not. The only way to comment out multiple lines is to start every line with #.

15. Comments, Booleans, and None

> **Note**
>
> You may be tempted to comment out multiple lines of code by making those lines a triple-quoted string. This is ugly and confusing. Try not to do this.

15.2 Booleans

Booleans represent the values for true and false. You have already seen them in previous code examples, such as the result of `.startswith`:

```
>>> 'bar'.startswith('b')
True
```

You can also assign those values to variables:

```
>>> a = True
>>> b = False
```

> **Note**
>
> The actual name of the boolean class in Python is `bool`, not boolean:
>
> ```
> >>> type(True)
> <class 'bool'>
> ```
>
> It can be useful to convert other types to booleans. In Python, the `bool` class can do that. Converting from one type to another is called *casting*. However, this is usually unnecessary due to the implicit casting Python performs when evaluating conditionals. The conditional statement will do this casting for you.

In Python parlance, it is common to hear of objects behaving as "truthy" or "falsey"—that means that non-boolean types can implicitly behave as though they were booleans. If you are unsure what the behavior might be, pass in the type to the `bool` class for an explicit conversion (or cast).

For strings, an empty string is "falsey", while non-empty values coerce to True:

```
>>> bool('')
False
>>> bool('0')   # The string containing 0
True
```

In data engineering, you might be streaming records from a data source and you want to process or transform records only if they contain valid data.

15.2. Booleans

Let's say we're streaming product SKUs (Stock Keeping Units) from an e-commerce database, and you want to validate that the SKU field isn't empty before further processing:

```
>>> sku = 'P12345'
>>> if sku:
...     print(f"Processing SKU: {sku}")
... else:
...     print("Invalid or missing SKU")
Processing SKU: P12345
```

When working with larger data streams, it's critical to have efficient checks. You might be tempted to check the length or convert it to a boolean to ensure it's not empty:

```
>>> if len(sku) > 0:
...     print(f"Processing SKU: {sku}")
Processing SKU: P12345
```

Or even:

```
>>> if bool(sku):
...     print(f"Processing SKU: {sku}")
Processing SKU: P12345
```

However, there's no need for such conversions or additional checks in Python. Given that a non-empty string is truthy by default, you can simplify your check:

```
>>> if sku:
...     print(f"Processing SKU: {sku}")
Processing SKU: P12345
```

This straightforward check enhances code readability and maintains efficiency, which is especially crucial in data-intensive tasks like data streaming and processing.

> **Note**
>
> The built-in types, int, float, str, and bool, are classes. Even though their capitalization (lowercase) makes it look as if they were functions, they are classes. Invoking help(str) will confirm this:
>
> ```
> >>> help(str)
> Help on class str in module builtins:
> class str(object)
>  |  str(object='') -> str
> ```

103

15. Comments, Booleans, and None

```
 |  str(bytes_or_buffer[, encoding[, errors]]) -> str
 |
```

This is one of those slight inconsistencies with Python. User-defined classes typically follow PEP8, which suggests camel-cased naming of classes.

For numbers, zero coerces to False while other numbers have "truthy" behavior:

```
>>> bool(0)
False
>>> bool(4)
True
```

While explicit casting via the bool function is available, it is usually overkill, because variables are implicitly coerced to booleans when used in conditional statements. For example, container types, such as *lists* and *dictionaries*, when empty, behave as "falsey". On the flip side, when they are populated, they act as "truthy".

> **Note**
>
> Be careful when parsing content that you want to turn into booleans. Strings that are non-empty evaluate to True. One example of a string that might bite you is the string 'False' which evaluates to True:
>
> ```
> >>> bool('False')
> True
> ```

Here is a table of truthy and falsey values:

Truthy	Falsey
True	False
Most objects	None
1	0
3.2	0.0
[1, 2]	[] (empty list)
{'a': 1, 'b': 2}	{} (empty dict)
'string'	"" (empty string)
'False'	
'0'	

15.2. Booleans

Note

When working with data structures, it's common to check the truthiness of variables or to determine if a data structure, like a string, dictionary, or list has data or not. Avoid complicating these checks with unnecessary comparisons or conversions.

Do not test boolean values to check if they are equal to True. Do not explicitly cast expressions to boolean results. If you have a variable, done, containing a boolean, this is sufficient:

```
if done:
    # do something
```

While this is overkill:

```
if done == True:
    # do something
```

As is this:

```
if bool(done):
    # do something
```

Similarly, if you have a list and need to distinguish between an empty and non-empty list, this is sufficient:

```
members = []
if members:
    # do something if members
    # have values
else:
    # member is empty
```

Likewise, this test is superfluous. It is not necessary to determine the truthiness of a list by its length:

```
if len(members) > 0:
    # do something if members
    # have values
else:
    # member is empty
```

Keep your checks succinct and to the point; it improves readability and simplifies your code.

If you wish to define the implicit truthiness for user-defined objects, the .__bool__ method specifies this behavior. It can return True, or False. If this

15. Comments, Booleans, and None

magic method is not defined, the `.__len__` method is checked for a non-zero value. If neither method is defined, an object defaults to True:

```
>>> class Nope:
...     def __bool__(self):
...         return False

>>> n = Nope()
>>> bool(n)
False
```

If this is confusing right now, feel free to come back to this example after reading about classes.

15.3 Truthiness in Pandas Series

While we've covered the basics of truthiness in Python's built-in types, working with data in a data engineering or data analysis setting often involves using libraries like pandas. The concept of truthiness extends to pandas Series and DataFrames, but with a few intricacies.

Pandas Series are one-dimensional arrays that can hold any data type, and they come with their own truthiness behavior. Let's consider a basic example:

```
>>> import pandas as pd
>>> series = pd.Series([1, 2, 0, None])
```

When attempting to check the truthiness of a Series directly:

```
>>> if series:
...     print("Series is truth")
Exception raised:
    Traceback (most recent call last):
    ...
    ValueError: The truth value of a Series is ambiguous. Use a.empty,
    a.bool(), a.item(), a.any() or a.all().
```

You'll get a `ValueError` with a message like `The truth value of a Series is ambiguous`. This is because pandas does not know if you're checking if any of the values are truthy, all of them are, or some other condition.

Instead, you'll need to use methods like `.any` or `.all`:

```
>>> if series.any():
...     print("At least one element in the series is truthy.")
At least one element in the series is truthy.

>>> if series.all():
...     print("All elements in the series are truth.")
```

15.4. None

This is a specific behavior to be aware of when working with Series in pandas.

15.4 None

None is an instance of NoneType. Other languages have similar constructs such as *nil*, *NULL*, or *undefined*. Variables can be assigned to None to indicate that they are waiting to hold a real value. None coerces to False in a boolean context:

```
>>> bool(None)
False
```

> **Note**
>
> A Python function defaults to returning None if no return statement is specified:
>
> ```
> >>> def hello():
> ...     print("hi")
> >>> result = hello()
> hi
> >>> print(result)
> None
> ```

> **Note**
>
> None is a *singleton* (Python only has one copy of None in the interpreter). The id for this value will always be the same:
>
> ```
> >>> a = None
> >>> id(a)
> 140575303591440
> >>> b = None
> >>> id(b)
> 140575303591440
> ```

Any variable pointing to None will be pointing to the same object. If you wanted to know if a variable is set to None, you typically use is to check for *identity* with these variables rather than using == to check for *equality*:

```
>>> a is b
True
>>> a is not b
False
```

15. Comments, Booleans, and None

is is faster than == and connotes to the programmer that identity is being compared rather than the value.

You can put the is expression in an if statement:

```
>>> if a is None:
...     print("A is not set!")
A is not set!
```

Since None evaluates to False in a boolean context, you could also do the following:

```
>>> if not a:
...     print("A is not set!")
A is not set!
```

But, you should be careful as other values also evaluate to False, such as 0, [], or '' (empty string). Checking against None is explicit.

15.5 np.nan

np.nan stands for 'Not a Number' and is a special floating-point value recognized by all systems that use the standard IEEE floating-point representation. It's part of the NumPy library in Python and is used to represent undefined or unrepresentable values, especially in data analysis.

In a boolean context, np.nan always coerces to True:

```
>>> import numpy as np
>>> bool(np.nan)
True
```

Note

When conducting numerical operations, any mathematical operation with np.nan always yields np.nan:

```
>>> np.nan + 1
nan
>>> np.nan * 2
nan
```

This behavior is often useful in data science, as it allows us to carry on with computations in the presence of missing data.

By definition, np.nan is not equal to itself:

```
>>> np.nan == np.nan
False
```

To check if something is np.nan, use the np.isnan function or is.

```
>>> a = np.nan
>>> a == np.nan
False
>>> a is np.nan
True
>>> np.isnan(a)
True
```

15.6 Summary

In this chapter, you learned about comments in Python. Comments are started with a hash, and any content following the hash until the end of the line is ignored. There are no multi-line comments.

The chapter also discussed True, False, and boolean coercion. Most values are True in a boolean context (when used in an if statement). The False values are zero, None, and empty sequences.

Finally, the None object was mentioned. It is a singleton that is used to indicate that you have a variable that may be assigned a value in the future. It is also the result of a function that does not explicitly return a value.

15.7 Exercises

1. Create a variable, age, set to your age. Create another variable, old, which uses a condition to test whether you are older than 18. The value of old should be True or False.
2. Create a variable, name, set to your name. Create another variable, second_half, that tests whether the name would be classified in the second half of the alphabet. What do you need to compare it to?
3. Create a list, names, with the names of people in a class. Write code to print 'The class is empty!' or 'Class has enrollments.', based on whether there are values in names. (See the tip in this chapter for details).
4. Create a variable, car, set to None. Write code to print 'Taxi for you!', or 'You have a car!', based on whether or not car is set (None is not the name of a car).

Chapter 16

Conditionals and Whitespace

Programming is filled with decisions. In Python, decisions are made using conditionals. Whether determining if one number is larger than another or checking if a specific item is in a list, conditionals play a pivotal role in guiding a program's flow. In this chapter, we explore conditionals and whitespace in shaping this logic.

16.1 Operations

In addition to the boolean values, True and False, in Python, you can also use expressions to get boolean values. If you have two numbers, you might want to compare them to check if they are greater than or less than each other. The operators, > and <, do this respectively:

```
>>> 5 > 9
False
```

Here is a table of comparison operations to create boolean values:

Operator	Meaning
>	Greater than
<	Less than
>=	Greater than or equal to
<=	Less than or equal to
==	Equal to
!=	Not equal to
is	Identical object
is not	Not identical object

These operations work on most types. If you create a custom class that defines the appropriate magic methods, your class can use them as well:

111

16. Conditionals and Whitespace

```
>>> name = 'Matt'
>>> name == 'Matt'
True
>>> name != 'Fred'
True
>>> 1 > 3
False
```

> **Note**
>
> The "rich comparison" magic methods, __gt__, __lt__, __ge__, __le__, __eq__, and __ne__ correspond to >, <, >=, <=, ==, and != respectively. Defining all of these can be somewhat tedious and repetitive. For classes where these comparisons are commonly used, the functools.total_ordering class decorator gives you all of the comparison functionality as long as you define __eq__ and __le__. The decorator will automatically derive the remainder of the comparison methods. Otherwise, all six methods should be implemented:
>
> ```
> >>> import functools
> >>> @functools.total_ordering
> ... class Abs:
> ...     def __init__(self, num):
> ...         self.num = abs(num)
> ...     def __eq__(self, other):
> ...         return self.num == abs(other.num)
> ...     def __lt__(self, other):
> ...         return self.num < abs(other.num)
> >>> five = Abs(-5)
> >>> four = Abs(-4)
> >>> five > four  # not using less than!
> True
> ```
>
> Decorators are considered an intermediate subject and are not covered in this beginning book.

16.2 Combining conditionals

Conditional expressions are combined using *boolean logic*. This logic consists of the and, or, and not operators.

Boolean Operator	Meaning
x and y	Both x and y must evaluate to True for true result
x or y	If x or y is True, result is true

112

16.2. Combining conditionals

Boolean Operator	Meaning
not x	Negate the value of x (True becomes False and vice versa)

Below is a simple example of setting a grade based on a score using and to test whether the score is between two numbers:

```
>>> score = 91
>>> if score > 90 and score <= 100:
...     grade = 'A'
```

> **Note**
>
> Python allows you to do the above example using a *range comparison* like this:
>
> ```
> >>> if 90 < score <=100:
> ...     grade = 'A'
> ```
>
> Either style works, but range comparisons are not common in other languages.

Here is an example for checking if a given name is a member of a band:

```
>>> name = 'Paul'
>>> beatle = False
>>> if name == 'George' or \
...    name == 'Ringo' or \
...    name == 'John' or \
...    name == 'Paul':
...     beatle = True
... else:
...     beatle = False
```

> **Note**
>
> In the above example, the \ at the end of "'George' or \" indicates that the statement will be continued on the next line.
>
> Like most programming languages, Python allows you to wrap conditional statements in parentheses. Because they are not required in Python, most developers leave them out unless they are needed for operator precedence. But another subtlety of using parentheses is that they serve as a hint to the interpreter when a statement is still open and will be continued on the next line. Hence the \ is not needed in that case:
>
> ```
> >>> name = 'Paul'
> ```

113

16. Conditionals and Whitespace

```
>>> beatle = False
>>> if (name == 'George' or
...      name == 'Ringo' or
...      name == 'John' or
...      name == 'Paul'):
...     beatle = True
... else:
...     beatle = False
```

Note

An idiomatic Python version of checking membership is listed below. To check if a value is found across a variety of values, you can throw the values in a set and use the `in` operator. Here we are using a set literal to represent the members of the Beatles and then checking if the name is in the set. Sets are discussed in a later chapter, *Containers: Lists, Tuples, and Sets*:

```
>>> beatles = {'George', 'Ringo', 'John', 'Paul'}
>>> beatle = name in beatles
```

A later chapter will discuss sets further.

Here is an example of using the `not` keyword in a conditional statement:

```
>>> last_name = 'unknown'
>>> if name == 'Paul' and not beatle:
...     last_name = 'Revere'
```

16.3 If Statements

Booleans (`True` and `False`) are often used in *conditional* statements. Conditional statements are instructions that say, "if this statement is true, perform a block of code, otherwise execute some other code." Branching statements are used frequently in Python. Sometimes, the "if statement" will check values that contain booleans, other times it will check *expressions* that evaluate to booleans. Another common check is for implicit coercion to "truthy" or "falsey" values:

```
>>> debug = True
>>> if debug:    # checking a boolean
...     print("Debugging")
Debugging
```

16.4 Else Statements

An else statement can be used in combination with an if statement. The body of the else statement will execute only if the if statement evaluates to False. Here is an example of combining an else statement with an if statement. The school below appears to have grade inflation:

```
>>> score = 87
>>> if score >= 90:
...     grade = 'A'
... else:
...     grade = 'B'
```

Note that the *expression*, score >= 90, is evaluated by Python and turns into a False. Because the "if statement" was false, the statements under the else block are executed, and the grade variable is set to 'B'.

16.5 More Choices

The previous example does not work for most schools. You can add more intermediate steps if needed using the elif keyword. elif is an abbreviation for "else if". Below is a complete grading scheme:

```
>>> score = 87
>>> if score >= 90:
...     grade = 'A'
... elif score >= 80:
...     grade = 'B'
... elif score >= 70:
...     grade = 'C'
... elif score >= 60:
...     grade = 'D'
... else:
...     grade = 'F'
```

The if, elif, and else statements above each have their own block. Python will start from the top trying to find a statement that evaluates to True, when it does, it runs the block and then continues executing at the code following all of the elif and else blocks. If none of the if or elif statements are True, it runs the block for the else statement.

> **Note**
>
> The if statement can have zero or more elif statements. The else statement is optional. If it exists, there can only be one.

16. Conditionals and Whitespace

16.6 Whitespace

A peculiarity you may have noticed is the colon (:) following the boolean expression in the if statement. The lines immediately after the if statement were indented by four spaces. The indented lines are the *block* of code executed when the if expression evaluates to True.

In other languages, an if statement might look like this:

```
if (score >= 90) {
    grade = 'A';
}
```

In many of these languages, the curly braces denote the boundaries of the if block. Any code between these braces is executed when the score is greater than or equal to 90.

Python, unlike those other languages, uses two things to denote blocks:

- a colon (:)
- indentation

If you have programmed in other languages, learning the whitespace rules in Python is easy. All you have to do is replace the left curly bracket with a colon and consistently indent until the block's end.

> **Note**
>
> What is consistent indentation? Typically, either tabs or spaces are used to indent code. The Python interpreter only cares about consistency on a per-file basis. It is possible to have a project with different files that each use different indentation schemes, but this would be silly.
>
> In Python, using four spaces is the preferred way to indent code. This is described in PEP 8[a]. If you mix tabs and spaces in the same file, you will eventually run into problems.
>
> Although spaces are preferred, it is better to be consistent if you are working on code that already uses tabs. In that case, continue using tabs with the code.
>
> The python3 executable will complain with a TabError when you mix tabs and spaces.
>
> ---
> [a]https://www.python.org/dev/peps/pep-0008/#tabs-or-spaces

16.7 Pandas Chains

You will chain multiple methods together when you do more advanced Pandas operations.

The code might look like this:

```
dataframe.sample(...).filter(...).assign(...).rename(...)
```

Often, it makes the code much easier to read by wrapping it with parentheses and putting each operation on its own like this:

```
(dataframe
    .sample(...)
    .filter(...)
    .assign(...)
    .rename(...)
)
```

In this case, the first and last parentheses act as operator precedence controls (and not method invocation parentheses). Inside the parentheses, we can add new lines and indent as we please.

When using precedence parentheses to do method chaining in Python, you can freely use newlines and indentation for clarity. The Python interpreter sees the entire expression as one line of code. This is a great way to write readable, complex data transformations.

16.8 Summary

This chapter discussed the `if` statement. This statement can be used to create arbitrarily complex conditions when combining expressions with and, or, and not.

Blocks, indentation, and whitespace were also discussed. Sometimes when people encounter Python, the required whitespace rules may seem like a nuisance. I've run across such people in my training. When asked if and why they indent code in other languages, they reply, "Of course, it makes code more readable". In Python, you emphasize readability, and enforcing whitespace tends to aid readability.

16.9 Exercises

1. Write an if statement to determine whether a variable holding a year is a leap year. (See the *Numbers* chapter exercises for the rules for leap years).
2. Write an if statement to determine whether a variable holding an integer is odd.
3. Write an if statement. Look at the indented block and check if your editor indented with tabs or spaces. If it is indented with tabs, configure your editor to indent with spaces. Some editors show tabs differently, if yours does not distinguish between tabs and spaces, an easy way to check if the spacing is a tab is to cursor over it. If the cursor jumps four or eight characters, then it inserted a tab character.

Chapter 17

Containers: Lists, Tuples, and Sets

Many types discussed so far have been *scalars*, which hold a single value. Integers, floats, and booleans are all scalar values.

Containers hold multiple objects (scalar types or even other containers). This chapter will discuss some of these types—lists, tuples, and sets.

17.1 Lists

Lists, as the name implies, hold a list of objects. In Python, a list may hold any type of item and even items with different types. However, in practice, you only store a single item type in a list. Another way to think of a list is that it can provide an order to a sequence of items. They are a *mutable type*, meaning you can add, remove, and alter their contents. There are two ways to create empty lists: one is to invoke the list class (sometimes called the constructor), and the other is to use the square bracket literal syntax—[and]:

```
>>> names = list()
>>> other_names = []
```

If you want to have prepopulated lists, you can provide the values in between the square brackets, using the *literal syntax*:

```
>>> other_names = ['Fred', 'Charles']
```

> **Note**
>
> The list class can also create prepopulated lists, but it is somewhat redundant because you have to pass a sequence (often in the form of a list) into it:
>
> ```
> >>> other_names = list(['Fred', 'Charles'])
> ```

17. Containers: Lists, Tuples, and Sets

Typically, this class is used to coerce other sequence types into a list. For example, a string is a sequence of characters. If you pass a string into `list`, you get back a list of the individual characters:

```
>>> list('Matt')
['M', 'a', 't', 't']
```

Lists, like other types, have methods that you can call on them (use `dir([])` to see a complete list of them). For example, to add items to the end of a list, use the `.append` method:

```
>>> names.append('Matt')
>>> names.append('Fred')
>>> names
['Matt', 'Fred']
```

Remember that lists are mutable. Python does not return a new list when you append to a list. Notice that the call to `.append` did not return a list (the REPL didn't print anything out). Rather, it returns None and updates the list in place. (In Python, the default return value is None for a function or a method. There is no way to have a method that doesn't return anything).

17.2 Sequence Indices

A list is one of the *sequence* types in Python. Sequences hold ordered collections of objects. To work effectively with sequences, it is crucial to understand what an *index* is. Every item in a list has an associated index, which describes its location in the list. For example, the ingredients in potato chips are potatoes, oil, and salt, typically listed in that order. Potatoes are the first ingredient on the list because they the are largest component, oil is the second largest component, and salt is the third.

In many programming languages, the first item in a sequence is at index 0, the second item is at index 1, the third at index 2, and so on. Counting beginning with zero is called *zero-based indexing*.

You can access an item in a list using the bracket notation and the index of said item:

```
>>> names[0]
'Matt'
>>> names[1]
'Fred'
```

Zero-based indexing, where the first element of a list or array is accessed with the index 0, is a common convention in many programming languages, including Python. This approach has both historical and logical justifications.

Historically, the origin of zero-based indexing can be traced back to low-level programming and the way memory allocation works: an array's name

17.3 List Insertion

in memory gives the address of the start, and adding the index provides the offset. Hence, an offset of 0 naturally retrieves the first element.

Logically, zero-based indexing aligns with mathematical concepts making certain computations more straightforward. By starting our counting from zero, we create a consistent, mathematical, and intuitive foundation for array manipulations, ensuring that both novice and seasoned programmers can quickly grasp and harness the power of data structures in Python.

17.3 List Insertion

To insert an item at a certain *index*, use the `.insert` method. Calling `.insert` will shift any items following that index to the right:

```
>>> names.insert(0, 'George')
>>> names
['George', 'Matt', 'Fred']
```

The syntax for replacement at an index is the bracket notation:

```
>>> names[1] = 'Henry'
>>> names
['George', 'Henry', 'Fred']
```

To append items to the end of a list, use the `.append` method:

```
>>> names.append('Paul')
>>> names
['George', 'Henry', 'Fred', 'Paul']
```

> **Note**
>
> CPython's underlying implementation of a list is a C array of pointers. You could imagine it as a row of boxes. This provides quick random access to indices at a given box. Also, appending and removing at the end of a list is quick (O(1)).
>
> While inserting and removing from the middle of a list is slower (O(n)). You need to make sure there is not an empty box in the middle, so you need to shuffle the other items to fill in the gap.
>
> If you find yourself inserting and popping from the front of a list, `collections.deque` is a better data structure to use.

17.4 List Deletion

To remove an item, use the `.remove` method:

17. Containers: Lists, Tuples, and Sets

```
>>> names.remove('Paul')
>>> names
['George', 'Henry', 'Fred']
```

You can also delete by index using the bracket notation:

```
>>> del names[1]
>>> names
['George', 'Fred']
```

17.5 Sorting Lists

A common operation on lists is *sorting*. The .sort method orders the values in the list. This method sorts the list *in place*. It does not return a new, sorted copy of the list. Rather, it updates the list with the items reordered:

```
>>> names.sort()
>>> print(names)
['Fred', 'George']
```

If the previous order of the list was important, you can make a copy of it before sorting. A more general option for sorting sequences is the sorted function. The sorted function works with any sequence. It returns a new list that is ordered:

```
>>> old = [5, 3, -2, 1]
>>> nums_sorted = sorted(old)
>>> print(nums_sorted)
[-2, 1, 3, 5]

>>> print(old)
[5, 3, -2, 1]
```

Note that the original list, old is not changed.

Be careful about what you sort. Python wants you to be explicit. In Python 3, when you try to sort a list that contains heterogeneous types, you might get an error:

```
>>> things = [2, 'abc', 'Zebra', '1']
>>> things.sort()
Traceback (most recent call last):
    ...
TypeError: '<' not supported between instances of 'str' and 'int'
```

Both the .sort method and sorted function allow arbitrary control of sorting by passing in a function for the key parameter. The key parameter can

17.5. Sorting Lists

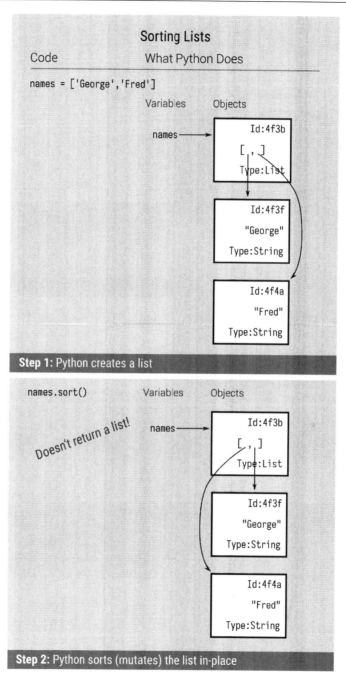

Figure 17.1: This illustrates sorting a list with the .sort method. Note that the list is sorted in place. The result of calling the .sort method is the list is mutated, and the method returns None.

17. Containers: Lists, Tuples, and Sets

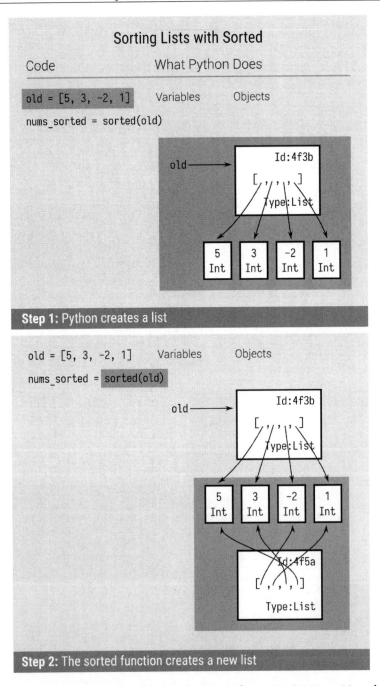

Figure 17.2: This illustrates sorting a list by using the sorted function. Note that the list is not modified, rather a new list is created. Also, note that Python reused the items of the list. It did not create new items.

17.5. Sorting Lists

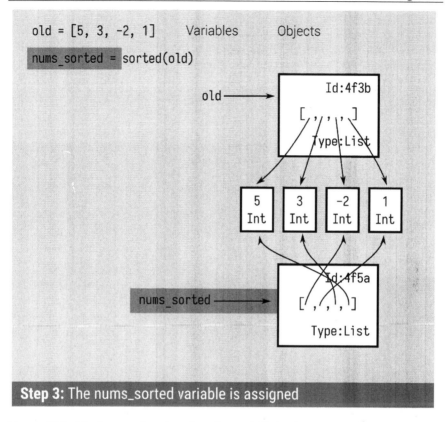

Figure 17.3: Final steps showing that the variable assignment is used to create a variable pointing to the new list. Note that the sorted function works with any sequence, not only lists.

be any callable (function, class, method) that takes a single item and returns something that can be compared.

In this example, by passing in str as the key parameter, every item in the list is sorted as if it were a string:

```
>>> things.sort(key=str)
>>> print(things)
['1', 2, 'Zebra', 'abc']
```

You can also reverse the order of the sort by passing in reverse=True:

```
>>> things.sort(key=str, reverse=True)
>>> print(things)
['abc', 'Zebra', 2, '1']
```

17. Containers: Lists, Tuples, and Sets

17.6 Useful List Hints

As usual, there are other methods found on lists. Do not hesitate to open the Python interpreter and type in a few examples. Remember that `dir` and `help` are your friends.

> **Note**
>
> range is a built-in that constructs integer sequences. Unlike a list, that materializes the entire sequence, range is lazy. It only computes the next value when needed. This is useful when you need to iterate over a large sequence of numbers. The following will create the numbers zero through four:
>
> ```
> >>> nums = range(5)
> >>> nums
> range(0, 5)
> ```

Python 3 tends to be lazy. Note that `range` does not materialize the list, but rather gives you an iterable that will return those numbers when iterated over. By passing the result into `list`, you can see the numbers it would generate:

```
>>> list(nums)
[0, 1, 2, 3, 4]
```

Notice that `range` does not include 5 in its sequence. Many Python functions dealing with final indices mean "up to but not including". (Slices are another example of this you will see later).

If you need to start at a non-zero number, `range` will accept two parameters. When there are two parameters, the first is the starting number (including itself), and the second is the "up to but not including" number:

```
# numbers from 2 to 5
>>> nums2 = range(2, 6)
>>> nums2
range(2, 6)
```

`range` also has an optional third parameter—*stride*. A stride of one (which is the default) means the next number in the sequence that `range` returns should be one more than the previous. A stride of 2 would return every other number. Below is an example that returns only even numbers below eleven:

```
>>> even = range(0, 11, 2)
>>> even
range(0, 11, 2)
>>> list(even)
[0, 2, 4, 6, 8, 10]
```

> **Note**
>
> Remember how we said counting from 0 was mathematically based? The "up to but not including" construct builds on this and is more formally known as the *half-open interval* convention. It is commonly used when defining sequences of natural numbers. This construct has a few nice properties:
>
> - The difference between the end and start is the length when dealing with a sequence of consecutive numbers
> - Two subsequences can be spliced together cleanly without overlap

Python adopts this half-open interval idiom widely. Here is an example:

```
>>> a = range(0, 5)
>>> b = range(5, 10)
>>> both = list(a) + list(b)
>>> len(both)   # 10 - 0
10
>>> both
[0, 1, 2, 3, 4, 5, 6, 7, 8, 9]
```

If you are dealing with numeric sequences you might want to follow suit, especially when defining APIs.

Famous computer scientist, Edsger Dijkstra, posited the reasons for using zero-based indexing, and why it is the correct choice.[1] He ends by saying:

> Many programming languages have been designed without due attention to this detail.

Luckily, Python is not one of those languages.

> **Note**
>
> Python provides support for *generators*. Generators are a way to create lazy sequences. They are similar to range in that they do not materialize the entire sequence. They are beyond the scope of this book, but you can read more about them in my Intermediate Python book.

17.7 Tuples

Tuples (commonly pronounced as either "two"-ples or "tuh"-ples) are *immutable* sequences. You should think of them as ordered records. Once you create them, you cannot change them. To create a tuple using the *literal syntax*, use parentheses around the members and commas in between. There

---

[1] https://www.cs.utexas.edu/users/EWD/transcriptions/EWD08xx/EWD831.html

17. Containers: Lists, Tuples, and Sets

is also a `tuple` class that you can use to construct a new tuple from an existing sequence:

```
>>> row = ('George', 'Guitar')
>>> row
('George', 'Guitar')
>>> row2 = ('Paul', 'Bass')
>>> row2
('Paul', 'Bass')
```

You can create tuples with zero or one item in them. Though in practice, because tuples hold record-type data, this isn't super common. There are two ways to create an empty tuple, using either the `tuple` function or the literal syntax:

```
>>> empty = tuple()
>>> empty
()
>>> empty = ()
>>> empty
()
```

Here are three ways to create a tuple with one item in it:

```
>>> one = tuple([1])
>>> one
(1,)
>>> one = (1,)
>>> one
(1,)
>>> one = 1,
>>> one
(1,)
```

> **Note**
>
> Parentheses are used for denoting the calling of functions or methods in Python. They are also used to specify operator precedence. In addition, they may be used in tuple creation. This overloading of parentheses can lead to confusion. Here is the simple rule: if there is one item in the parentheses, then Python treats the parentheses as normal parentheses (for operator precedence), such as those that you might use when writing (2 + 3) * 8. If commas separate multiple items (without square brackets), then Python treats them as a tuple:
>
> ```
> >>> d = (3)
> >>> type(d)
> ```

128

```
<class 'int'>
```

In the above example, d might look like a tuple with parentheses, but Python claims it is an integer. For tuples with only one item, you need to put a comma (,) following the item—or use the `tuple` class with a single item list:

```
>>> e = (3,)
>>> type(e)
<class 'tuple'>
```

Having said all of this, how often in the real world do I use a single item tuple? Never. If I only need a single item, why stick it in a tuple?

Here are three ways to create a tuple with more than one item. Typically, you would use the last one to be Pythonic. Because it has parentheses it is easier to see that it is a tuple:

```
>>> p = tuple(['Steph', 'Curry', 'Guard'])
>>> p
('Steph', 'Curry', 'Guard')
>>> p = 'Steph', 'Curry', 'Guard'
>>> p
('Steph', 'Curry', 'Guard')
>>> p = ('Steph', 'Curry', 'Guard')
>>> p
('Steph', 'Curry', 'Guard')
```

Because tuples are immutable, you cannot append to them:

```
>>> p.append('Golden State')
Traceback (most recent call last):
  File "<stdin>", line 1, in <module>
AttributeError: 'tuple' object has no attribute 'append'
```

Note

Why the distinction between tuples and lists? Why not use lists since they appear to be a super-set of tuples.

The main difference between the objects is mutability. However, I like to think of the difference between them as hints to the reader of a program. A list hints that I have items of the same type and might want to have them in a different order. A tuple indicates that I have data that goes together and is often not of the same type.

17. Containers: Lists, Tuples, and Sets

> Because tuples are immutable, they can serve as keys in dictionaries. Tuples are often used to represent a record of data, such as the row of a database query, which may contain heterogeneous types of objects. Perhaps a tuple would contain a name, address, and age:
>
> ```
> >>> person = ('Matt', '123 North 456 East', 24)
> ```
>
> Tuples are used for returning multiple items from a function. Tuples also serve as a hint to the developer that this type is not meant to be modified.
>
> Tuples also use less memory than lists. If you have sequences that you are not mutating, consider using tuples to conserve memory.

17.8 Sets

Another container type found in Python is a *set*. A set is an unordered collection that cannot contain duplicates. Like a tuple, it can be instantiated with a list or anything you can iterate over. Unlike a list or a tuple, a set does not care about order. Sets are beneficial for two things: removing duplicates and checking membership. Because the lookup mechanism is based on the optimized hash function found in dictionaries, a lookup operation takes very little time, even on large sets.

> **Note**
>
> Because sets must be able to compute a hash value for each item in the set, sets can only contain items that are *hashable*. A hash is a semi-unique number for a given object. If an object is hashable, it will always generate the same hash number.
>
> In Python, mutable items are not hashable. This means that you cannot hash a list or dictionary. To hash your own user-created classes, you must implement __hash__ and __eq__.

Sets can be specified by passing in a sequence into the set class (another coercion class that appears as a function):

```
>>> digits = [0, 1, 1, 2, 3, 4, 5, 6,
...     7, 8, 9]
>>> digit_set = set(digits)   # remove extra 1
```

They can also be created with a literal syntax using { and }:

```
>>> digit_set = {0, 1, 1, 2, 3, 4, 5, 6,
...     7, 8, 9}
```

As was mentioned, a set is great for removing duplicates. When a set is created from a sequence, any duplicates are removed. The extra 1 was removed from digit_set:

17.8. Sets

```
>>> digit_set
{0, 1, 2, 3, 4, 5, 6, 7, 8, 9}
```

To check for membership, you use the in operation:

```
>>> 9 in digit_set
True
>>> 42 in digit_set
False
```

> **Note**
>
> There is a contains protocol in Python. If a class (set or list, or user-defined class) implements the __contains__ method (or the iteration protocol), you can use in to check for membership. Due to how sets are implemented, membership tests against them can be much quicker than tests against a list.

Below, a set called odd is created. This set will aid in the following examples:

```
>>> odd = {1, 3, 5, 7, 9}
```

Sets provide *set operations*, such as union (|), intersection (&), difference (-), and xor (^).

The *difference* (-) operator removes items in one set from another:

```
>>> odd = {1, 3, 5, 7, 9}
>>> # set difference
>>> even = digit_set - odd
>>> even
{0, 8, 2, 4, 6}
```

Notice that the order of the result is somewhat arbitrary at a casual glance. If the order is important, a set is not the data type you should use.

The *intersection* (&) operation (you can think of it as the area where two roads intersect) returns the items found in both sets:

```
>>> prime = set([2, 3, 5, 7])
# those in both
>>> prime_even = prime & even
>>> prime_even
{2}
```

The *union* (|) operation returns a set composed of all the items from both sets, with duplicates removed:

131

```
>>> numbers = odd | even
>>> print(numbers)
{0, 1, 2, 3, 4, 5, 6, 7, 8, 9}
```

Xor (^) is an operation that returns a set of items that only are found in one set or the other, but not both:

```
>>> first_five = set([0, 1, 2, 3, 4])
>>> two_to_six = set([2, 3, 4, 5, 6])
>>> in_one = first_five ^ two_to_six
>>> print(in_one)
{0, 1, 5, 6}
```

> **Note**
>
> Why use a set instead of a list? Remember that sets are optimized for membership testing and removing duplicates. If you find yourself performing unions or differences among lists, look into using a set instead.

Sets are also much quicker for testing membership. The in operator runs faster for sets than lists. However, this speed comes at a cost. Sets do not keep the elements in order, whereas lists and tuples do. If the order is important to you, use a data structure that remembers the order.

17.9 Summary

This chapter discussed a few of the built-in container types. You saw lists, which are ordered mutable sequences. Remember that a list method does not return a new list but typically will change the list in place. Lists will support inserting any item, but you typically put items of the same type in a list.

You also saw tuples. Tuples are also ordered like lists. Unlike lists, however, tuples do not support mutation. In practice, you use them to represent a record of data, like a row retrieved from a database. When they are representing records, they might hold different types of objects.

Finally, sets were introduced. Sets are mutable, but they are unordered. They are used to remove duplicates and check membership. Because of their hashing mechanism, these set operations are fast and efficient. But it requires that the items in the set are hashable.

17.10 Exercises

1. Create a list. Append the names of your colleagues and friends to it. Has the id of the list changed? Sort the list. What is the first item in the list? What is the second item in the list?

17.10. Exercises

2. Create a tuple with your first name, last name, and age. Create a list, people, and append your tuple to it. Make more tuples with the corresponding information from your friends and append them to the list. Sort the list. When you learn about functions, you can use the key parameter to sort by any field in the tuple, first name, last name, or age.
3. Create a list of the names of first names your friends. Create a list with the top ten common names. Use set operations to see if any of your friends have common names.
4. Go to Project Gutenberg[11] and find a page of text from Shakespeare. Paste it into a triple-quoted string. Create another string with a paragraph of text from Ralph Waldo Emerson. Use the string's .split method to get a list of words from each. Using set operations find the common words and words unique to both authors.
5. Tuples and lists are similar but have different behavior. Use set operations to find the attributes of a list object that are not in a tuple object.

Chapter 18

NumPy Sequences

We just explored Python lists. In this section, we will explore into one such type of container provided by the NumPy library – the NumPy arrays.

18.1 NumPy Arrays

NumPy arrays, like Python lists, hold a sequence of items. However, they are explicitly designed for numerical computations and have several advantages over lists for such tasks. A significant difference is that NumPy arrays are homogenous, i.e., they hold items of a single type. Furthermore, they provide many mathematical operations that can be performed on the whole array simultaneously.

A NumPy array can be created using the np.array function. You can pass a Python list (or other sequence-like objects) to this function to create an array.

Imagine you have temperature readings over a week, and you want to analyze them. You can store these readings in a NumPy array:

```
>>> import numpy as np
>>> temps = np.array([68, 72, 75, 69, 71, 73, 74])
>>> temps
array([68, 72, 75, 69, 71, 73, 74])
```

> **Note**
>
> NumPy arrays are different from Python lists. While you can create a NumPy array from a Python list, the resulting array is an instance of the numpy.ndarray class, not the list class.

NumPy arrays, like lists, have an associated index for each item, starting from zero. Each temperature in the array has a position number. We can use this number to look at specific temperatures:

18. NumPy Sequences

```
>>> temps[0]
68

>>> temps[3]
69
```

18.2 NumPy Array Operations

One of the coolest parts about NumPy arrays is how they let you do things to all the temperatures simultaneously, something regular Python lists can't do. Let's say you want to convert all those Fahrenheit readings into Celsius:

```
>>> celsius_temps = (temps - 32) * 5/9
>>> celsius_temps
array([20.        , 22.22222222, 23.88888889, 20.55555556, 21.66666667,
       22.77777778, 23.33333333])
```

> **Note**
>
> This ability to perform operations on all elements at once is often referred to as "vectorization," and it allows for faster execution and more readable code.

If we were to do something similar with a Python list, the code would be much more complicated:

```
>>> py_temps = [68, 72, 75, 69, 71, 73, 74])
>>> celsius_temps = []
>>> for temp in py_temps:
...     celsius_temps.append((temp - 32) * 5/9)

>>> celsius_temps
[20.0, 22.22222222222222, 23.88888888888889, 20.555555555555557,
 21.666666666666668, 22.77777777777778, 23.333333333333332]
```

By using NumPy arrays, we can perform operations on all the elements at once, which is much more efficient and readable.

18.3 NumPy Array Shape

NumPy arrays can have any number of dimensions, and the size of each dimension is stored in the array's shape attribute. For a 1-dimensional array, the shape will be a tuple with a single item:

```
>>> temps.shape
(7,)
```

18.4. Statistical Methods

We can also reshape an array without changing its data. For example, we can reshape our array into a 2D array (a matrix):

```
>>> arr_2d = temps.reshape(7, 1)
>>> arr_2d
array([[68],
       [72],
       [75],
       [69],
       [71],
       [73],
       [74]])

>>> arr_2d.shape
(7, 1)
```

18.4 Statistical Methods

NumPy offers a rich set of statistical methods for performing computations on arrays. Imagine you want to explore the temperature data.

To get a sense of the average temperature throughout the week, you'd use *mean*. The mean gives the average value across the dataset. Let's find out our average temperature:

```
>>> np.mean(temps)
71.71428571428571
```

When analyzing data, we're often interested in the middlemost value or the *median*. In the context of our temperature data, the median can help us identify the temperature that sits right between the hottest and coolest days:

```
>>> np.median(temps)
72.0
```

Understanding how spread out our temperatures were during the week is equally important. This is where *standard deviation* comes in handy. A higher standard deviation would indicate that the temperatures varied significantly throughout the week:

```
>>> np.std(temps)
2.3733211036908783
```

Additionally, you can gain insights into the week's temperature by looking at the *sum, minimum,* and *maximum* values. These functions let you know the total temperatures recorded, the coolest day, and the hottest day, respectively:

18. NumPy Sequences

```
>>> np.sum(temps)
502
>>> np.min(temps)
68
>>> np.max(temps)
75
```

18.5 Manipulating Arrays with NumPy

Suppose you've been recording daily temperatures for two weeks, and you've collected 14 data points. Using NumPy, you can easily manipulate and analyze this data. Let's start by defining our temperature data:

```
>>> import numpy as np
>>> temperatures = np.array([72, 75, 78, 77, 73, 80, 79, 76, 75, 74, 71, 70,
...     68, 72])
```

Imagine you'd like to *reshape* this data to view it week by week. You can rearrange this flat array into a 2x7 matrix, where each row represents a week:

```
>>> weeks = np.reshape(temperatures, (2, 7))
>>> weeks
array([[72, 75, 78, 77, 73, 80, 79],
       [76, 75, 74, 71, 70, 68, 72]])
```

Sometimes, you might be interested in a sequential list of temperatures, but focusing on weekdays across the weeks. This can be achieved using the np.ravel function:

```
>>> np.ravel(weeks)
array([72, 75, 78, 77, 73, 80, 79, 76, 75, 74, 71, 70, 68, 72])
```

In certain analyses, you might want to compare temperatures of specific days across the two weeks. For instance, compare all Mondays, all Tuesdays, etc. The np.transpose function can help:

```
>>> np.transpose(weeks)
array([[72, 76],
       [75, 75],
       [78, 74],
       [77, 71],
       [73, 70],
       [80, 68],
       [79, 72]])
```

Lastly, if you want to examine temperature trends by looking at the data in reverse — perhaps to see if temperatures are dropping towards the end of the two weeks — you can use np.flip:

```
>>> np.flip(temperatures)
array([72, 68, 70, 71, 74, 75, 76, 79, 80, 73, 77, 78, 75, 72])
```

18.6 Mathematical Methods

NumPy's suite of mathematical functions offers robust tools to manipulate and compare datasets. This section will explore the practical application of these functions on a hypothetical two-week temperature dataset from two cities.

Let's consider two weeks of daily temperature data from two cities: CityA and CityB:

```
>>> import numpy as np
>>> np.random.seed(42)
>>> temp_a = np.random.randint(15, 30, size=14)
>>> temp_b = np.random.randint(10, 35, size=14)

>>> temp_a
array([21, 18, 27, 29, 25, 22, 27, 19, 21, 24, 17, 21, 25, 25])


>>> temp_b
array([33, 30, 13, 17, 33, 12, 31, 30, 11, 33, 21, 15, 11, 30])
```

To gain insights into daily regional climate variations between the two cities, we could subtract them:

```
>>> temp_diff = np.subtract(temp_a, temp_b)
>>> temp_diff
array([-12, -12,  14,  12,  -8,  10,  -4, -11,  10,  -9,  -4,   6,  14,
        -5])
```

Sometimes, recorded temperature data needs adjustments. Perhaps a sensor was miscalibrated, or an external factor affected the readings. NumPy makes such adjustments easy and efficient. We could use np.add to adjust our temperature data with a daily temperature delta.

After a review, we identified that our temperature recordings for CityA were consistently lower each day. The corrections are as follows (for 14 days):

```
>>> daily_deltas = np.array([0.5, 0.6, 0.7, 0.5, 0.6, 0.5, 0.7, 0.6,
...      0.5, 0.6, 0.7, 0.5, 0.6, 0.7])
```

These daily deltas represent how much we need to adjust the temperature for each day. To apply these adjustments, run this code:

18. NumPy Sequences

```
>>> corrected_a = np.add(temp_a, daily_deltas)
>>> corrected_a
array([21.5, 18.6, 27.7, 29.5, 25.6, 22.5, 27.7, 19.6, 21.5, 24.6, 17.7,
       21.5, 25.6, 25.7])
```

Once we've applied these corrections, we might be interested in understanding how much each observed value deviated from its corrected counterpart.

We can compute:

```
>>> deviation = np.divide((temp_a - corrected_a),
...     corrected_a) * 100
>>> deviation
array([-2.3255814 , -3.22580645, -2.52707581, -1.69491525, -2.34375   ,
       -2.22222222, -2.52707581, -3.06122449, -2.3255814 , -2.43902439,
       -3.95480226, -2.3255814 , -2.34375   , -2.72373541])
```

The deviation percentages array will then offer a clear picture of the deviations for each day, expressed as percentages.

The square root of temperature can be applicable in some thermodynamics scenarios:

```
>>> np.sqrt(temp_a)
array([4.58257569, 4.24264069, 5.19615242, 5.38516481, 5.        ,
       4.69041576, 5.19615242, 4.35889894, 4.58257569, 4.89897949,
       4.12310563, 4.58257569, 5.        , 5.        ])
```

We can compute the natural logarithm of these temperatures using np.log. This is often used as a transformation for machine learning:

```
>>> log_temperatures = np.log(temp_a)
>>> log_temperatures
array([3.04452244, 2.89037176, 3.29583687, 3.36729583, 3.21887582,
       3.09104245, 3.29583687, 2.94443898, 3.04452244, 3.17805383,
       2.83321334, 3.04452244, 3.21887582, 3.21887582])
```

Now, if we take the exponential of these logged values using np.exp, we should retrieve our original temperature values:

```
>>> np.exp(log_temperatures)
array([21., 18., 27., 29., 25., 22., 27., 19., 21., 24., 17., 21., 25.,
       25.])
```

As expected, applying the exponential function to the log-transformed temperatures brings us back to our original values, illustrating the inverse relationship between the two functions.

18.7 Summary

To summarize, we covered the following topics about NumPy arrays:

A NumPy array is a robust data structure that holds a collection of items of the same type, making it ideal for numerical computations. Arrays are created using the np.array() function and can be manipulated in many ways. Unlike Python lists, operations can be performed on entire arrays at once. NumPy arrays have a shape attribute that stores the size of each dimension, and arrays can be reshaped using the reshape method. NumPy provides many valuable methods for arrays, like .sum, .max, and .min.

18.8 Exercises

1. Create a NumPy array of 10 elements, all being 0.
2. Given the array: python   arr = np.array([2, 5, 7, 8, 9, 12]) Write a code snippet that would access the value 8 in arr.
3. Given the array: python   arr = np.array([1, 2, 3, 4, 5]) Find the sum and product of all elements in arr.
4. Use NumPy functions to calculate the square root, and exponent of all elements in the array arr.

Chapter 19

Pandas Series

Python's pandas library offers powerful data structures to handle various data manipulation tasks. The most fundamental of these structures is the Series, a one-dimensional array-like object capable of holding any data type (integers, strings, floats, Python objects, etc.). It is essentially a column in an Excel sheet.

19.1 Series

A Series in pandas, like a list, can hold different types of items. You can create an empty Series or a prepopulated Series using the pd.Series constructor.

```
>>> import pandas as pd
>>> ser = pd.Series()
>>> other_ser = pd.Series(['Fred', 'Charles'])

>>> other_ser
0    Fred
1    Charles
dtype: object
```

> **Note**
>
> While a Series is similar to a list, it offers much more functionality and is equipped with more powerful methods. For instance, it comes with built-in methods to calculate statistical properties such as mean, median, and standard deviation.
>
> You might be wondering why we would want a Series if we have NumPy? Pandas is focused on dealing with tabular data, and it has a lot of functionality for dealing with data that is missing, or has been corrupted. It also has a lot of functionality for dealing with time series data. If you just need to deal with matrices, then NumPy is probably the better choice. If you have tabular data, then Pandas is the better choice.

19. Pandas Series

19.2 Series Indices

Like lists, every item in a Series has an associated index describing its location. You can access an item in a Series using the bracket notation and the index of the item:

```
>>> other_ser[0]
'Fred'
```

```
>>> other_ser[1]
'Charles'
```

In addition to positional indexing, pandas also allows you to use labels as indices, these labels can be set when creating the Series by setting the name parameter:

```
>>> labeled_ser = pd.Series(['Fred', 'Charles'],
...                         index=['Person 1', 'Person 2'])
```

```
>>> labeled_ser
Person 1      Fred
Person 2    Charles
dtype: object
```

```
>>> labeled_ser['Person 1']
'Fred'
```

```
>>> labeled_ser['Person 2']
'Charles'
```

Generally, I don't manually set index values. But it is good to be aware of them and Pandas often *aligns* the index before performing operations.

19.3 Series Insertion and Deletion

The Series object does not directly support methods for insertion of elements as lists do. However, we can achieve similar functionality using other methods.

To append a new item, we can use the pd.concat function which returns a new Series with the appended data:

```
>>> new_ser = pd.concat([other_ser, pd.Series(['George'])])
>>> print(new_ser)
0      Fred
1    Charles
0    George
dtype: object
```

> **Note**
>
> Notice that the indices of the original Series are preserved. If you want to reset the index, use the `ignore_index=True`:
>
> ```
> >>> pd.concat([other_ser, pd.Series(['George'])],
> ...    ignore_index=True)
> 0      Fred
> 1   Charles
> 2    George
> dtype: object
> ```

To delete an item from a Series, we can use the drop method:

```
>>> new_ser = new_ser.drop(0)
>>> print(new_ser)
1   Charles
dtype: object
```

Notice that this dropped both items with index 0. This is because the drop method drops all items with the specified index, not by position.

19.4 Sorting Series

The `.sort_values` method orders the values in the series. Here we will sort the names alphabetically:

```
>>> names = pd.Series(['Fred', 'George', 'Charles'])
>>> names
0      Fred
1    George
2   Charles
dtype: object

>>> names_sorted = names.sort_values()
>>> names_sorted
2   Charles
0      Fred
1    George
dtype: object`
```

This method returns a new Series with sorted values, leaving the original Series unaltered. Be aware that the index values are moved along with the values.

19. Pandas Series

19.5 Useful Series Hints

pandas provides many powerful methods to manipulate and analyze data in a Series. Do not hesitate to use the `dir` and `help` functions to explore them.

If you want to perform element-wise operations on a Series, you can directly use the math operators:

```
>>> num_series = pd.Series([1, 2, 3])
>>> num_series + 5
0    6
1    7
2    8
dtype: int64
```

As with most pandas functions, these operations return a new Series and leave the original Series unchanged.

A Series has the ability to handle missing (or NaN) values. You can check for missing values using the `.isna` method:

```
>>> ser = pd.Series([1, None, 3])
>>> ser
0    1.0
1    NaN
2    3.0
dtype: float64

>>> ser.isna()
0    False
1     True
2    False
dtype: bool
```

You can replace missing values using the `.fillna` method:

```
>>> ser.fillna(0)
0    1.0
1    0.0
2    3.0
dtype: float64
```

In this case, the missing value was replaced by 0. Notice that the datatype of the Series changed to float since NaN is considered a float in pandas.

Remember, pandas Series is a versatile and powerful data structure. While we've covered some of the basic operations, there's a lot more you can do with it. Please refer to the pandas documentation for more details.

19.6 Summary

Pandas Series is a powerful and versatile data structure representing a one-dimensional array-like object of any data type. It is a key component of the pandas library and is used widely in data manipulation and analysis tasks.

In this chapter, we have learned how to create a Series, access and modify its elements, and perform various operations such as sorting, finding maximum and minimum values, and dealing with missing (or NaN) values. Many more operations can be performed on a Series, and I encourage you to explore them.

Like Python lists, a Series uses zero-based indexing and can contain items of different data types. However, a Series provides additional functionality like handling missing data, alignment by index labels, and vectorized operations, which make them superior for data analysis tasks.

19.7 Exercises

1. Create a pandas Series with integers from 1 to 10. Print the Series.

2. Using the Series created in the first exercise, print the element at index 5.

3. Change the element at index 5 to 15 in the Series created in the first exercise.

4. Print the minimum and maximum values of the Series created in the first exercise.

5. Add 5 to all elements of the Series created in the first exercise and print the resulting Series.

Chapter 20

Iteration

A common idiom when dealing with sequences is to loop over the contents of the sequence. You might want to filter out one of the items, apply a function, or print it out. The for loop is one way to do this. This chapter will cover looping and repetition constructs in Python.

20.1 The For Loop

Here is an example of collecting the uppercase strings in from a list:

```
>>> uppers = []
>>> for letter in ['c', 'a', 't']:
...     uppers.append(letter.upper())

>>> print(uppers)
['C', 'A', 'T']
```

During a for loop, Python makes a new variable, letter, that holds the item of iteration. Note that the value of letter is not the index position but rather the string. This variable is not cleaned up by Python after the for loop is done.

If we inspect letter, we can see that it is pointing to the last item in the list:

```
>>> print(letter)
t
```

> **Note**
>
> Be aware that a for loop construct contains a colon (:) followed by the indented code. (The indented code is the *block* of the for loop).

20. Iteration

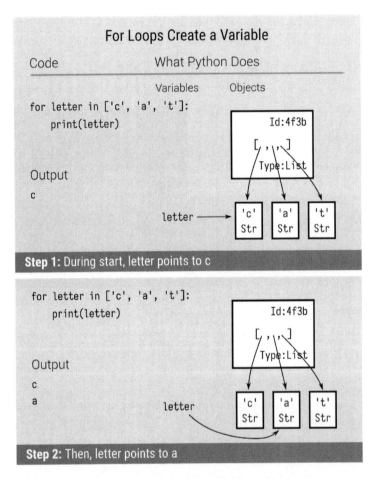

Figure 20.1: This illustrates how a for loop creates a variable. A new variable, letter, is created. At first, it points to 'c', which is printed. Then the loop continues, and the variable points to 'a'.

20.2. Looping with an index

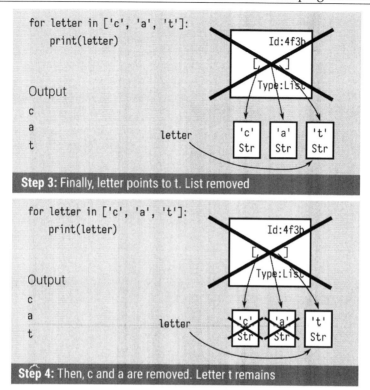

Figure 20.2: The for loop continues with the final loop. After 't' is printed, the loop exits. At this point, the list literal is garbage collected. Because the only thing pointing to 'c' and 'a' was the list, those are also garbage collected. However, the letter variable is still pointing to 't'. Python doesn't clean up this variable. It hangs around after the for loop is done.

20.2 Looping with an index

In languages like C, when you loop over a sequence, you do not loop over the items in the sequence. Rather, you loop over the indices. You can pull out the items at those index values using those indices. Here is one way to do that in Python using the built-in functions range and len:

```
>>> animals = ["cat", "dog", "bird"]
>>> for index in range(len(animals)):
...     print(index, animals[index])
0 cat
1 dog
2 bird
```

20. Iteration

The above code is a *code smell*. A code smell indicates issues with the code where the code may not be wrong, but its design could benefit from refinement or restructuring. It indicates that you are not using Python as you should. Usually, the reason for iterating over a sequence is to get access to the items in the sequence, not the indices. But occasionally, you will also need the index position of the item. Python provides the built-in enumerate function that makes the combination of range and len unnecessary. The enumerate function returns a tuple of (index, item) for every item in the sequence:

```
>>> animals = ["cat", "dog", "bird"]
>>> for index, value in enumerate(animals):
...     print(index, value)
0 cat
1 dog
2 bird
```

Because the tuple is a pair of index and value, you can use *tuple unpacking* to create two variables, index and value, directly in the for loop. You need to put a comma between the variable names. As long as the tuple has the same length as the number of variables you include in the for loop, Python will happily create them for us.

20.3 Breaking Out of a Loop

You may need to stop processing a loop early without going over every item in the loop. The break keyword will jump out of the nearest loop you are in. Below is a program that adds numbers until the first negative one. It uses the break statement to stop processing when it comes across a negative number:

```
>>> numbers = [3, 5, 9, -1, 3, 1]
>>> result = 0
>>> for item in numbers:
...     if item < 0:
...         break
...     result += item

>>> print(result)
17
```

> **Note**
>
> The line:
>
> ```
> result += item
> ```
>
> uses what is called *augmented assignment*. It is similar to writing:

```
result = result + item
```

The augmented assignment is slightly quicker as the lookup for the result variable only occurs once. Another added benefit is that it is easier to type.

Note

The `if` block inside the `for` block is indented eight spaces. Blocks can be nested, and each level needs to be indented consistently.

20.4 Skipping over Items in a Loop

Another common looping idiom is to skip over items. If the body of the `for` loop takes a while to execute, but you only need to execute it for For certain items in the sequence, the `continue` keyword is handy. The `continue` statement tells Python to disregard processing of the current item in the for loop and "continue" from the top of the for block with the next value in the loop.

Here is an example of summing all positive numbers:

```
>>> numbers = [3, 5, 9, -1, 3, 1]

>>> result = 0
>>> for item in numbers:
...     if item < 0:
...         continue
...     result = result + item

>>> print(result)
21
```

20.5 The In Statement can be used for Membership

We have seen the `in` statement in a `for` loop. In Python, the `in` statement can also be used to check for membership. If you want to know if a list contains an item, you can use the `in` statement to check that:

```
>>> animals = ["cat", "dog", "bird"]
>>> 'bird' in animals
True
```

If you want the index location, use the `.index` method:

```
>>> animals.index('bird')
2
```

20.6 Removing Items from Lists During Iteration

It was mentioned previously that lists are mutable. Because they are mutable you can add or remove items from them. Also, lists are sequences, so you can loop over them. Do not mutate the list at the same time that you are looping over it.

For example, if you wanted to filter a list of names so it only contained 'John' or 'Paul', this would be the wrong way to do it:

```
>>> names = ['John', 'Paul', 'George',
...    'Ringo']

>>> for name in names:
...     if name not in ['John', 'Paul']:
...         names.remove(name)

>>> names
['John', 'Paul', 'Ringo']
```

What happened? Python assumes that lists will not be modified while they are being iterated over. When the loop got to 'George', it removed the name from the list. Internally, Python tracks the index location of the for loop. At that point, there are only three items in the list, 'John', 'Paul', and 'Ringo'. But the for loop internally thinks it is on index location 3 (the fourth item), and there is no fourth item so the loop stops, leaving 'Ringo' in.

There are two alternatives to the above construct of removing items from a list during iteration. The first is to collect the items to be removed during a pass through the list. In a subsequent loop, iterate over only the items that need to be deleted (names_to_remove), and remove them from the original list (names):

```
>>> names = ['John', 'Paul', 'George',
...    'Ringo']

>>> names_to_remove = []
>>> for name in names:
...     if name not in ['John', 'Paul']:
...         names_to_remove.append(name)
>>> for name in names_to_remove:
...     names.remove(name)

>>> names
['John', 'Paul']
```

Another option is to iterate over a copy of the list. This can be done relatively painlessly using the [:] slice copy construct that is covered in the chapter on slicing:

```
>>> names = ['John', 'Paul', 'George',
...  'Ringo']
>>> for name in names[:]:  # copy of names
...     if name not in ['John', 'Paul']:
...         names.remove(name)

>>> names
['John', 'Paul']
```

20.7 Else Clauses

A `for` loop can also have an `else` clause. Any code in an `else` block will execute if the `for` loop completes (i.e. did not hit a `break` statement). Below is sample code that checks if numbers in a loop are positive:

```
>>> positive = False
>>> for num in items:
...     if num < 0:
...         break
... else:
...     positive = True
```

Note that `continue` statements do not have any effect on whether an `else` block is executed.

The `else` statement is somewhat oddly named. For a `for` loop, it indicates that the whole sequence was processed. A typical use of an `else` statement in a `for` loop is to indicate that an item was not found.

Suppose you're a software engineer working with a list of passwords, and you need to check if any password in the list is less than 8 characters long (which is considered insecure). Here's how you could do that:

```
passwords = ['myPassword', 'abc123', 'qwerty']

for password in passwords:
    if len(password) < 8:
        print(f"The password '{password}' is too short.")
        break
else:
    print("All passwords are of adequate length.")
```

In this case, the output will be "The password 'abc123' is too short." because 'abc123' is less than 8 characters long. If all the passwords in the list are at least 8 characters long, you will see 'All passwords are of adequate length.' as the output.

20. Iteration

20.8 List Comprenhensionshs

Because doing a mapping operation (calling a function on each item in a list) is so common, Python has a syntactic sugar for doing mapping operations called a list comprehension. Another common operation is to filter a list. And list comprehensions support these as well.

Let's assume we have city temperatures stored in a list. Every item in the list is a tuple of the city name and the temperature in Fahrenheit.

Here's the data:

```
>>> city_temperatures = [('Las Vegas', 104), ('Atlanta', 90),
...     ('Detroit', 85), ('Seattle', 80), ('Paris', 75), ('Tokyo', 75),
...     ('Portland', 60), ('Miami', 95), ('Boston', 60), ('Los Angeles', 85),
...     ('New York', 75), ('Chicago', 90), ('San Francisco', 70)]
```

If we wanted the names of the cities, we could use a normal for loop like this:

```
>>> city_names = []
>>> for city_temp in city_temperatures:
...     city_names.append(city_temp[0])

>>> city_names
['Las Vegas', 'Atlanta', 'Detroit', 'Seattle', 'Paris', 'Tokyo', 'Portland',
 'Miami', 'Boston', 'Los Angeles', 'New York', 'Chicago', 'San Francisco']
```

We can convert that to a single-line list comprehension by realizing that this code is following a standard pattern. We're looping over a list, and for each item in the list, we're doing something with it and appending to a list. In general, this is called a *mapping operation*. The mapping step is what we are doing to each item, in this case pulling out the first item of the tuple.

If you have a mapping operation that looks like this:

```
>>> old_list = [1, 2, 3, 4, 5]
>>> new_list = []
>>> for item in old_list:
...     new_list.append(some_function(item))
```

You can write it as a list comprehension like this:

```
>>> new_list = [some_function(item) for item in old_list]
```

For example, we can convert the above code to a list comprehension like this:

```
>>> city_names = [city_temp[0] for city_temp in city_temperatures]
```

20.9. Filtering with Comprehensions

Let's do another mapping example by converting the temperatures to Celsius. Folks who don't know about list comprehensions will often do something like this:

```
>>> celsius_temperatures = []
>>> for city_temp in city_temperatures:
...     celsius_temperatures.append((city_temp[0],
...                                  (city_temp[1] - 32) * 5 / 9))

>>> celsius_temperatures
[('Las Vegas', 40.0), ('Atlanta', 32.22222222222222),
('Detroit', 29.444444444444443), ('Seattle', 26.666666666666668),
('Paris', 23.88888888888889), ('Tokyo', 23.88888888888889),
('Portland', 15.555555555555555), ('Miami', 35.0),
('Boston', 15.555555555555555), ('Los Angeles', 29.444444444444443),
('New York', 23.88888888888889), ('Chicago', 32.22222222222222),
('San Francisco', 21.11111111111111)]
```

But now we notice that we are looping over a sequence, and for each item in the sequence, we are doing something with it, and appending to a list. That's a mapping operation, so we can convert it to a list comprehension like this:

```
>>> celsius_temperatures = [(city_temp[0], (city_temp[1] - 32) * 5 / 9)
...                         for city_temp in city_temperatures]
```

Note that because the comprehension is within parentheses, I can split it across multiple lines without having to worry about using a backslash to escape the newline. This is a common pattern when you have a long list comprehension.

20.9 Filtering with Comprehensions

Let's look at an example of filtering. Suppose we want to filter out any temperatures that are less than 80 degrees. Here's how we could do that with a for loop:

```
>>> hot_temperatures = []
>>> for city_temp in city_temperatures:
...     if city_temp[1] >= 80:
...         hot_temperatures.append(city_temp)

>>> hot_temperatures
[('Las Vegas', 104), ('Atlanta', 90), ('Detroit', 85), ('Seattle', 80),
('Miami', 95), ('Los Angeles', 85), ('Chicago', 90)]
```

In this case, this is a common pattern called a *filter*. We are filtering out any temperatures that are less than 80 degrees. We can convert this to a list comprehension like this:

```
>>> hot_temperatures = [city_temp for city_temp in city_temperatures
...                     if city_temp[1] >= 80]
```

I put the if statement on the next line, but that is not required.

List comprehensions are used all over the place in Python. They are a very powerful tool that you should be familiar with. Just remember to look for the mapping or filtering pattern.

I'll end with one more example that combines both mapping and filtering. Suppose we want to filter out any temperatures that are less than 80 degrees, and convert the remaining temperatures to Celsius. Here's how we could do that with a for loop:

```
>>> hot_temperatures = []
>>> for city_temp in city_temperatures:
...     if city_temp[1] >= 80:
...         hot_temperatures.append((city_temp[0],
...                                  (city_temp[1] - 32) * 5 / 9))
```

The list comprehension version looks like this:

```
>>> hot_temperatures = [(city_temp[0], (city_temp[1] - 32) * 5 / 9)
...                     for city_temp in city_temperatures
...                     if city_temp[1] >= 80]
```

```
>>> hot_temperatures
[('Las Vegas', 40.0), ('Atlanta', 32.22222222222222),
 ('Detroit', 29.444444444444443), ('Seattle', 26.666666666666668),
 ('Miami', 35.0), ('Los Angeles', 29.444444444444443),
 ('Chicago', 32.22222222222222)]
```

20.10 While Loops

Python will let you loop over a code block as long as a condition holds. This is called a *while loop*, and you use the while statement to create it. A while loop is followed by an expression that evaluates to True or False. Then, a colon follows it. Remember what follows a colon (:) in Python? Yes, an indented block of code. This block of code will continue to repeat as long as the expression evaluates to True. This allows you to create an infinite loop easily.

You usually try to avoid infinite loops because they cause your program to "hang"-forever caught in the processing of a loop with no way out. One exception to this is a server that loops forever, continuing to process requests.

20.11. While Example

Another exception seen in more advanced Python is an infinite generator. A generator behaves like a lazy list and only creates values when you loop over it. If you are familiar with stream processing, you could think of it as a stream. (I don't cover generators in this book, but I do in my more advanced book.)

Typically, if you have an object that supports iteration, you use a for loop to iterate over the items. You use while loops when you don't have easy access to an iterable object.

A common example is counting down:

```
>>> n = 3
>>> while n > 0:
...     print(n)
...     n = n - 1
3
2
1
```

You can also use the break statement to exit a while loop:

```
>>> n = 3
>>> while True:
...     print(n)
...     n = n - 1
...     if n == 0:
...         break
```

20.11 While Example

In many real-world situations, especially in domains like medical imaging or proprietary research, labeled data can be scarce or expensive to obtain. Imagine you are training a machine learning model to identify rare medical conditions from X-rays. Each label might need to be verified by an expert radiologist, which is both time-consuming and costly.

In such scenarios, you would want to maximize the utility of each labeled example. One way to achieve this is through active learning. The basic idea behind active learning is to iteratively train a model and use it to identify which data points, when labeled, would be most valuable for improving the model further.

The provided code is a simplified version of this approach. After each training iteration, it identifies and removes data points that the model is already confident about, under the assumption that they are no longer contributing significantly to the model's learning. By repeatedly refining the training set, we hope to retain and focus on the more "challenging" or "informative" examples that help the model improve.

```python
import xgboost as xgb
from sklearn.datasets import load_diabetes
```

20. Iteration

```python
from sklearn.model_selection import train_test_split
from sklearn.metrics import mean_squared_error
import numpy as np

# Load the dataset
data = load_diabetes()
X, y = data.data, data.target

# Splitting the dataset
X_train, X_val, y_train, y_val = train_test_split(X, y, test_size=0.2,
        random_state=42)

# Initial parameters
params = {
    'objective': 'reg:squarederror',
    'eval_metric': 'rmse',
    'n_estimators': 50,
    'learning_rate': 0.05
}

prev_rmse = float('inf')
tolerance = 0.01

while True:
    model = xgb.XGBRegressor(**params)
    model.fit(X_train, y_train)

    y_pred_train = model.predict(X_train)
    y_pred = model.predict(X_val)

    rmse = np.sqrt(mean_squared_error(y_val, y_pred))

    if prev_rmse - rmse < tolerance:
        break

    # Get the absolute errors and their indices
    errors = np.abs(y_train - y_pred_train)

    # Drop the top 10% of data points that the model is most confident about
    confident_indices = np.argsort(errors)[:int(0.1 * len(errors))]

    X_train = np.delete(X_train, confident_indices, axis=0)
    y_train = np.delete(y_train, confident_indices)

    prev_rmse = rmse
```

```
print(f'{X_train.shape=}')
```

In a full-fledged active learning system, instead of just discarding the confidently predicted points, you'd typically use the model to scan through a pool of unlabeled data and identify which points, if labeled by an expert, would be most beneficial for the next training iteration.

In essence, this strategy helps achieve better model performance with fewer labeled examples, maximizing data efficiency, and prioritizing the labeling of the most informative data points when labeled data is a precious resource.

20.12 Assignment Expressions

Python 3.8 introduced a feature called "assignment expressions", also known as the walrus operator. Sometimes, when programming, you create a variable and then do a check (with an `if` or a `while` statement) to verify the value. Then, you might call the code to fetch the variable again.

Here is simplified code from a business intelligence application I wrote years ago. It reads some number of rows in the database. If there are no rows returned, the process is done. Otherwise, it processes the rows and asks for more data:

```
done = False
while not done:
    items = result.fetchmany(count)
    done = len(items) == 0
    if not done:
        for item in items:
            process(item)
```

Using the new walrus operator, this could be re-written as:

```
while len(items := result.fetchmany(count)) != 0:
    for item in items:
        process(item)
```

The walrus operator is the `:=` syntax (supposedly, the colon looks like eyes and the equal sign looks like the tusks of a sideways walrus, hence the name). Normally, when we create a variable with the assignment operator (`=`) the result does not evaluate to anything. It creates the variable but does not return a value. The walrus operator is different in this respect. In addition to creating the `items` variable, it evaluates to the value of that variable so the conditional can check the length of `items`.

Here is another example of code that might benefit from the walrus operator. It is a prompt to ask the user to input text that is not empty:

20. Iteration

```
txt = input('> ')
while txt == '':
    print("please type something")
    txt = input('> ')
```

With the walrus operator, we can cut out some of the lines:

```
while (txt:= input('> ')) == '':
    print("please type something")
```

20.13 Summary

This chapter discussed using the `for` loop to iterate over a sequence. You saw that you can loop over lists. You can also loop over strings, tuples, dictionaries, and other data structures. You can define your own classes that respond to the `for` statement by implementing the `.__iter__` method.

A `for` loop creates a variable during iteration. This variable is not garbage collected after the for loop, it sticks around. If your `for` loop is inside of a function, the variable will be garbage collected when the function exits.

The `enumerate` function was introduced. This function returns a sequence of tuples of index item pairs for the sequence passed into it. If you need to get the index location as well as the item of iteration, use `enumerate`.

Finally, you saw how to break out of loops, continue to the next item of iteration, and use `else` statements. These constructs enable you to adeptly configure your looping logic.

20.14 Exercises

1. Create a list with the names of friends and colleagues. Calculate the average length of the names.
2. Create a list with the names of friends and colleagues. Search for the name John using a for loop. Print `not found` if you didn't find it. (Hint: use `else`).
3. Create a list of tuples of first names, last names, and ages for your friends and colleagues. If you don't know the age, put in `None`. Calculate the average age, skipping over any `None` values. Print out each name, followed by `old` or `young` if they are above or below the average age.

Chapter 21

Dictionaries

A dictionary is a built-in Python data structure for mapping keys to values. They are also known as *associative arrays* or *hash tables* in other languages. They are similar to lists, except each item is a key-value pair. The key can be any Python type, usually numbers or strings. The value can be any Python value.

We use them to look up values by key. For example, if you have a dictionary of English to Spanish words, you can look up the Spanish equivalent of an English word quickly if you know the English word.

In this chapter, you will learn about dictionaries and how to use them in Python.

21.1 Overview

Dictionaries are a highly optimized built-in type in Python.

I like to compare a Python dictionary to an English dictionary. An English dictionary has words and definitions. The dictionary allows fast lookup of the word to find the definition. You can quickly look up any word by doing a binary search (open the dictionary to the midpoint, determine which half the word is in, and repeat).

A Python dictionary also has words and definitions, but you call them *keys* and *values* respectively. The purpose of a Python dictionary is to provide a fast lookup of the keys.

Python's dictionaries can search for words even quicker than binary search by using *hashing*. When you store a key-value pair in the dictionary, the word undergoes a hashing process, transforming it into a hash code, a unique integer derived from the key. This hash code is then used to determine the "bucket" where the key-value pair should be stored within the dictionary's underlying data structure. Since this determination is based on the key's hash value, accessing the value associated with a key is extremely fast. Collisions, scenarios where two keys produce the same hash code, are handled by the dictionary internally, ensuring that the dictionary remains efficient and accurate.

21. Dictionaries

You can quickly look for a key and pull out its associated value. Like an English dictionary, where it would take a long time to find the word if you only had a definition (if you didn't know the word beforehand), looking up the value in a Python dictionary is slow.

In Python 3.6, there is a feature that is new for dictionaries. The keys are now sorted by insertion order. If you are writing Python code that needs to work in prior versions, you will need to remember that before 3.6, keys had an arbitrary order (that allowed Python to do quick lookups but wasn't particularly useful to end users).

21.2 Dictionary Assignment

Dictionaries provide a link from a *key* to a *value*. (Other languages call them *hashes, hash maps, maps,* or *associative arrays*). Suppose you wanted to store name information about an individual. You saw how you could use a tuple to represent a record. A dictionary is another mechanism. Because dictionaries are built into Python, you can use a literal syntax to create one. This one has first and last names:

```
>>> info = {'first': 'Pete', 'last': 'Best'}
```

> **Note**
>
> An alternate way to create a dictionary is with the built-in dict class. If you pass a list of tuple pairs into the class, it will return a dictionary:
>
> ```
> >>> info = dict([('first', 'Pete'),
> ...              ('last', 'Best')])
> ```
>
> You can also use named parameters when you call dict:
>
> ```
> >>> info = dict(first='Pete', last='Best')
> ```
>
> If you use named parameters, the parameters must be valid Python variable names, and they will be converted to strings.

You can also use index operations to insert values into the dictionary. Let's insert the age and occupation:

```
>>> info['age'] = 20
>>> info['occupation'] = 'Drummer'
```

In the above example, the keys are 'first', 'last', 'age', and 'occupation'. For example, 'age' is the *key* that maps to the integer 20, the *value*. You can quickly look up the value for 'age' by performing a lookup with an index operation:

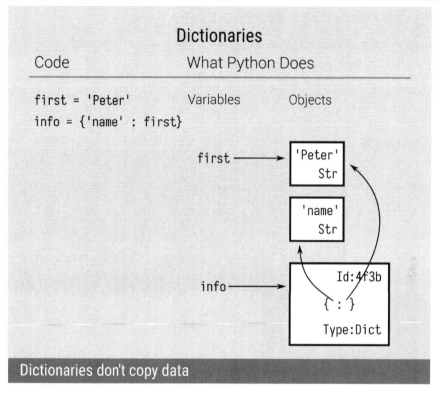

Figure 21.1: This illustrates the creation of a dictionary. In this case, you use an existing variable for the value. Note that the dictionary does not copy the variable but points to it (increasing the reference count).

```
>>> info['age']
20
```

Conversely, finding the key with the value 20 is a slow operation. It would be like giving someone a definition of an English Dictionary and asking what word has that definition.

The above example illustrates the literal syntax for creating a populated dictionary. It also shows how the square brackets (index operations) are used to insert items into a dictionary and pull them out. When combined with the *assignment operator* (=), an index operation associates a key with a value. When the index operation has no assignment, it looks up the value for a given key.

21. Dictionaries

21.3 Retrieving Values from a Dictionary

As you have seen, the square bracket literal syntax (also called an *index operation*) can pull a value out of a dictionary when you use the brackets without assignment:

```
>>> info['age']
20
```

Be careful, though, if you try to access a key that does not exist in the dictionary, Python will throw an exception:

```
>>> info['Band']
Traceback (most recent call last):
  File "<stdin>", line 1, in <module>
KeyError: 'Band'
```

Because Python likes to be explicit and fail fast, raising an exception is the desired behavior. The KeyError indicates that the 'Band' key is not in the dictionary. It would be bad if Python returned an arbitrary value for a key that was not in the dictionary. Doing so could allow errors to propagate further in your program and mask a logic error.

21.4 The In Operator

We saw using the in operator with lists. You can use the in operator to quickly check if a key is in a dictionary:

```
>>> 'Band' in info
False
>>> 'first' in info
True
```

As you have seen, in also works with sequences. You can use the in statement with a list, set, or string to check for membership:

```
>>> 5 in [1, 3, 6]
False
>>> 't' in {'a', 'e', 'i'}
False
>>> 'P' in 'Paul'
True
```

> **Note**
>
> Python 3 removed the .has_key method, which provided the same functionality as the in statement but is specific to a dictionary. Hooray for steps forward toward consistency!

> The in statement will work with most containers. For the curious, Python uses the .__contains__ method to implement the in statement. The containers that implement this dunder method include lists, sets, strings, and dictionaries. Later we will see how to create your own class. You can define your own classes that respond to this statement. Your class must define the .__contains__ method or be iterable.

21.5 Dictionary Shortcuts

The .get method of a dictionary will retrieve a value for a key. .get also accepts an optional parameter to provide a default value if the key is not found. If you wanted the genre to default to 'Rock', you could do the following:

```
>>> genre = info.get('Genre', 'Rock')
>>> genre
'Rock'
```

> **Note**
>
> The .get method of dictionaries is one way to get around the KeyError that is thrown when trying to use the bracket notation to pull out a key not found in the dictionary.
>
> It is OK to use this method because you are being explicit about what will happen when the key is missing. You should prefer to fail fast when you aren't specific about the failing case.

21.6 Setdefault

A practical but somewhat confusingly named method of dictionaries is the .setdefault method. The method has the same signature as .get and initially behaves like it, returning a default value if the key does not exist. In addition, it also sets the value of the key to the default value if the key is not found. Because .setdefault returns a value, if you initialize it to a mutable type, such as a dictionary or list, you can mutate the result in place.

.setdefault can be used to provide an accumulator or counter for a key. For example, if you wanted to count the number of people with the same name, you could do the following:

```
>>> names = ['Ringo', 'Paul', 'John',
...          'Ringo']
>>> count = {}
>>> for name in names:
...     count.setdefault(name, 0)
...     count[name] += 1
```

21. Dictionaries

Without the .setdefault method, a bit more code is required:

```
>>> names = ['Ringo', 'Paul', 'John',
...          'Ringo']
>>> count = {}
>>> for name in names:
...     if name not in count:
...         count[name] = 1
...     else:
...         count[name] += 1
>>> count['Ringo']
2
```

> **Note**
>
> Performing these counting types of operations was so common that later the collections.Counter class was added to the Python standard library. This class can perform the above operations much more succinctly:
>
> ```
> >>> import collections
> >>> count = collections.Counter(['Ringo', 'Paul',
> ...     'John', 'Ringo'])
> >>> count
> Counter({'Ringo': 2, 'Paul': 1, 'John': 1})
> >>> count['Ringo']
> 2
> >>> count['Fred']
> 0
> ```

Here is a somewhat contrived example illustrating mutating the result of .setdefault. Assume you want to have a dictionary mapping a name to bands that they played in. If a person named Paul is in two bands, the result should map Paul to a list containing both of those bands:

```
>>> band1_names = ['John', 'George',
...    'Paul', 'Ringo']
>>> band2_names = ['Paul']
>>> names_to_bands = {}
>>> for name in band1_names:
...     names_to_bands.setdefault(name,
...         []).append('Beatles')
>>> for name in band2_names:
...     names_to_bands.setdefault(name,
...         []).append('Wings')

>>> names_to_bands['Paul']
['Beatles', 'Wings']
```

21.7. Deleting Keys

> **Note**
>
> The `collections` module from the Python standard library includes a useful class—`defaultdict`. This class behaves like a dictionary but also allows setting a key's default value to an arbitrary *factory*. If the default factory is not `None`, this function or class is called to initialize a value for the key whenever a key is missing.
>
> The previous example re-written with `defaultdict` is the following:
>
> ```
> >>> from collections import defaultdict
> >>> names_to_bands = defaultdict(list)
> >>> for name in band1_names:
> ...     names_to_bands[name].append('Beatles')
> >>> for name in band2_names:
> ...     names_to_bands[name].append('Wings')
>
> >>> print(names_to_bands['Paul'])
> ['Beatles', 'Wings']
> ```
>
> Using `defaultdict` is slightly more readable than using `setdefault`.

21.7 Deleting Keys

Another operation on dictionaries is the removal of keys and their corresponding values. To remove an item from a dictionary, use the `del` statement:

```
>>> names_to_bands
defaultdict(<class 'list'>, {'John': ['Beatles'], 'George': ['Beatles'],
    'Paul': ['Beatles', 'Wings'], 'Ringo': ['Beatles']})

>>> # remove 'Ringo' from the dictionary
>>> del names_to_bands['Ringo']

>>> names_to_bands
defaultdict(<class 'list'>, {'John': ['Beatles'], 'George': ['Beatles'],
    'Paul': ['Beatles', 'Wings']})
```

This is an operation that I find I rarely use. However, it is good to have this functionality should you need it.

> **Note**
>
> Python will prevent you from adding to or removing from a dictionary while you are looping over it. Python will throw a `RuntimeError`:

21. Dictionaries

```
>>> data = {'name': 'Matt'}
>>> for key in data:
...     del data[key]
Traceback (most recent call last):
  ...
RuntimeError: dictionary changed size during iteration
```

21.8 Dictionary iteration

Dictionaries also support iteration using the for statement. By default, when you iterate over a dictionary, you get back the keys.

Suppose we have the following dictionary representing the grades of different students in a math class:

```
>>> student_grades = {
...     'Alice': 95,
...     'Bob': 87,
...     'Charlie': 78,
...     'Dave': 92,
...     'Eva': 88,
... }
```

We could calculate the average score like this:

```
>>> total = 0
>>> for name in student_grades:
...     total += student_grades[name]
>>> print(f'The average was: {total / len(student_grades):.1f}')
The average was: 88.0
```

> **Note**
>
> The dictionary has a method—.keys—that will also list out the keys of a dictionary. In Python 3, the .keys method returns a *view*. The view is a window into the current keys found in the dictionary. You can iterate over it, like a list. But, unlike a list, it is not a copy of the keys. If you remove a key from the dictionary later, the view will reflect that change. A list would not.

To iterate over the values of a dictionary, iterate over the .values method:

```
>>> for value in student_grades.values():
...     print(value)
95
87
78
```

170

21.8. Dictionary iteration

```
92
88
```

The result of .values is also a view. It reflects the current state of the values found in a dictionary.

To retrieve both key and value during iteration, use the .items method, which returns a view:

```
>>> for key, value in student_grades.items():
...     print(key, value)
Alice 95
Bob 87
Charlie 78
Dave 92
Eva 88
```

If you materialize the view into a list, you will see that the list is a sequence of (key, value) tuples—the same thing that dict accepts to create a dictionary:

```
>>> list(student_grades.items())
[('Alice', 95), ('Bob', 87), ('Charlie', 78), ('Dave', 92), ('Eva', 88)]
```

Remember that a dictionary is ordered based on key insertion order. If a different order is desired, you will need to sort the sequence of iteration.

The built-in function sorted will return a new sorted list, given a sequence:

```
>>> for name in sorted(student_grades.keys()):
...     print(name)
Alice
Bob
Charlie
Dave
Eva
```

The sorted function has an optional argument, reverse, to flip the order of the output:

```
>>> for name in sorted(student_grades,
...                    reverse=True):
...     print(name)
Eva
Dave
Charlie
Bob
Alice
```

21. Dictionaries

> **Note**
>
> It is possible to have keys of different types. The only requirement for a key is that it has to be *hashable*. For example, a list isn't hashable because you can mutate it, and Python can't generate a consistent hash value for it. If you used a list as a key and then mutated that key, should the dictionary return the value based on the old list, the new one, or both? Python refuses to guess here and makes you use keys that don't change.

It would be possible to insert items into a dictionary using both integers and strings as keys:

```
>>> weird = {1: 'first',
...     '1': 'another first'}
```

Typically, you don't mix key types because it is confusing to readers of the code and also makes sorting keys harder. Python 3 won't sort mixed type lists without a key function telling Python explicitly how to compare different types. This is one of those areas where Python gives you the ability to do something, but that doesn't mean you should. In the words of Python core developer Raymond Hettinger:

> Many "Can I do x in Python" questions equate to "Can I stop a car on train tracks when no trains are coming?" Yes you can, No you shouldn't
>
> –@raymondh

21.9 Merging Dictionaries

You can combine two dictionaries into a single dictionary. This is an area where you can do this in many ways. Assume we had a dictionary mapping objects to their color:

```
>>> color = {'phone': 'black',
...     'pen': 'yellow'}
```

If we had another dictionary with objects and colors, we could merge them together:

```
>>> color2 = {'car': 'red',
...     'pen': 'blue'}
```

One way to merge the dictionaries is to use the dictionary unpack operator, **:

```
>>> {**color, **color2}
{'phone': 'black', 'pen': 'blue', 'car': 'red'}
```

Another way is with the .update method. Note that this method mutates the dictionary it is called on. It does not return a new dictionary!:

```
>>> color.update(color2)
>>> color
{'phone': 'black', 'pen': 'blue', 'car': 'red'}
```

A third way was introduced in Python 3.9 (PEP 584) called dictionary union. It is implemented with the pipe operator, |,. It does not mutate either dictionary, but returns a new object:

```
>>> color = {'phone': 'black',
...          'pen': 'yellow'}
>>> color2 = {'car': 'red',
...          'pen': 'blue'}
>>> color | color2
{'phone': 'black', 'pen': 'blue', 'car': 'red'}
```

Note that because the 'pen' key is duplicated, the order of the operands matter. The last key seen will overwrite the previous keys:

```
>>> color2 | color
{'car': 'red', 'pen': 'yellow', 'phone': 'black'}
```

21.10 Dictionary Comprehensions

Much like list comprehensions, dictionary comprehensions are a way to create dictionaries using a single line of code. If you find yourself creating a dictionary in a loop, a dictionary comprehension is one alternative to consider.

Here is an example of looping over a dictionary of stock prices and updating the prices by 10%:

```
>>> prices = {'GOOG': 490.10,
...          'AAPL': 123.50,
...          'IBM': 91.50,
...          'MSFT': 52.13}

>>> prices2 = {}
>>> for key, value in prices.items():
...     prices2[key] = value * 1.1

>>> prices2
{'GOOG': 539.1100000000001,
 'AAPL': 135.85000000000002,
 'IBM': 100.65000000000002,
 'MSFT': 57.343}
```

21. Dictionaries

This is a *mapping* operation. We are mapping the old value to a new value that is 10% higher. This is a perfect use case for a dictionary comprehension. The construction of a dictionary comprehension is similar to a list comprehension, but with a colon separating the key and value.

Here's my steps:
1 - Create a new empty dictionary, prices2. 2 - Place the for loop inside the curly braces without the colon. 3 - Place the key and value expressions at the start of the new dictionary. Insert a colon between them.

The three steps would look like this:
1 - prices2 = {} 2 - prices2 = {for key, value in prices.items()} 3 - prices2 = {key: value * 1.1 for key, value in prices.items()}

21.11 Dictionaries with Pandas

When working with pandas, we often use dictionaries. This section will look at several scenarios where dictionaries are particularly valuable in dealing with pandas data structures, such as DataFrames and Series.

A DataFrame is a tabular data structure that contains rows and columns. Each column in a DataFrame is a Series. DataFrames in pandas are used to represent tabular data such as stock prices, flight schedules, and sports scores. Series are used to represent a single column of data.

Renaming columns in a DataFrame is often necessary for various reasons - to improve clarity, ensure a consistent naming convention, and so on. This is an ideal scenario where a dictionary can come in handy. The keys in the dictionary represent the current column names, and their corresponding values denote the new column names.

```
>>> import pandas as pd
>>> df = pd.DataFrame({
...      'A': [1, 2, 3],
...      'B': [4, 5, 6],
...      'C': [7, 8, 9]
... })

>>> rename_dict = {'A': 'Alpha', 'B': 'Beta', 'C': 'Gamma'}
>>> df.rename(columns=rename_dict, inplace=True)
>>> df
   Alpha  Beta  Gamma
0      1     4      7
1      2     5      8
2      3     6      9
```

21.12 Dict Comprehensions with Pandas

Let's assume I have a dataframe and some of the columns are 64 bit integers. I want to convert them to 32 bit integers. I can use a dictionary comprehension to do this:

```
>>> import pandas as pd
>>> df = pd.DataFrame({
...     'name': ['Alice', 'Bob', 'Charlie'],
...     'B': [4, 5, 6],
...     'C': [7, 8, 9]
... })

>>> df
      name  B  C
0    Alice  4  7
1      Bob  5  8
2  Charlie  6  9
```

Notice that column B and C are 64 bit integers:

```
>>> df.dtypes
name     object
B         int64
C         int64
dtype: object
```

I don't need 64 bit integers for these columns. I can convert them to unsigned 8 bit integers without losing any information. The .astype method can be used to convert the data type of a column. You need to pass it a dictionary where the keys are the column names and the values are the data types. We will use a dictionary comprehension to convert all the columns that are currently 64 bit integers to 8 bit integers:

```
>>> df8 = (df
...     .astype({col: 'uint8' for col in df.select_dtypes('int64').columns})

>>> df8
      name  B  C
0    Alice  4  7
1      Bob  5  8
2  Charlie  6  9

>>> df8.dtypes
name     object
B         uint8
C         uint8
dtype: object
```

21.13 Using the Assign Method with Column Names that Contain Spaces

Pandas' .assign method can be used to add new columns to your DataFrame or modify existing ones. If these column names contain spaces or special characters, a dictionary is especially useful. Here we will add a column with a space in it:

```
>>> df = pd.DataFrame({
...     'Alpha': [1, 2, 3],
...     'Beta': [4, 5, 6],
... })
>>> df = df.assign(**{'Gamma Delta': [7, 8, 9]})
>>> df
   Alpha  Beta  Gamma Delta
0      1     4            7
1      2     5            8
2      3     6            9
```

Here, the ** operator is used to unpack the dictionary. The key ('Gamma Delta') becomes the column name, and its corresponding value is set as the column's value.

21.14 Value Mapping

Dictionaries are also very useful when you want to map values in a Series or DataFrame. For instance, you may have categorical data represented as text that you wish to map to corresponding numeric values. This can come up in machine learning when the model only accepts numeric input but the data is encoded as strings. In this case, you can create a dictionary with the keys being the text categories and the values being the numeric values to map to.

```
>>> s = pd.Series(['cat', 'dog', 'cat', 'dog',
...                'bird', 'cat', 'bird', 'cat'])
>>> s
0     cat
1     dog
2     cat
3     dog
4    bird
5     cat
6    bird
7     cat
dtype: object

>>> category_dict = {'cat': 1, 'dog': 2, 'bird': 3}
```

```
>>> s = s.map(category_dict)
>>> s
0    1
1    2
2    1
3    2
4    3
5    1
6    3
7    1
dtype: int64
```

Dictionaries in pandas are versatile tools that can greatly simplify data manipulation processes. From renaming columns and creating new columns to mapping values, dictionaries provide an efficient and practical solution for handling data with pandas.

21.15 Summary

This chapter discussed the dictionary. This data structure is important because it is a building block in Python. Classes, namespaces, and modules in Python are all implemented using a dictionary under the covers.

Dictionaries provide quick lookup or insertion for a key. You can also do a lookup by value, but it is slow. If you find yourself doing this operation often, it is a code smell that you should use a different data structure.

You saw how to mutate a dictionary. You can insert and remove keys from a dictionary. You can also check a dictionary for membership using the in statement.

You looked at some fancier constructs, using .setdefault to insert and return values in one operation. You saw that Python includes specialized dictionary classes, Counter and defaultdict in the collections module.

Because dictionaries are mutable, you can delete keys from them using the del statement. You can also iterate over a dictionary's keys using a for loop.

Remember that Python 3.6 introduced ordering to the dictionary. The keys are ordered by insertion order, not alphabetic or numeric order.

We showed some examples where dictionaries are used with pandas.

21.16 Exercises

1. Create a dictionary, info, that holds your first name, your last name, and your age.

2. Create an empty dictionary, phone, that will hold details about your phone. Add the screen size, memory, OS, brand, etc. to the dictionary.

21. Dictionaries

3. Write a paragraph in a triple-quoted string. Use the `.split` method to create a list of words. Create a dictionary to hold the count for every word in the paragraph.

4. Count how many times each word is used in a paragraph of text from Ralph Waldo Emerson.

5. Write code that will print out the anagrams (words that use the same letters) from a paragraph of text.

6. The *PageRank* algorithm created the Google search engine. The algorithm gives a score to each page based on incoming links. It takes one input: a list of pages that link to other pages. Each page initially gets a score set to 1. Then multiple iterations of the algorithm are run, typically ten. For each iteration:

   - A page transfers its score divided by the number of outgoing links to each page that it links to.
   - The score transferred is multiplied by a *damping factor*, typically set to .85.

   Write some code to run 10 iterations of this algorithm on a list of tuples of source and destination links, ie:

   ```
   links = [('a', 'b'), ('a', 'c'), ('b', 'c')]
   ```

Chapter 22

Functions

We have come a long way without discussing functions, a basic building block of Python programs. Functions are discrete units of code isolated into their own block. We will explore functions in this chapter.

22.1 Black Boxes

You have been using built-in functions along the way such as dir, help, (and the classes that behave like coercion functions—float, int, dict, list, and bool).

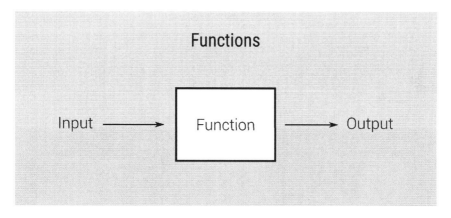

Figure 22.1: A function is like a box. It can take input and return output. It can be passed around and reused.

One way to think of a function is as a black box to which you can send input and get output out of it. (Though neither input nor output are required). The black box can then perform a series of operations using the input and return the output (it implicitly returns None if the function ends without return being called). An advantage of a function is that it enables code reuse. Once a function is defined, you can call it multiple times. If you have code that you

22. Functions

repeatedly run in your program, rather than copying and pasting it, you can put it in a function once, and then call that function multiple times. This gives you less code to reason about, making your programs easier to understand. It is also easier to change code (or fix bugs) later as you only have to do it in one place.

Here is a simple example of a function. This function, named add_2, takes a number as input, adds 2 to that value, and returns the result:

```
>>> def add_2(num):
...     '''
...     return 2 more than num
...     '''
...     result = num + 2
...     return result
```

What are the different components of a function? This whole group of code is known as a *function definition*. First, you see the def statement, which is short for *define* (i.e., define a function). Following def is a required space (one space is fine) and then the function name—add_2. This is the name that is used to *invoke* the function. Synonyms for invoke include call, execute, or run the function. When Python creates a function, it will create a new variable using the function's name.

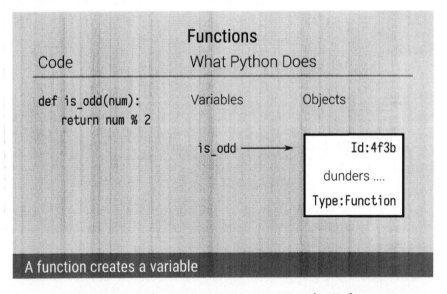

Figure 22.2: This illustrates the creation of a function. Note that Python creates a new function object, and then points a variable to it using the name of the function. Use the dir function on the function name to see the attributes of the newly created function.

Following the function name is a left parenthesis followed by num and a right parenthesis. You do not need to put a space before the parentheses. The names between the parentheses (there can be an arbitrary number of names; in this case, there is only one) are the input *parameters*. These are the objects that you pass into a function.

After the closing parentheses comes a colon (:). Whenever you see a colon at the end of a line in Python, you should immediately think the colon is followed by an indented block—similar to the body of the `for` loops shown previously. Everything that is indented is the *body* of the function. It is also called a *block of code*.

The body of a function is where the logic lives. You might recognize the first three lines of indented code as a triple-quoted string. This is not a comment, though it appears to have comment-like text. It is a string. Python allows you to place a string immediately after the `:`. If you place a string in this location, it is called a *docstring*. A docstring is a string used solely for documentation. It should describe the block of code following it. The docstring does not affect the logic of the function.

> **Note**
>
> The `help` function has been emphasized throughout this book. It is important to note that the `help` function gets its content from the *docstring* of the object passed into it. If you call `help` on `add_2`, you should see the following:
>
> ```
> >>> help(add_2)
> Help on function add_2 in module
> __main__:
> add_2()
>     return 2 more than num
> (END)
> ```

Providing docstrings can be helpful to you as a reminder of what your code does. If they are accurate, the docstrings are invaluable to anyone trying to use your code.

The function's logic comes following the docstring (note that a docstring is optional). The `result` is calculated. Finally, the function uses a `return` statement to indicate that it has output. A `return` statement is not necessary, and if it is missing a function will return `None` by default when it finishes running. Furthermore, you can use more than one return statement, and they do not even have to be at the end of the function. For example, a conditional block may contain a return statement inside of an `if` block and another in an `else` block.

To recap, the main parts of a function are:

- the `def` keyword
- a function name
- function parameters between parentheses
- a colon (:)

- indentation
    - docstring
    - logic
    - return statement

Creating functions is easy. They allow you to reuse code, making it shorter and easier to understand. They are useful for removing global state by keeping short-lived variables inside of the function body. Use functions to improve your code.

22.2 Invoking functions

When you call or execute a function, you are *invoking* a function. If you type the function name, it will not run (it just shows that the function name is a variable pointing to a function object).

```
>>> add_2
<function add_2 at 0x102145d80>
```

In Python, you invoke functions by adding parentheses following the function name. This code invokes the newly defined function add_2:

```
>>> add_2(3)
5
```

To invoke a function, list its name followed by a left parenthesis, the input parameters, and a right parenthesis. The number of parameters should match the number of parameters in the function declaration. Notice that the REPL implicitly prints the result—the integer 5. The result is what the return statement passes back.

You can pass in whatever object you want to the add_2 function. However, if that object doesn't support adding a number, you will get an exception. For example, if you pass a string in, you will see a TypeError:

```
>>> add_2('hello')
Traceback (most recent call last):
  ...
TypeError: can only concatenate str (not "int") to str
```

22.3 Scope

Python looks for variables in various places. We call these places *scopes* (or *namespaces*). When looking for a variable (remember that functions are also variables in Python, as are classes, modules, and more), Python will look in the following locations, in this order:

22.3. Scope

- Local scope - Variables that are defined inside of functions.
- Global scope - Variables that are defined at the global level.
- Built-in scope - Variables that are predefined in Python.

In the following code is a function that will look up variables in each of the three scopes:

```
>>> x = 2  # Global
>>> def scope_demo():
...     y = 4  # Local to scope_demo
...     print("Local: {}".format(y))
...     print("Global: {}".format(x))
...     print("Built-in: {}".format(dir))
>>> scope_demo()
Local: 4
Global: 2
Built-in: <built-in function dir>
```

Note that after `scope_demo` is invoked, the local variable y is garbage collected and no longer available in the global scope:

```
>>> y
Traceback (most recent call last):
  ...
NameError: name 'y' is not defined
```

However, the global variable x is still around:

```
>>> x
2
```

Variables defined inside of a function or method will be local. In general, you should try to avoid global variables. They make it harder to reason about code. Global variables are common in books, blogs, and documentation because using them requires writing less code and allows you to focus on concepts without them being wrapped in a function. Using functions and classes are some of the tools that help you remove global variables, make your code more modular, and easier to understand.

> **Note**
>
> Python will allow you to override variables in the global and built-in scope. At the global level, you could define your own variable called `dir`. At that point, the built-in function, `dir`, is *shadowed* by the global variable. You could also do this within a function, and create a local variable that shadows a global or built-in:
>
> ```
> >>> def dir(x):
> ```

22. Functions

```
...     print("Dir called")
>>> dir('')
Dir called
```

You can use the del statement to delete variables in the local or global scope. In practice though, you don't see this, as it is better to avoid shadowing built-ins in the first place:

```
>>> del dir
>>> dir('')
['__add__', '__class__', '__contains__', ... ]
```

> **Note**
>
> You can use the locals and globals functions to list these scopes. These return dictionaries with their current scope in them:
>
> ```
> >>> def foo():
> ...     x = 1
> ...     print(locals())
> >>> foo()
> {'x': 1}
> ```

The __builtins__ variable lists the built-in names. If you access its __dict__ attribute, you will get a dictionary similar to globals and locals.

```
>>> print(dir(__builtins__))
['ArithmeticError', 'AssertionError', 'AttributeError', ...
'UserWarning', 'ValueError', 'Warning', 'ZeroDivisionError', ...
'__IPYTHON__', '__build_class__', '__debug__', '__doc__', ...
'abs', 'aiter', 'all', 'anext', 'any', 'ascii', 'bin', ...
'str', 'sum', 'super', 'tuple', 'type', 'vars', 'zip']
```

22.4 Multiple Parameters

Functions can have as few or as many parameters as they need. Below is a function that takes two parameters and returns their sum:

```
>>> def add_two_nums(a, b):
...     return a + b
```

Note that Python is a dynamic language, and you don't specify the types of the parameters. This function can add two integers:

```
>>> add_two_nums(4, 6)
10
```

It can also add floats:

```
>>> add_two_nums(4.0, 6.0)
10.0
```

Strings too:

```
>>> add_two_nums('4', '6')
'46'
```

Note that the strings use + to perform string *concatenation* (joining two strings together).
Even lists!

```
>>> add_two_nums(['matt'], ['harrison'])
['matt', 'harrison']
```

However, if you try to add a string and a number, Python will complain:

```
>>> add_two_nums('4', 6)
Traceback (most recent call last):
  ...
TypeError: Can't convert 'int' object to str implicitly
```

This is an instance where Python wants you to be more explicit about what operation is desired, and it isn't going to guess for you. If you wanted to add a string type to a number, you might want to convert them to numbers first (using float or int). Likewise, it might be useful to convert from numbers to strings if concatenation is the desired operation. Python does not implicitly choose which operation to perform. Instead, it throws an error, which should force the programmer to resolve the ambiguity.

22.5 Default Parameters

One cool feature of Python functions is *default parameters*. As the name implies, default parameters allow you to specify the default values for function parameters if they are not provided when the function is called. The default parameters are then optional, though you can override them if necessary.

Consider a function that generates a greeting message for an online platform. Typically, you'd want to greet users with a standard message like "Hello". However, sometimes you might want to customize that greeting based on the time of day or another factor:

```
>>> def greet_user(name, greeting="Hello"):
...     """Generate a greeting message.
...     Default is a general 'Hello'."""
```

22. Functions

```
...     return f"{greeting}, {name}!"
>>> greet_user("Alice")
'Hello, Alice!'

>>> greet_user("Bob", "Good Morning")
'Good Morning, Bob!'
```

In the above example, the greet_user function uses a default parameter for the greeting. If the greeting is not provided, it defaults to "Hello". However, if a custom greeting is provided when calling the function, it will use that instead. This provides flexibility and simplifies the function's usage in most common scenarios.

> **Note**
>
> Default parameters must be declared after non-default parameters. Otherwise, Python will give you a SyntaxError:
>
> ```
> >>> def add_n(num=3, n):
> ...     return num + n
> Traceback (most recent call last):
>   ...
>   File "<doctest c01-build.md[565]>", line 1
>     def add_n(num=3, n):
>                       ^
> SyntaxError: non-default argument follows
> default argument
> ```
>
> Because default parameters are optional, Python forces you to declare required parameters before optional ones. The above code wouldn't work with an invocation like add_n(4) because the required parameter is missing.

> **Note**
>
> Do not use mutable types (lists, dictionaries) for default parameters unless you know what you are doing. Due to how Python works, the default parameters are created only once—at function definition time, not at function execution time. If you use a mutable default value, you will end up re-using the same instance of the default parameter during each function invocation.
>
> Suppose you are designing a function for an e-commerce website to add items to a user's shopping cart. If you use a mutable default parameter for the cart, every user might end up sharing the same cart:
>
> ```
> >>> def add_to_cart(item, cart=[]):
> ```

```
...     cart.append(item)
...     return cart
>>> add_to_cart('laptop')
['laptop']
>>> add_to_cart('smartphone')
['laptop', 'smartphone']
```

Instead of adding the 'smartphone' to a new cart, it got added to the cart that already contained the 'laptop'. This can lead to serious issues on an e-commerce platform, where each user expects to have their own independent cart.

To avoid such issues, always initialize mutable default parameters within the function:

```
>>> def add_to_cart(item, cart=None):
...     if cart is None:
...         cart = []
...     cart.append(item)
...     return cart
>>> add_to_cart('laptop')
['laptop']
>>> add_to_cart('smartphone')
['smartphone']
```

Now, each function invocation creates a separate cart, ensuring that items don't get mixed between different users or sessions.

The following code:

```
...     if cart is None:
...         cart = []
```

Can also be written as a single line using a *conditional expression*:

```
...     cart = cart if cart is not None else []
```

22.6 Lambda Functions

In Python, a lambda function is an *anonymous function*, meaning a function declared with no name. It is a small and restricted function having no more than one line. Like a normal function, a lambda function can have multiple arguments but only one expression, which is evaluated and returned.

The syntax of a lambda function is:

```
lambda arguments: expression
```

22. Functions

Lambda functions can have any number of arguments but only one expression. The expression is evaluated and returned.

22.7 Examples of Lambda Functions

If we had an add function written like this:

```
>>> def add(a, b):
...     return a + b
```

We could re-write it like this:

```
>>> add = lambda a, b: a + b
```

Following the `lambda` keyword, we place the parameters. We follow that with a colon. On the right of the colon is what the function returns. (without using the `return` keyword). Note that there is no `return` statement in the lambda function. The single expression after the colon is the return value.

> **Note**
>
> In the above example, the lambda function is not strictly 'anonymous' because we created a variable to store it. The next example will show creating a label inside a call to a function. This example will be anonymous because we are just passing along the function, there is no global variable to store it.

22.8 Using Lambda Functions with Python Built-ins

Lambda functions are beneficial with built-in Python functions like `sorted`, `max`, and `min`, or pandas methods like `.assign`, `.apply`, `.pipe`, and `.map`.

Consider the following scenario: You have a list of strings representing salaries and wish to identify the highest salary. While each entry is a string, for comparison purposes, you'd like to treat them as integers.

```
>>> salary = ['1', '9999', '1000000']

>>> max(salary)   # maximum based on string comparison
'9999'

>>> # maximum when treated as an integer value
>>> max(salary, key=lambda val: int(val))
'1000000'
```

In this case, the `max` function can accept a `key` argument that defines how to determine the "largeness" of each entry. Using a lambda function that converts each string to an integer, `max` can effectively compare the true numerical values of the salaries, yielding the expected highest salary, '1000000'.

If you're not used to them, lambda functions can seem strange initially, but they can be very powerful when used correctly. They are an excellent tool to have in your Python toolbox.

22.9 Using Functions with Pandas

Functions are a powerful tool for code reuse and logic encapsulation in Python, and they can also be applied to pandas DataFrames and Series. In this section, we'll look at some of the main ways you can use functions when working with pandas, focusing on the .assign, .rename, and .pipe methods.

The .assign method can be used to add new columns to a DataFrame in pandas. Combined with a function, it allows us to create or modify columns based on a computation or transformation applied to the existing data.

Here's an example where we create a new column, *mpg*, calculated from the columns in the DataFrame.

```
>>> import pandas as pd
>>> data = pd.DataFrame({
...     'distance_miles': [100, 200, 120, 150],
...     'fuel_gallons': [4, 10, 5, 7.5]
... })
>>> data
   distance_miles  fuel_gallons
0             100           4.0
1             200          10.0
2             120           5.0
3             150           7.5
```

Now, we'll define a function to perform the miles per gallon calculation and use the .assign method to add a new column to our DataFrame:

```
>>> def calc_mpg(df):
...     return df['distance_miles'] / df['fuel_gallons']

>>> data.assign(mpg=calc_mpg)
   distance_miles  fuel_gallons   mpg
0             100           4.0  25.0
1             200          10.0  20.0
2             120           5.0  24.0
3             150           7.5  20.0
```

In this example, the calc_mpg function calculates the miles per gallon. The .assign method then adds a new column to the DataFrame using this calculation.

22. Functions

> **Note**
>
> We could also use a lambda to write the previous code.
>
> ```
> >>> data.assign(
> ...     mpg=lambda df: df['distance_miles'] / df['fuel_gallons'])
>    distance_miles  fuel_gallons   mpg
> 0             100           4.0  25.0
> 1             200          10.0  20.0
> 2             120           5.0  24.0
> 3             150           7.5  20.0
> ```

22.10 Using Rename with Functions

The .rename method can alter a DataFrame's index labels or column names. Combined with a function, it allows us to change these names based on a function that processes the current names.

Consider this example:

```
>>> df = pd.DataFrame({
...     'A': [1, 2, 3],
...     'B': [4, 5, 6],
...     'C': [7, 8, 9]
... })

>>> df.rename(columns=lambda col: col.lower())
   a  b  c
0  1  4  7
1  2  5  8
2  3  6  9
```

Here, we pass a lambda function to .rename, which converts each column name to lowercase.

22.11 Using Pipe with Functions

The .pipe method can be used to apply a function (or a sequence of functions) to the whole DataFrame. This can be particularly handy for creating data processing pipelines, where raw data is transformed through a series of steps before it is used for analysis or modeling.

Let's consider an example where we have a DataFrame of temperatures in degrees Celsius, and we want to convert these to Fahrenheit and Kelvin. We can define functions for these conversions and then use the .pipe method to apply them.

First, let's create a DataFrame with temperatures in Celsius:

```
>>> df = pd.DataFrame({
...     'temp_celsius': [0, 20, 37, 100]
... })
>>> df
   temp_celsius
0             0
1            20
2            37
3           100
```

Now, let's define our conversion functions:

```
>>> def celsius_to_fahrenheit(df):
...     return df.assign(temp_fahrenheit =
...         df['temp_celsius'] * 9/5 + 32)

>>> def celsius_to_kelvin(df):
...     return df.assign(temp_kelvin =
...         df['temp_celsius'] + 273.15)
```

We can now use the .pipe method to apply these functions to our DataFrame:

```
>>> (df
...  .pipe(celsius_to_fahrenheit)
...  .pipe(celsius_to_kelvin)
... )
   temp_celsius  temp_fahrenheit  temp_kelvin
0             0             32.0       273.15
1            20             68.0       293.15
2            37             98.6       310.15
3           100            212.0       373.15
```

Using functions with pandas provides a powerful way to express complex data transformations succinctly and readably. They make your code easier to understand, test, and maintain, and they help you take full advantage of the power of pandas and Python.

22.12 Naming Conventions for Functions

Function naming conventions are similar to variable naming conventions (and are also found in the PEP 8[1] document). One notable convention from PEP 8 is the use of *snake case* for function naming. This style is touted for its readability. Following this convention, function names should:

---

[1] https://peps.python.org/pep-0008/

- be entirely lowercase
- use underscores to separate words (e.g., has_time_overlap)
- not start with numbers (e.g., avoid 1st_function_name)
- not override or shadow built-in names (e.g., avoid naming a function print or int)
- not use Python reserved keywords (e.g., avoid class or def)
- In contrast, some languages like Java use *camel case* naming conventions. For example, while you might encounter a method named hasTimeOverlap in Java, in Python, it would more likely be has_time_overlap.

That said, PEP 8 also emphasizes consistency. If you're contributing to a codebase with a different style, it's essential to be consistent with the existing convention. A notable exception in Python's standard library is the unittest module. Its naming mirrors Java-style conventions, a vestige from its origins as a port from the Java library, JUnit.

22.13 Summary

Functions allow you to encapsulate change and side effects within their body. In this chapter, you learned that functions can take input and return output. There can be multiple input parameters, and you can also provide default values.

Remember that Python is based on objects, and when you create a function, you also create a variable with the function name that points to it.

Functions can also have a docstring, a string written immediately after the declaration. These strings present documentation when the function is passed into the help function.

22.14 Exercises

1. Write a function, is_odd, that takes an integer and returns True if the number is odd and False if the number is not odd.
2. Write a function, is_prime, that takes an integer and returns True if the number is prime and False if the number is not prime.
3. Write a binary search function. It should take a sorted sequence and the item it is looking for. It should return the index of the item if found. It should return -1 if the item is not found.
4. Write a function that takes camel-cased strings (i.e. *ThisIsCamelCased*), and converts them to snake case (i.e. *this_is_camel_cased*). Modify the function by adding an argument, separator, so it will also convert to kebab case (i.e. *this-is-camel-case*) as well.

Chapter 23

Indexing and Slicing

Python provides two constructs to pull data from sequence-like types (lists, tuples, and even strings). These are the *indexing* and *slicing* constructs. Indexing allows you to access single items from a sequence, while slicing allows you to pull a sub-sequence from a sequence.

23.1 Indexing

We have seen indexing with lists and dictionaries. For example, if you have a list containing pets, you can pull out animals by index:

```
>>> my_pets = ["dog", "cat", "bird"]
>>> my_pets[0]
'dog'
```

> **Note**
>
> Remember that in Python, indices start at 0. If you want to pull out the first item, reference it by 0, not 1. This is called *zero-based indexing*.

Python has a cool feature where you can reference items using negative indices. -1 refers to the last item, -2 is the second to last item, etc. This is commonly used to pull off the last item in a list:

```
>>> my_pets[-1]
'bird'
```

Guido van Rossum, the creator of Python, tweeted to explain how to understand negative index values:

> [The] proper way to think of [negative indexing] is to reinterpret a[-X] as a[len(a)-X]
>
> –@gvanrossum

23. Indexing and Slicing

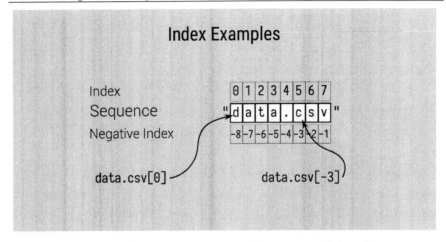

Figure 23.1: This illustrates positive and negative index positions.

You can also perform an index operation on a tuple or a string:

```
>>> ('Fred', 23, 'Senior')[1]
23
>>> 'Fred'[0]
'F'
```

Some types, such as sets, don't support index operations. If you want to define your own class that supports index operations, you should implement the .__getitem__ method.

23.2 Slicing Sub Lists

In addition to accepting an integer to pull out a single item, a *slice* may be used to pull out a sub-sequence. A slice may contain the start index, an optional end index, and an optional *stride*, all separated by a colon.

Here is a slice that pulls out the first two items of a list:

```
>>> my_pets = ["dog", "cat", "bird"]   # a list
>>> print(my_pets[0:2])
['dog', 'cat']
```

Remember that Python uses the *half-open interval* convention. The list goes up to but does not include the end index. As mentioned, the range function also behaves similarly with its second parameter, stop.

The first index is optional when you slice with a colon (:). If the first index is missing, the slice defaults to starting from the first item of the list (the zeroth item):

23.2. Slicing Sub Lists

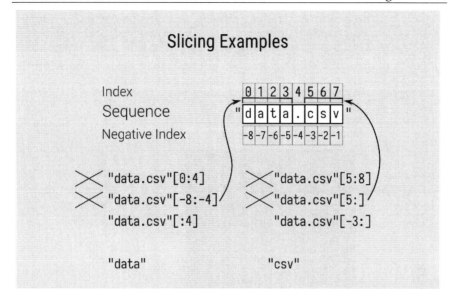

Figure 23.2: This illustrates slicing off the first four characters of a string. Three options are shown. The last option is the preferred way. You don't need the zero index since it is the default. Using negative indices is just silly. Slicing off the final three characters is shown as well. Again, the final example is the idiomatic way to do it. The first two assume the string has a length of eight, while the final code will work with any string that has at least three characters.

```
>>> print(my_pets[:2])
['dog', 'cat']
```

You can also use negative indices when slicing. A negative index can be used in the start location or ending location. The index -1 represents the last item. If you slice up to the last item, you will get everything but that item:

```
>>> my_pets[0:-1]
['dog', 'cat']
>>> my_pets[:-1]    # defaults to start at 0
['dog', 'cat']
>>> my_pets[0:-2]
['dog']
```

The final index is also optional. If the final index is missing, the slice defaults to the end of the list:

```
>>> my_pets[1:]
['cat', 'bird']
>>> my_pets[-2:]
['cat', 'bird']
```

23. Indexing and Slicing

Finally, you can use the default values for the start and end indices. If both indices are missing, the slice returned will run from the start to the end (which will contain a copy of the list). This is a construct you can use to quickly copy lists in Python:

```
>>> print(my_pets[:])
['dog', 'cat', 'bird']
```

23.3 Striding Slices

Slices also allow for an optional *stride* following the starting and ending indices. The default value for an unspecified stride is 1. A stride of 1 means take every item from a sequence between the indices. A stride of 2 would take every second item. A stride of 3 would take every third item:

```
>>> my_pets = ["dog", "cat", "bird"]
>>> dog_and_bird = my_pets[0:3:2]
>>> print(dog_and_bird)
['dog', 'bird']
>>> zero_three_six = [0, 1, 2, 3, 4, 5, 6][::3]
>>> print(zero_three_six)
[0, 3, 6]
```

> **Note**
>
> Again, the range function has a similar third parameter that specifies stride:
>
> ```
> >>> list(range(0, 7, 3))
> [0, 3, 6]
> ```

Strides can be negative. A -1 stride means moving backward from right to left. To use a negative stride, you should make the start slice greater than the end slice. The exception is if you leave out the start and end indices, a stride of -1 will reverse the sequence:

```
>>> my_pets[0:2:-1]
[]
>>> my_pets[2:0:-1]
['bird', 'cat']
>>> print([1, 2, 3, 4][::-1])
[4, 3, 2, 1]
```

The next time you are in a job interview, and they ask you to reverse a string, you can do it in a single line by tacking a slice onto the end of the string:

```
>>> 'emerih'[::-1]
'hireme'
```

Of course, they will probably want you to do it in C. Tell them that you want to program in Python!

23.4 Slicing in pandas

Pandas allows you to select rows from a DataFrame based on their positions. This can be accomplished using .iloc, which allows purely integer-based indexing. Its syntax is .iloc[row_selection, column_selection].

Let's take a look at a few examples. First, we need to create a DataFrame to work with.

```
>>> import pandas as pd
>>> df = pd.DataFrame({
...     'Name': ['Alice', 'Bob', 'Charlie', 'Dave'],
...     'Age': [25, 32, 18, 48],
...     'Height': [5.5, 6.0, 5.8, 5.9],
...     'Weight': [130, 150, 140, 170]
... })

>>> df
      Name  Age  Height  Weight
0    Alice   25     5.5     130
1      Bob   32     6.0     150
2  Charlie   18     5.8     140
3     Dave   48     5.9     170
```

To select the first three rows of our DataFrame, we can use the slice :3 with iloc.

```
>>> df.iloc[:3]
      Name  Age  Height  Weight
0    Alice   25     5.5     130
1      Bob   32     6.0     150
2  Charlie   18     5.8     140
```

When you use .iloc in pandas, you can pass in a slice to select rows and another slice to select columns. In this example, we pass in : as a row selector and 1:3 as the column selector. The : will select all of the rows. 1:3 will select the columns in positions 1 through (but not including) 3. *Name* is in position 0, *Age* is in 1, and *Height* is in 2.

```
>>> df.iloc[:, 1:3]
   Age  Height
```

23. Indexing and Slicing

```
0   25    5.5
1   32    6.0
2   18    5.8
3   48    5.9
```

The following command selects the first three rows and the first two columns.

```
>>> df.iloc[:3, :2]
     Name  Age
0   Alice   25
1     Bob   32
2 Charlie   18
```

Note that negative indexing works as well. It starts counting from the end. For instance, -1: gets the last row, and :-1 gets all but the last row.

```
>>> df.iloc[-1:]
   Name  Age  Height  Weight
3  Dave   48     5.9     170

>>> df.iloc[:-1]
     Name  Age  Height  Weight
0   Alice   25     5.5     130
1     Bob   32     6.0     150
2 Charlie   18     5.8     140
```

23.5 Summary

You use indexing operations to pull single values out of sequences. This makes it easy to get a character from a string or an item from a list or tuple.

If you want subsequences, you can use the slicing construct. Slicing follows the half-open interval and gives you the sequence up to but not including the last index. You can skip elements in a slice if you provide an optional stride.

Python has a nice feature that allows you to use negative values to index or slice relative to the end of the sequence. This lets you do your operations relative to the length of the sequence, and you don't have to worry about calculating the length of the sequence and subtracting from that.

23.6 Exercises

1. Create a variable with your name stored as a string. Use indexing operations to pull out the first character. Pull out the last character. Will your code to pull out the last character work on a name of arbitrary length?

23.6. Exercises

2. Create a variable, `filename`. Assuming that it has a three-letter extension, and using slice operations, find the extension. For `README.txt`, the extension should be `txt`. Write code using slice operations that will give the name without the extension. Does your code work on filenames of arbitrary length?
3. Create a function, `is_palindrome`, to determine if a supplied word is the same if the letters are reversed.

Chapter 24

File Input and Output

Reading and writing files is common in programming. Python makes these operations easy. You can read both text and binary files. You can also read a file by the number of bytes, lines, or even the whole file at once. There are similar options available for writing files.

24.1 Opening Files

The Python function, open, returns a file object. This function has many optional parameters:

```
open(filename, mode='r', buffering=-1, encoding=None,
    errors=None, newline=None, closefd=True, opener=None)
```

> **Note**
>
> Windows paths use \ as a separator, which can be problematic. Python strings also use \ as an escape character. If you had a directory named "test" and wrote "C:\test", Python would treat \t as a tab character.
>
> The remedy for this is to use raw strings to represent Windows paths. Put an r in front of the string:
>
> r"C:\test"

We typically are only concerned with a few parameters. The first parameter, the filename, is required. The second parameter is the mode, which determines if you are reading or writing a file and if the file is a text file or a binary file. There are various modes.

Mode	Meaning
'r'	Read text file (default)
'w'	Write text file (overwrites if exists)

201

24. File Input and Output

Mode	Meaning
'x'	Write text file, throw `FileExistsError` if it exists.
'a'	Append to text file (write to end)
'rb'	Read binary file
'wb'	Write binary (overwrite)
'w+b'	Open binary file for reading and writing
'xb'	Write binary file, throw `FileExistsError` if it exists.
'ab'	Append to a binary file (write to end)

It can also be helpful to be specific about the file encoding. We will discuss that in the next chapter when we discuss Unicode.

For details on the rest of the options to the `open` function, pass it into `help`. This function has very detailed documentation.

Typically, when dealing with text files, we use `'r'` as the mode to *read* a file and `'w'` to *write* a file. Here, we open the file `/tmp/a.txt` on a UNIX system for writing. Python will create that file or overwrite it if it already exists:

```
>>> a_file = open('/tmp/a.txt', 'w')
```

The file object, returned from the `open` call, has various methods for reading and writing. This chapter discusses the most commonly used methods. To read the full documentation on a file object, pass it to the `help` function. It will list all of the methods and describe what they do.

> **Note**
>
> /tmp is where Unix systems place temporary files. If you are on Windows, you can inspect the `Temp` variable by typing:
>
> `c:\> ECHO %Temp%`
>
> The value is usually:
>
> `C:\Users\<username>\AppData\Local\Temp'`

24.2 Reading Text Files

Python provides multiple ways to read data from files. We deal with strings if you open a file in text mode (the default). We read strings from the file, or we write strings to it. If we open a file in binary mode (using a `'rb'` for reading or `'wb'` for writing), we will read and write *byte* strings.

If you want to read a single line from an existing text file, use the `.readline` method. If we don't specify a mode, Python will default to reading a text file (mode of r).

Let's read the UNIX password file:

24.2. Reading Text Files

```
>>> passwd_file = open('/etc/passwd')
>>> passwd_file.readline()
'root:x:0:0:root:/root:/bin/bash'
```

Be careful if you open a file for reading that does not exist, Python will throw an error:

```
>>> fin = open('bad_file')
Traceback (most recent call last):
  ...
IOError: [Errno 2] No such file or
directory: 'bad_file'
```

> **Note**
>
> The open function returns a *file object* instance. This object has methods to read and write data.
>
> Common variable names for file objects are fin (file input), fout (file output), fp (file pointer, used for either input or output) or names such as passwd_file. Useful names like fin and fout can indicate whether the file is used for reading or writing, respectively.

As illustrated above, the .readline method will return one line of a file. You can call it repeatedly to retrieve every line or use the .readlines method to return a list containing all the lines.

To read all the contents of a file into one string, use the .read method:

```
>>> passwd_file = open('/etc/passwd')
>>> print(passwd_file.read())
root:x:0:0:root:/root:/bin/bash
bin:x:1:1:bin:/bin:/bin/false
daemon:x:2:2:daemon:/sbin:/bin/false
adm:x:3:4:adm:/var/adm:/bin/false
```

You should always close your files when you are done with them by calling .close:

```
>>> passwd_file.close()
```

Closing your files is easy. A bit later, you will dig into why you should make sure you close them.

24.3 Reading Binary Files

Pass in `'rb'` (read binary) as the mode to read a binary file. When you read a binary file, you will not get strings but byte strings. Don't worry, as the interface for byte strings is very similar to strings. Here are the first eight bytes of a PNG file. To read eight bytes, you will pass 8 to the `.read` method:

```
>>> bfin = open('img/dict.png', 'rb')
>>> bfin.read(8)
b'\x89PNG\r\n\x1a\n'
```

Notice the b in front of the string, specifying that this is a byte string. You can also use `.readline` on binary files, and it will read until it gets to a `b'\n'`. Binary strings versus regular strings will be discussed in a later chapter.

24.4 Iteration with Files

Iteration over sequences was discussed previously. In Python, it is easy to iterate over the lines in a file. When dealing with a text file, you can iterate over the `.readlines` method to get a line at a time:

```
>>> fin = open('/etc/passwd')
>>> for line in fin.readlines():
...     print(line)
```

However, because `.readlines` returns a list, Python will need to read the whole file to create that list, which could be problematic. Say the file was a large log file. It could potentially consume all of your memory to read it. Python has a trick up its sleeve, though. Python allows you to loop over the file instance itself to iterate over the lines of the file. When you iterate directly over the file, Python is lazy and only reads the lines of text as needed:

```
>>> fin = open('/etc/passwd')
>>> for line in fin:
...     print(line)
```

How can you iterate directly over the file instance? Python has a dunder method, `.__iter__`, that defines the behavior for looping over an instance. It just so happens that for the file class, the `.__iter__` method iterates over the lines in the file.

The `.readlines` method should be reserved for when you are sure that you can hold the file in memory and you need to access the lines multiple times. Otherwise, directly iterating over the file is preferred.

24.5 Writing Files

You must first open the file in *write* mode to write to a file. If mode is set to `'w'`, the file is opened for writing text data:

```
>>> fout = open('/tmp/names.txt', 'w')
>>> fout.write('George')
```

If the file exists, the above method will try to overwrite the file /tmp/names.txt. Otherwise, the file will be created. Permission Error will be thrown if you don't have permission to access the file. If the path is bad, you will see a FileNotFoundError.

Two methods used to place data in a file are .write and .writelines. The .write method takes a string as a parameter and writes it to the file. The .writelines method takes a sequence containing string data and writes it to the file.

> **Note**
>
> To include newlines in your file, you must explicitly pass them to the file methods. On Unix platforms, strings passed into .write should end with \n. Likewise, each of the strings in the sequence passed into .writelines should end in \n. On Windows, the newline string is \r\n.
>
> To program in a cross-platform manner, the linesep string found in the os module defines the correct newline string for the platform:
>
> ```
> >>> import os
> >>> os.linesep    # Unix platform
> '\n'
> ```

> **Note**
>
> If you are trying this out on the interpreter right now, you may notice that the /tmp/names.txt file is empty even though you told Python to write George in it. What is going on?
>
> File output is *buffered* by the operating system. To optimize writes and preserve the lifetime of the storage media, the operating system will only write data after a certain threshold has been passed. On Linux systems, this is normally 4K bytes.
>
> To force writing the data, you can call the .flush method, which *flushes* the pending data to the storage media.
>
> A more heavy-handed mechanism to ensure that data is written is to call the .close method. This informs Python that you are done writing to the file:
>
> ```
> >>> fout2 = open('/tmp/names2.txt',
> ...              'w')
> ```

24. File Input and Output

```
>>> fout2.write('John\n')
>>> fout2.close()
```

24.6 Closing Files

As mentioned previously, calling .close will write the file buffers out to the storage media. The best practice in Python is to always close files after you finish using them (whether for writing or reading).

Here are a few reasons why you should explicitly close your files:

- If you have a file in a global variable, it will never be closed while your program is executing.
- cPython will automatically close your files for you if they are garbage collected. Other Python implementations may not.
- Unless you call .flush, you won't know when your data is written.
- Your operating system probably has a limit of open files per process.
- Some operating systems won't let you delete an open file.

Python usually takes care of garbage collection for you, and you don't have to worry about cleaning up objects. Opening and closing files are exceptions. Python will automatically close the file for you when the file object goes out of scope. But this is a case where you shouldn't rely on garbage collection. Be explicit and clean up after yourself. Make sure you close your files!

Python 2.5 introduced the with statement to the language. The with statement is used with *context managers* to enforce conditions that occur before and after a block is executed. The open function also serves as a context manager to ensure that a file is opened before the block is entered and closed when it is exited. Below is an example:

```
>>> with open('/tmp/names3.txt', 'w') as fout3:
...     fout3.write('Ringo\n')
```

This is the equivalent of:

```
>>> fout3 = open('/tmp/names3.txt', 'w')
>>> fout3.write('Ringo\n')
>>> fout3.close()
```

Notice that the with line ends with a colon. When a line ends with a colon in Python, you always indent the following code. The indented content following a colon is called a *block* or the body of the context manager. In the above example, the block consists of writing Ringo to a file. Then the block finishes. You can't see it in the above example, but you know a with block ends when the code is dedented. At this point, the context manager executes the exit logic. The exit logic for the file context manager tells Python to automatically close the file for you when the block is finished.

24.7. Designing Around Files

> **Note**
>
> Use the with construct for reading and writing files. It is a good practice to close files; if you use the with statement when using files, you do not have to worry about closing them. The with statement automatically closes the file for you.

24.7 Designing Around Files

You have seen how to use functions to organize and compartmentalize complicated programs. One benefit to using functions is that you can reuse those functions throughout your code. Here is a tip for organizing functions that deal with files.

Assume that you want to write code that takes a filename and creates a sequence of the lines from the file with the line number inserted before every line. At first thought, it might seem that you want the API (application programming interface) for your functions to accept the filename of the file that you want to modify, like this:

```
>>> def add_numbers(filename):
...     results = []
...     with open(filename) as fin:
...         for num, line in enumerate(fin):
...             results.append(f'{num}-{line}')
...     return results
```

This code will work okay. But what will happen when you need to insert line numbers in front of lines from a source other than a file? If you want to test the code, now you can access the file system. One solution is to refactor the add_numbers function to only open the file in a context manager and then call another function, add_nums_to_seq. This new function contains logic that operates on a sequence rather than depending on a filename. Since a file behaves as a sequence of strings, you preserve the original functionality:

```
>>> def add_numbers(filename):
...     with open(filename) as fin:
...         return add_nums_to_seq(fin)

>>> def add_nums_to_seq(seq):
...     results = []
...     for num, line in enumerate(seq):
...         results.append(f'{num}-{line}')
...     return results
```

Now you have a more general function, add_nums_to_seq, that is easier to test and reuse because instead of depending on a filename, it depends on a sequence. You can pass in a list of strings or create a fake file to pass into it.

24. File Input and Output

Consider the original add_numbers function. Testing this function means we'd always have to create an actual file, write specific content, and then run our function. This approach makes testing cumbersome and slows it down, as file operations are typically much slower than in-memory operations.

By refactoring and introducing add_nums_to_seq, we can test the core logic of numbering lines without touching the file system. This means tests can be faster and more focused. We can pass a list of strings directly to add_nums_to_seq and validate its output. For instance:

```python
def test_add_nums_to_seq():
    assert add_nums_to_seq(["a", "b", "c"]) == ["0-a", "1-b", "2-c"]
```

Our initial design is tied to files. But what if the source of our data changes? What if we want to number lines from data coming from a network socket, a database, or an API response?

By separating the core logic from the file operation, add_nums_to_seq can work with any sequence, making it flexible and adaptable to different data sources. This separation of concerns also ensures that any changes to how we source our data won't affect our core logic of adding numbers to sequences.

> **Note**
>
> Other types also implement the file-like interface (read and write). Any time you find yourself coding with a filename, ask yourself if you may want to apply the logic to other sequence-like things. If so, use the previous example of refactoring the functions to create code that is much easier to reuse and test.

24.8 CSV files in Pandas

Loading data from CSV files is a common task when using pandas.

Let's create a CSV file using the .write method:

```
>>> data = '''Name,Age,City
... John,28,New York
... Anna,24,Paris
... Peter,35,Berlin
... Linda,32,London'''

>>> with open('myfile.csv', 'w') as fout:
...     fout.write(data)
```

The pandas .read_csv function will create a DataFrame from a CSV file. Here's an example:

```
>>> import pandas as pd
>>> df = pd.read_csv('myfile.csv')
```

```
>>> df.head()
    Name  Age      City
0   John   28  New York
1   Anna   24     Paris
2  Peter   35    Berlin
3  Linda   32    London
```

In this example, `'myfile.csv'` is the name of the CSV file that we want to load. This file must be in the same directory as the Python script or notebook you're running. If it's in a different directory, you'll have to specify the full path to the file.

If you have a file object instead of a filename, you can pass that to read_csv as well. Here's how you could do this:

```
>>> with open('myfile.csv', 'r') as f:
...     df = pd.read_csv(f)
>>> df.head()
    Name  Age      City
0   John   28  New York
1   Anna   24     Paris
2  Peter   35    Berlin
3  Linda   32    London
```

In this case, the open function returns a file object, which is then passed to read_csv. This can be useful in situations where you need more control over how the file is opened, such as when working with files in unusual formats.

The read_csv function has many more options[1] that allow you to control how the CSV file is loaded. You can specify a column to use as the index, specify the data type of each column, handle missing values, and much more. Pandas has the ability to load other types of files as well, such as Excel spreadsheets, Parquet files, and JSON files. [2]

24.9 Summary

Python provides a single function to interact with both text and binary files, open. Specifying the mode lets you tell Python whether you want to read or write to the file. When you are dealing with text files, you read and write strings. When you are dealing with binary files, you read and write byte strings.

Make sure you close your files. Using the with statement is the idiomatic way to do this. Finally, make sure your functions deal with sequences of data instead of filenames, as this makes your code more generally useful.

---
[1] See https://pandas.pydata.org/docs/reference/api/pandas.read_csv.html
[2] See https://pandas.pydata.org/pandas-docs/stable/user_guide/io.html

24. File Input and Output

24.10 Exercises

1. Write a function to write a comma-separated value (CSV) file. It should accept a filename and a list of tuples as parameters. The tuples should have a name, address, and age. The file should create a header row followed by a row for each tuple. If the following list of tuples was passed in:

   ```
   [('George', '4312 Abbey Road', 22),
    ('John', '54 Love Ave', 21)]
   ```

   it should write the following in the file:

   ```
   name,address,age
   George,4312 Abbey Road,22
   John,54 Love Ave,21
   ```

2. Write a function that reads a CSV file. It should return a list of dictionaries, using the first row as key names, and each subsequent row as values for those keys. For the data in the previous example, it would return:

   ```
   [{'name': 'George', 'address': '4312 Abbey Road', 'age': 22},
    {'name': 'John', 'address': '54 Love Ave', 'age': 21}]
   ```

Chapter 25

Unicode

We've seen strings all over the place, but we haven't discussed one of the most significant changes in Python 3: Unicode strings! Python 2 supported Unicode strings, but you needed to create them explicitly. This is no longer the case. Everything is Unicode.

25.1 Background

What is Unicode? It is a standard for representing glyphs (the characters that create most written language, symbols, and emoji). The standard can be found on the Unicode website[1] and is frequently updated. The standard consists of various documents or charts that map *code points* (hexadecimal numbers such as 0048 or 1F600) to glyphs (such as H or 😀), and names (*LATIN CAPITAL H* and *GRINNING FACE*). The code points and names are unique, though many glyphs may look similar visually.

Here is a condensed history. As computers became prevalent, different providers had different schemes to map binary data to string data. One *encoding*, ASCII, would use 7 bits of data to map to 128 symbols and control codes. That works fine in a Latin character-centric environment such as English. Having 128 different glyphs would provide enough space for lowercase characters, uppercase characters, digits, and standard punctuation.

As support for non-English languages became more common, ASCII was not sufficient. Windows systems through Windows 98 supported an encoding called Windows-1252, which supported various accented characters and symbols such as the Euro sign.

These encoding schemes provided a one-to-one mapping of bytes to a character. To support Chinese, Korean, and Japanese scripts, many more than 128 symbols were needed. Using four bytes provided support for over 4 billion characters. But this encoding came at a cost. For most people using

---

[1] https://unicode.org

25. Unicode

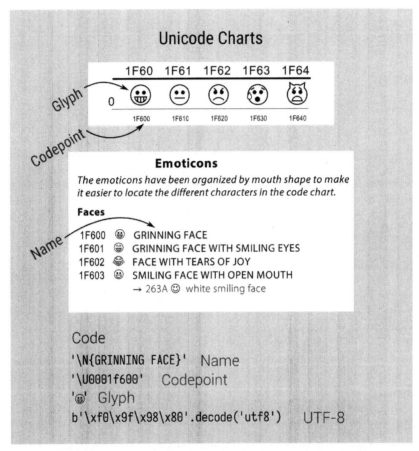

Figure 25.1: This illustrates how to read code charts found at unicode.org. The charts have tables listing glyphs by their hex code points. Following that table is another table with the codepoint, glyph, and name. You can use a glyph, the name, or the code point. If the code point has more than 4 digits, you need to use capital U and left pad with 0 until you have 8 digits. If it has 4 or fewer digits, you need to use a lowercase u and left pad with 0 until you have 4 digits. Also shown is an example of decoding the UTF-8 byte string to the corresponding glyph.

25.2. Basic steps in Python

only ASCII-centric characters, requiring those characters to be encoded in four times as much data seemed like a colossal waste of memory.

A compromise that provided both the ability to support all characters but not waste memory was to stop encoding characters to a sequence of bits. Instead, the characters were abstracted. Each character is mapped to a unique *code point* (that has a hex value and a unique name). Various encodings then mapped these code points to bit encodings. Unicode maps from a character to a code point—it is not the encoding. For different contexts, an alternate encoding might provide better characteristics.

One encoding, UTF-32, uses four bytes to store the character information. This representation is straightforward for low-level programmers, as indexing operations are trivial. But it uses four times the amount of memory as ASCII to encode a Latin sequence of letters.

The notion of variable-width encodings also helped alleviate memory waste. UTF-8 is one such encoding. It uses between one and four bytes to represent a character. In addition, UTF-8 is backward compatible with ASCII. UTF-8 is the most common encoding on the web and is an excellent choice for encoding since many applications and operating systems know how to deal with it.

> **Note**
>
> You can find the preferred encoding on your machine by running the following code. Here is mine on a Mac:
>
> ```
> >>> import locale
> >>> locale.getpreferredencoding(False)
> 'UTF-8'
> ```

Let's be clear. UTF-8 is an encoding of bytes for Unicode code points. Referring to UTF-8 as Unicode is a conflation and might indicate a fundamental misconception regarding character encodings. In fact, the term 'UTF-8' stands for Unicode Transformation Format - 8-bit, underscoring its role as an *encoding format specifically tailored for Unicode*.

Let's look at an example. The character named *SUPERSCRIPT TWO* is defined in the Unicode standard as code point *U+00b2*. It has a *glyph* (a written representation) of [2]. ASCII has no way to represent this character. Windows-1252 does. It is encoded as the hex byte *b2* (which happens to be the same as the code point, note that this is not guaranteed). In UTF-8, it is encoded as *c2 b2*. Likewise, UTF-16 encodes it as *ff fe b2 00*. There are multiple encodings for this Unicode code point.

25.2 Basic steps in Python

You can create Unicode strings in Python. You have been doing it all along. Remember, in Python 3, strings are Unicode strings. But you probably want to create a string that has a non-ASCII character. Below is the code for a string

213

with x squared (x²). If you can find the glyph you want to use, you can copy that character into your code:

```
>>> result = 'x²'
```

This works in general. However, you might have problems if your font does not support said glyph. Then you will get what is sometimes called *tofu* because it looks like an empty box or a diamond with a question mark (□). Another way to include non-ASCII characters is to use the hex Unicode code point following \u:

```
>>> result2 = 'x\u00b2'
```

Note that this string is the same as the previous string:

```
>>> result == result2
True
```

Finally, you can use the name of the code point inside of the curly braces in \N{}:

```
>>> result3 = 'x\N{SUPERSCRIPT TWO}'
```

All of these work. They all return the same Unicode string:

```
>>> print(result, result2, result3)
x² x² x²
```

The third option is a little verbose and requires a little more typing. But if you don't speak native code point or have font support, it is perhaps the most readable.

> **Note**
>
> The Python help documentation has an entry for Unicode. Type help(), then UNICODE. It doesn't discuss Unicode that much but rather the different ways to create Python strings.

25.3 Encoding

Perhaps one of the keys to grokking Unicode in Python is to understand that you *encode a Unicode string to a byte string*. You never encode a byte string. You *decode a byte string to a Unicode string*. Likewise, you never decode a Unicode string. Another way of looking at encoding and decoding is that encoding transforms a human-readable or meaningful representation into an abstract representation meant for storage (Unicode to bytes or letter to bytes), and decoding transforms that abstract representation back to a human-readable or meaningful representation.

Given a Unicode string, you can call the .encode method to see the representation in various encodings. Let's start off with UTF-8:

25.3. Encoding

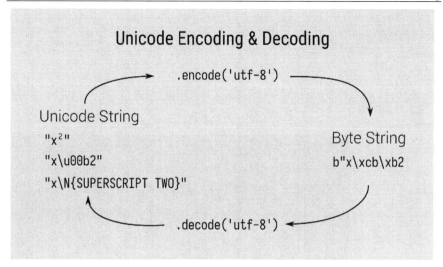

Figure 25.2: Image illustrates the *encoding* (in this case using UTF-8) of a Unicode string into its byte representation, and then the *decoding* of the same byte string back into Unicode (also using UTF-8). Note that you should be explicit when decoding, as there are other encodings that, if used, might produce erroneous data or mojibake (character transformation).

```
>>> x_sq = 'x\u00b2'
>>> x_sq.encode('utf-8')
b'x\xc2\xb2'
```

If Python does not support an encoding, it will throw a UnicodeEncodeError. This means that the Unicode code points are not supported in that encoding. For example, ASCII does not have support for the squared character:

```
>>> x_sq.encode('ascii')
Traceback (most recent call last):
  ...
UnicodeEncodeError: 'ascii' codec can't encode character
'\xb2' in position 1: ordinal not in range(128)
```

If you use Python long enough, you will probably encounter this error. It means that the specified encoding cannot represent all of the characters. If you are certain that you want to force Python to this encoding, there are a few different options you can provide to the errors parameter. To ignore characters Python can't encode, use errors='ignore':

```
>>> x_sq.encode('ascii', errors='ignore')
b'x'
```

25. Unicode

If you specify errors='replace', Python will insert a question mark for the unsupported bytes:

```
>>> x_sq.encode('ascii', errors='replace')
b'x?'
```

> **Note**
>
> The encodings module has a mapping of aliases of encodings that Python supports. There are many encodings in Python. Most modern applications try to stay in UTF-8, but if you need support for other encodings, there is a good chance that Python has support for it.
>
> This mapping is found in encodings.aliases.aliases. Alternatively, the documentation on the module at the Python website[a] has a table of the encodings.
>
> [a] https://docs.python.org/3/library/codecs.html

Here are some other possible encodings for this string:

```
>>> x_sq.encode('cp1026')    # Turkish
b'\xa7\xea'
>>> x_sq.encode('cp949')     # Korean
b'x\xa9\xf7'
>>> x_sq.encode('shift_jis_2004')    # Japanese
b'x\x85K'
```

Though Python supports many encodings, their usage is becoming rarer. Typically they are used for legacy applications. Today, most applications use UTF-8.

25.4 Decoding

Decoding has a specific meaning in Python. It means to take a sequence of bytes and create a Unicode string from them. In Python, you never encode bytes, you decode them (in fact there is no .encode method on bytes). If you can remember that rule, it can save a bit of frustration when dealing with non-ASCII characters.

Let's assume that you have the UTF-8 byte sequence for x^2:

```
>>> utf8_bytes = b'x\xc2\xb2'
```

When you are dealing with character data represented as bytes, you want to get it into a Unicode string as soon as possible. Typically, you will only deal with strings in your application and use bytes as a serialization mechanism (i.e. when persisting to files or sending over the network). If you received these bytes somehow and the framework or library that you were using did not convert it into a string for you, you could do the following:

25.4. Decoding

```
>>> text = utf8_bytes.decode('utf-8')
>>> text
'x²'
```

It's important to recognize that a sequence of bytes does not convey its encoding mechanism. While the byte sequence in the provided code is identifiable as UTF-8 due to its direct creation in that context, an arbitrary sequence received from an external source lacks this inherent clarity. Without explicit metadata or accompanying documentation, one should exercise caution in assuming its encoding schema.

> **Note**
>
> It is imperative to be informed of the specific encoding used. Absent this knowledge, there's a risk of applying an incorrect decoding mechanism, leading to data corruption. This phenomenon of character distortion is referred to as *mojibake*—a term derived from the Japanese language meaning "character mutation".
>
> Here are some examples of erroneous decoding. We are taking the UTF-8 bytes and trying to decode them with the wrong encoding. The results are, as you might expect, not good:
>
> ```
> >>> b'x\xc2\xb2'.decode('cp1026')   # Turkish
> 'İB¥'
> >>> b'x\xc2\xb2'.decode('cp949')    # Korean
> 'x쒲'
> >>> b'x\xc2\xb2'.decode('shift_jis_2004')  # Japanese
> 'xツ²'
> ```

But some encodings don't support all byte sequences. If you decode with the wrong encoding, sometimes instead of getting bad data, you get an exception. For example, ASCII does not support this byte sequence:

```
>>> b'x\xc2\xb2'.decode('ascii')
Traceback (most recent call last):
    ...
UnicodeDecodeError: 'ascii' codec can't decode byte 0xc2
in position 1: ordinal not in range(128)
```

A `UnicodeDecodeError` means that you were trying to convert a byte string to a Unicode string and the encoding did not have support to create Unicode strings for all of the bytes. Typically, this means that you are using the wrong encoding. For best results, try to determine and use the correct encoding.

If you really don't know the encoding, you can pass the `errors='ignore'` parameter, but then you are losing data. This should only be used as a last resort:

```
>>> b'x\xc2\xb2'.decode('ascii', errors='ignore')
'x'
```

25.5 Unicode and Files

When you read a text file, Python will give you Unicode strings. By default, Python will use the default encoding (locale.getpreferredencoding(False)) of the operating system. If you want to encode a text file in another encoding, you can pass that information to the encoding parameter to the open function.

Likewise, you can specify the encoding when you open a file for writing. Remember, you should treat encodings as a serialization format (used to transfer information over the internet or store the data in a file). Here are two examples of writing to a file. With the first file, no encoding is defined, and it, therefore, defaults to UTF-8 (per the system's default encoding). In the second example, CP949 (Korean) is set as the encoding parameter:

```
>>> with open('/tmp/sq.utf8', 'w') as fout:
...     fout.write('x²')
>>> with open('/tmp/sq.cp949', 'w', encoding='cp949') as fout:
...     fout.write('x²')
```

From the UNIX terminal, look at the files. You see that they have different contents because they use different encodings:

```
$ hexdump /tmp/sq.utf8
0000000 78 c2 b2
0000003
$ hexdump /tmp/sq.cp949
0000000 78 a9 f7
0000003
```

You can read the data back:

```
>>> data = open('/tmp/sq.utf8').read()
>>> data
'x²'
```

Remember that in Python, *explicit is better than implicit*. When dealing with encodings, you need to be specific. Python on a UTF-8 system will try and decode from UTF-8 when you read a file. This is fine if the file is encoded with UTF-8, but if it is not, you will either get mojibake or an error:

```
>>> data = open('/tmp/sq.cp949').read()
Traceback (most recent call last):
    ...
UnicodeDecodeError: 'utf-8' codec can't decode byte
0xa9 in position 1: invalid start byte
```

If you are explicit and tell Python that this file was encoded with the CP949 encoding, you will get the correct data from this file:

```
>>> data = open('/tmp/sq.cp949', encoding='cp949').read()
>>> data
'x²'
```

If you are dealing with text files that contain non-ASCII characters, make sure you specify their encoding.

25.6 Unicode in SQLite

SQLite is a powerful database system with support for Unicode. This makes SQLite a good option when dealing with international or multilingual data.

As discussed, Unicode is a standard that maps unique code points (hexadecimal numbers) to characters. Python 3 uses Unicode for all its strings, and SQLite also uses Unicode.

Let's imagine you're building a database for a multilingual application, and you have data in different languages that you want to store and retrieve accurately. In this case, ensuring your SQLite database can handle Unicode characters correctly is crucial.

Firstly, when creating a SQLite database, the database itself does not need to know or care about the encoding of the strings you are storing, because Python handles all the encoding and decoding operations.

Let's use the Python `sqlite3` module to create a SQLite database and populate it with Unicode data. Here is an example:

```
>>> import sqlite3
>>> conn = sqlite3.connect('multilang.db')
>>> cursor = conn.cursor()
>>> cursor.execute("DROP TABLE iF EXISTS Languages")
>>> cursor.execute("CREATE TABLE Languages (name TEXT, greeting TEXT)")
<sqlite3.Cursor object at 0x7f5b6c1a8b90>
>>> data = [('English', 'Hello World'),
...         ('French', 'Bonjour le monde'),
...         ('Spanish', '¡Hola Mundo!'),
...         ('German', 'Hallo Welt'),
...         ('Japanese', 'こんにちは世界'),
...         ('Python', '\N{SNAKE}')]
>>> cursor.executemany("INSERT INTO Languages VALUES (?, ?)", data)
<sqlite3.Cursor object at 0x7f5b6c1a8b90>
>>> conn.commit()
```

In this example, we've created a new SQLite database named `multilang.db`. Inside this database, we've created a table named *Languages*, and populated it with the names of several languages and a greeting in each language. Note that we're using Unicode strings for non-English greetings.

25. Unicode

25.7 Retrieving Unicode from SQLite Database

Let's retrieve the data we've just inserted into our SQLite database. Here is how you can do it. First, we run our query:

```
>>> cursor.execute("SELECT * FROM Languages")
<sqlite3.Cursor object at 0x7f5b6c1a8b90>
```

Then we pull out all of the rows from the result:

```
>>> rows = cursor.fetchall()
>>> for row in rows:
...     print(row)
...
('English', 'Hello World')
('French', 'Bonjour le monde')
('Spanish', '¡Hola Mundo!')
('German', 'Hallo Welt')
('Japanese', 'こんにちは世界')
('Python', '🐍')
```

Finally, we close the connection when we are done.

```
>>> conn.close()
```

When you run this code, it will print the name of each language and its greeting, correctly displaying the Unicode characters for non-English greetings.

Note that SQLite will always return Unicode strings when you fetch data from the database.

25.8 Non-ASCII Data and Pandas

Encoding considerations become paramount when dealing with data sets encompassing a range of character sets. Let's explore a scenario involving a CSV file, *students.csv*, encoded in *cp1252* (a legacy Windows encoding). The file comprises the following entries:

```
name,country
José,Spain
François,France
Jürgen,Germany
```

This CSV file includes non-ASCII characters in the names.

Attempting to load this file into a pandas DataFrame without specifying the encoding can produce unintended results:

```
>>> import pandas as pd

# Attempt to read the CSV file without specifying the encoding
>>> students = pd.read_csv('students.csv')
Traceback (most recent call last):
  ...
UnicodeDecodeError: 'utf-8' codec can't decode byte 0xe9
in position 16: invalid continuation byte
```

As you can see, pandas wasn't able to read the file because, by default, it assumes the file is UTF-8 encoded.

Now let's specify `'cp1252'` as the encoding when reading the file:

```
>>> students = pd.read_csv('students.csv', encoding='cp1252')

>>> print(students.head())
       name   country
0      José     Spain
1  François    France
2    Jürgen   Germany
```

By specifying the correct encoding, pandas is now able to interpret and display the characters correctly.

25.9 Summary

Unicode is a mapping of code points to glyphs. In Python, strings can hold Unicode glyphs. You can *encode* the Unicode string to a byte string using various encodings. You never decode Python strings.

When you read a text file, you can specify the encoding to ensure you get a Unicode string containing the correct characters. When you write text files, you can use the encoding parameter to declare the encoding to use.

UTF-8 is the most popular encoding these days. Unless you have a reason to use another encoding, you should default to using UTF-8.

25.10 Exercises

1. Go to http://unicode.org and download a chart with code points. Choose a non-ASCII character and write Python code to print the character by both the code point and name.
2. Various Unicode characters appear to be upside-down versions of ASCII characters. Find a mapping of these characters (they should be a search away). Write a function that takes a string with ASCII characters and returns the upside-down version of that string.
3. Write the upside-down version of your name to a file. What are some of the possible encodings that support your name? What are some encodings that don't?

25. Unicode

4. ASCII does not support Smart quotes (or curly quotes). Write a function that takes an ASCII string as input and returns a string where the double quotes are replaced with smart quotes. For example, the string *Python comes with "batteries included"* should become *Python comes with "batteries included"* (if you look closely, you will see that with smart quotes, the left quotes curve differently than the right quotes).
5. Write a function that takes text with old-school emojis in it (:), :P, etc.). Using the emoji chart[1], add code to your function that replaces the text emojis with Unicode versions found in the chart.

---

[1] http://unicode.org/emoji/charts/full-emoji-list.html

Chapter 26

Classes

Strings, dictionaries, files, and integers are all objects. Even functions are objects. In Python, almost everything is an object. There are some exceptions. Keywords (such as in) are not objects. Also, variable names are not objects, but they do point to them. This chapter will delve deeper into what an object is.

26.1 Objects

"Object" is a somewhat ambiguous term. One definition of "Object-Oriented Programming" is using structures to group data (state) and methods (functions to alter state). Many object-oriented languages such as C++, Java, and Python use *classes* to define an object's state and the methods to alter that state. Whereas classes are the definition of the state and methods, *instances* are occurrences of said classes. Generally, when C++ or Java programmers say *object* they mean an instance of a class.

In Python, str is the name of the class used to store strings. The str class defines the methods of strings.

You can create an instance of the str class, b, by using Python's literal string syntax:

```
>>> b = "I'm a string"
>>> b
"I'm a string"
```

You will see many terms thrown about to talk about b. You may hear, "b is a string", "b is an object", "b is an instance of a string", or "b is a variable that points to a string". The latter is perhaps the most specific. But, b is not a string class.

26. Classes

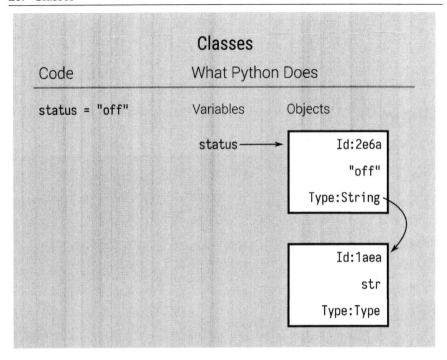

Figure 26.1: This illustrates a string object. All objects have types, which are really just the class of the object. In this case, the class is str.

> **Note**
>
> The str class can also be used to create strings but is typically used for casting. Strings literals are built into the language, so passing in a string literal into the str class would be redundant.
>
> You wouldn't say:
>
> ```
> >>> c = str("I'm a string")
> ```
>
> Because Python automatically creates a string when you put quotes around characters. The term *literal* means this is a special syntax built into Python to create strings.
>
> On the flip side, if you have a number that you want to convert to a string, you could call str:
>
> ```
> >>> num = 42
> >>> answer = str(num)
> >>> answer
> '42'
> ```

26.1. Objects

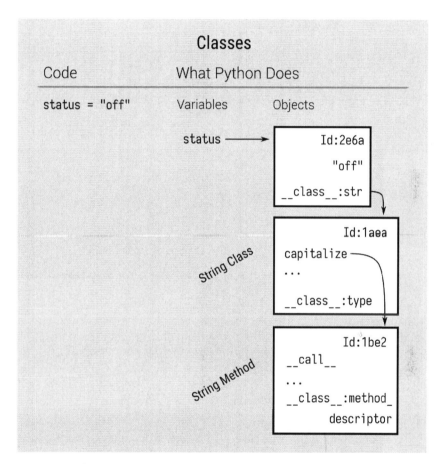

Figure 26.2: This illustrates an updated version of a string object. Type has been changed to __class__, because when you inspect the object, the __class__ attribute points to the object's class. Note that this class has various methods; this image only shows capitalize, but there are many more. Methods are also objects, as shown in the image.

26. Classes

It is said that Python comes with "batteries included"—it has libraries and classes predefined for your use. These classes tend to be generic. You can define your own classes that deal specifically with your problem domain. You can create customized objects that contain state, as well as logic to change that state.

26.2 Planning for a Class

First of all, classes are not always needed in Python. Sometimes, a simple function or a collection of functions can serve the purpose more efficiently. Classes typically represent entities, whether tangible items or abstract concepts. However, simple descriptors like speed or color might not warrant a class.

To decide whether you need a class, consider the following guiding questions:

1. **Naming**: Does the entity have a distinctive name or identifier?
2. **Properties/Attributes**:
    - What attributes does the entity possess?
    - Which attributes remain constant across instances?
    - Which ones might vary with individual instances?
3. **Behaviors/Methods**: What actions or behaviors are associated with the entity?

Imagine working at a ski resort, and you wish to represent the functioning of chairlifts. For those unfamiliar, a chairlift comprises multiple chairs that skiers sit on, transporting them from the base to the peak of a hill.

To decide on the need for a class:

1. **Naming**: Our entity is distinctly named: `Chair`
2. **Properties/Attributes**:
    - **Constant Attributes**: Chair number, maximum capacity, safety bar presence, type of seating (padded or not).
    - **Variable Attributes**: Current number of occupants.
3. **Behaviors/Methods**: Actions might include loading or unloading skiers at specific points. For simplicity, we can overlook actions like adjusting the safety bar.

By this breakdown, we realize that a chair on a chairlift has distinct attributes and behaviors, making it a suitable candidate for a class. Note that while designing this class, we're not concerned with the chair's material or the year it was built. Your class does not need to model everything and you can decide the level of relevant abstraction.

26.3 Defining a Class

Here is a Python class to represent a chair on a chairlift. Below is a simple class definition. The comments are numbered for discussion following the code:

```
>>> class Chair:                        # 1
...     ''' A Chair on a chairlift '''  # 2
...     max_occupants = 4               # 3
...
...     def __init__(self, id):         # 4
...         self.id = id                # 5
...         self.count = 0
...
...     def load(self, number):         # 6
...         self.count += number
...
...     def unload(self, number):       # 7
...         self.count -= number
```

The class statement in Python defines a class. You need to name it (1), followed by a colon. Remember that in Python, you indent following a colon (unless it is a slice). Note that you indented consistently below the class definition. All lines 2-7 are indented. Also, note that the name of the class was capitalized.

> **Note**
>
> The recommended naming convention for class names is *capital camelcase*. Because Chair is a single word, you might not have noticed. Unlike functions where words are joined together with underscores, in camel casing, you capitalize the first letter of each word and then shove them together. Normally class names are nouns. In Python, they cannot start with numbers. The following are examples of class names, both good and bad:
>
> - Kitten   # good
> - SnowLeopard   # good - camel case
> - jaguar   # bad - starts with lowercase
> - White_Tiger   # bad - has underscores
> - whiteTiger   # bad - starts with lowercase
> - 9Lives   # illegal - starts with a number
>
> See PEP 8 [a] for further insight into class naming.

> Note that, sadly, many of the built-in types do not follow this rule: str, int, float, etc.
>
> [a]https://www.python.org/dev/peps/pep-0008/

You can insert a docstring immediately following the class declaration (2). This is just a string. Note that if it is a triple-quoted string, it may span multiple lines. Docstrings are optional, but they are useful to your code's readers and appear when you use the help function to inspect your code in the REPL. Use them judiciously, and they will pay great dividends.

Inside the indented body of the class, you can create *class attributes* (3). A class attribute is used to hold a state that is shared among all class instances. In this example, any chair you create will have a maximum of four occupants. (Skiers call these types of chairlifts quads). There are advantages to creating class attributes. Because the class sets this number, you don't have to repeat yourself and set the value each time you create a chair. On the flip side, you have hard-coded your chair to only support four seats on it. Later, you will see how to override the class attribute.

Next, you see a def statement (4). It looks like you are defining a function inside of the class body. And you are, except when you define a function directly inside of a class body, you call it a *method*. Because this method has a special name, __init__, you call it a *constructor*. It has two parameters, self and id. Most methods have self as the first parameter. You can interpret self as being the instance of the class.

A constructor is called when you create an instance of a class. If you consider a class to be a factory that provides a template or blueprint for instances, then the constructor initializes the state for the instances. The constructor takes an instance as input (the self parameter), and updates it inside the method. Python takes care of passing around the instance for us. This can be confusing and will be discussed later.

Inside the body of the constructor (5) (it is indented because it follows a colon), you attach two attributes that will be unique to the instance, id and count. On most chairlifts, each chair on the chairlift has a unique number painted on the chair. The id represents this number. Also, a chair may hold several skiers—you store this in the count attribute and initialize it to zero. Note that the constructor does not return anything, but rather it updates values that are unique to the instance.

> **Note**
>
> Remember that id is a built-in function in Python, but you can also use that as an attribute name in a class. You will still have access to the id function. Every time you want to access the id attribute, you will do a lookup on the instance. If the instance was named chair, you would get the id by calling chair.id. So, this is not shadowing the built-in function and is ok.

26.3. Defining a Class

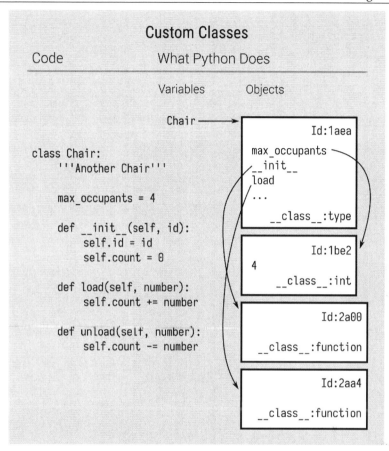

Figure 26.3: This illustrates what happens when you define a class. Python will create a new type for you. Any class attributes or methods will be stored as attributes of the new class. Instance attributes (id and count) are not found in the class as they will be defined on the instances.

You can tell that the constructor logic is finished when you see that the indentation level has changed and is stepped back out. You see another method defined (6), load. This method represents an action that an instance of the class can perform. In this case, a chair may load passengers onto it, and this method tells the instance what to do when that happens. Again, self (the instance), is the first parameter of the method. The second parameter, number, is the number of people that get on the chair. Given that chairlifts are designed to accommodate multiple passengers—potentially up to four in this instance—we will use the load method to update the chair's occupancy. Internally, the method would modify the count attribute of the instance to reflect the number of passengers boarded.

26. Classes

Likewise, there is a corresponding method, unload (7), that should be called when skiers dismount at the top of the hill.

> **Note**
>
> Don't be intimidated by methods. You have already seen many methods, such as the .capitalize method defined on a string. Methods are functions that are attached to a class. Instead of calling the method by itself, you need to call it on an instance of the class:
>
> ```
> >>> 'matt'.capitalize()
> 'Matt'
> ```

In summary, creating a class is easy. You define the attributes you want. The attributes that are constant are put inside the class definition. The attributes that are unique to an instance are put in the constructor. You can also define methods that contain actions that modify the instance of the class. After the class is defined, Python will create a variable with the name of the class that points to the class:

```
>>> Chair
<class '__main__.Chair'>
```

You can inspect the class with the dir function. Note that the class attributes are defined in the class, and you can access them directly on the class:

```
>>> dir(Chair)
['__class__', '__delattr__', '__dict__', '__dir__', '__doc__',
'__eq__', '__format__', '__ge__', '__getattribute__', '__gt__',
'__hash__', '__init__', '__le__', '__lt__', '__module__',
'__ne__', '__new__', '__reduce__', '__reduce_ex__', '__repr__',
'__setattr__', '__sizeof__', '__str__', '__subclasshook__',
'__weakref__', 'load', 'max_occupants', 'unload']
>>> Chair.max_occupants
4
```

The figure in this section shows how the attributes and methods of the class are stored. We can also inspect them from the REPL. Because everything is an object in Python, they will all have a __class__ attribute:

```
>>> Chair.__class__
<class 'type'>
>>> Chair.max_occupants.__class__
<class 'int'>
>>> Chair.__init__.__class__
<class 'function'>
>>> Chair.load.__class__
```

```
<class 'function'>
>>> Chair.unload.__class__
<class 'function'>
```

The methods are also defined in the class, but the instance attributes are not. Because instance attributes are unique to the instance, they will be stored on the instance.

If you have docstrings defined in your class or its methods, you can inspect them with help:

```
>>> help(Chair)
  Help on class Chair in module __main__:

  class Chair(builtins.object)
   |  A Chair on a chairlift
   |
   |  Methods defined here:
   |
   |  __init__(self, id)
   |
   |  load(self, number)
   |
   |  unload(self, number)
   |
   |  ----------------------------------------------------------
   |
   |  Data descriptors defined here:
   |
   |  __dict__
   |      dictionary for instance variables (if defined)
   |
   |  __weakref__
   |      list of weak references to the object (if defined)
   |
   |  ----------------------------------------------------------
   |
   |  Data and other attributes defined here:
   |
   |  max_occupants = 4
```

26.4 Creating an Instance of a Class

Now that you have defined a class representing a chair, you can create *instances* of chairs. One way to think of the Chair class is to compare it to a factory. The factory takes in bare objects and churns out chair objects.

To be more specific, this is pretty much what the constructor method, __init__ does. You'll notice that self is the first parameter. This is the bare

26. Classes

object. Python assigns the __class__ attribute (pointing to the Chair class) to the object before passing it into the constructor.

To better understand classes, one might find a metaphor insightful. Imagine a scenario often depicted in animations where infants await their destined families sleeping in clouds. Upon the appropriate moment, a stork arrives to retrieve the infant from the cloud and ensures its safe delivery to the awaiting domicile of the respective family.

When you call the constructor, Python picks a baby up from the cloud (gets an object for you). It delivers it to the house, making it a family member (it sets the __class__ to Chair or whatever your class is). Once the baby is inside the house, you can mold her, cut her hair, etc. Remember that objects store the state and mutate the state.

Below is the code to create chair number 21 in Python. When you invoke the class (i.e., put parentheses after the class name), you tell Python that you want to call the constructor. Unlike some languages, you don't need to say new or add the variable type, you just add parentheses with the constructor parameters following the name of the class:

```
>>> chair = Chair(21)
```

Again, to be specific with terminology, the chair variable points to an object or instance. It does not point to a class. The object has a class, Chair. The instance has a few attributes, including count and id.

You can access an instance attribute from the instance, chair. Consider these examples:

```
>>> chair.count
0
>>> chair.id
21
```

Python has a hierarchy for looking up attributes:

1. First, Python will look for the attribute on the instance.

2. Next, Python will try to find the attribute on the class. Because instances know about their class, Python will look there next.

3. If that fails, Python will raise an AttributeError, an apt error for a missing attribute.

For example, the max_occupants attribute is stored on the class, but you can access it from the instance:

```
>>> chair.max_occupants
4
```

26.4. Creating an Instance of a Class

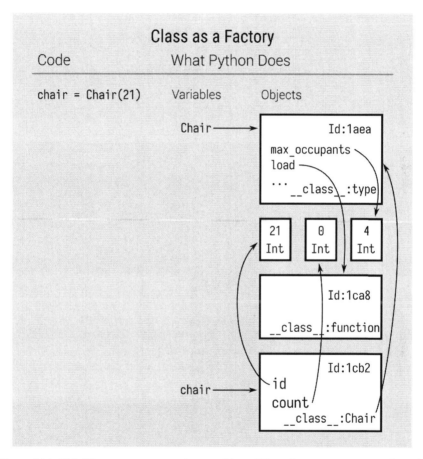

Figure 26.4: This illustrates constructing an object. When the constructor is called, the proverbial Python "stork" drops a baby object as self into the constructor. The baby object has the __class__ attribute set, but the constructor is free to alter the instance by adding attributes. This object will turn into chair.

26. Classes

When you run the above code, under the covers, Python is doing this for you:

```
>>> chair.__class__.max_occupants
4
```

Attribute lookup is different from variable lookup. Recall that Python looks for variables first in the local scope, then the global scope, then the built-in scope, and finally raises a `NameError` if it was unsuccessful. Attribute lookup occurs first on the instance, then the class, then the parent classes, and will raise an `AttributeError` if the attribute was not found.

26.5 Calling a Method on a Class

When you have an instance of a class, you can call methods on it. Methods—like functions—are invoked by adding parentheses with any arguments inside of them. Below, we will call the `.load` method to add 3 skiers to the chair:

```
>>> chair.load(3)
```

Here's a review of the syntax of method invocation. First, you list the instance, `chair`, which is followed by a period. A period means searching for an attribute in Python (unless it is following a number literal). When you see a period following an instance, remember that Python is going to search for what follows the period.

First, Python will look at the instance for `load`. This attribute was not found on the instance. Recall that only `count` and `id` were set on the instance inside of the constructor. But the instance has a link to its class. So if the search fails on the instance, Python will look for those attributes on the class. The `.load` method is defined on the `Chair` class, so Python returns that. The parentheses mean invoke or call the method. You are passing 3 in as a parameter to the method.

Recall that the declaration of `load` looked like this:

```
...     def load(self, number):      # 6
...         self.count += number
```

In the declaration, there were two parameters, `self` and `number`. But in the invocation, you only passed a single parameter, 3. Why the mismatch? The `self` parameter represents the instance, which is `chair` in your case. Python will call the `.load` method by inserting `chair` as the `self` parameter and 3 as the `number` parameter. In effect, Python handles passing around the `self` parameter for you automatically.

Note

When you call:

```
chair.load(3)
```

What happens under the covers is similar to this:

```
Chair.load(chair, 3)
```

You can try this out to validate that it works, but you wouldn't type this out in real life because it is harder to read, and also requires more typing.

26.6 Examining an Instance

If you have an instance and want to know what its attributes are, you have a few options. You can look up the documentation (if it exists). You can read the code where the class was defined. Or you can use `dir` to examine it for you:

```
>>> dir(chair)
['__class__', '__delattr__', '__dict__', '__dir__',
'__doc__', '__eq__', '__format__', '__ge__', '__getattribute__',
'__gt__', '__hash__', '__init__', '__le__', '__lt__',
'__module__', '__ne__', '__new__', '__reduce__', '__reduce_ex__',
'__repr__', '__setattr__', '__sizeof__', '__str__',
'__subclasshook__', '__weakref__', 'count', 'id', 'load',
'max_occupants', 'unload']
```

Recall that the `dir` function lists the attributes of an object. If you look at the documentation for `dir`, you see that the definition previously provided for `dir` is not quite correct. The documentation reads:

> return an alphabetized list of names comprising (some of) the attributes of the given object, *and of attributes reachable from it.*
>
> –help(dir) (emphasis added)

This function shows the attributes that are reachable from an object. The actual state of the instance is stored in the `__dict__` attribute, a dictionary mapping attribute names to values:

```
>>> chair.__dict__
{'count': 3, 'id': 21}
```

So, the instance really only stores `count` and `id`, the other attributes are available through the class. Where is the class stored? In the `__class__` attribute:

235

```
>>> chair.__class__
<class '__main__.Chair'>
```

It is important that an instance knows what its class is because the class stores the methods and class attributes.

26.7 Private and Protected

Some languages have the notion of private attributes or methods. These are methods that are meant to be implementation details, and end users can't call them. In fact, the language may prevent access to them.

Python does not try to prevent users from doing much of anything. Rather, it takes the attitude that you are an adult, and you should take responsibility for your actions. If you want to access something, you can do it. But you should be willing to accept the consequences.

Python programmers realize that it can be convenient to store state and methods that are implementation details. To signify to end users that they should not access these members, you prefix their name with an underscore. Here is a class that has a helper method, ._check, that is not meant to be called publicly:

```
>>> class CorrectChair:
...     ''' A Chair on a chairlift '''
...     max_occupants = 4
...
...     def __init__(self, id):
...         self.id = id
...         self.count = 0
...
...     def load(self, number):
...         new_val = self._check(self.count + number)
...         self.count = new_val
...
...     def unload(self, number):
...         new_val = self._check(self.count - number)
...         self.count = new_val
...
...     def _check(self, number):
...         if number < 0 or number > self.max_occupants:
...             raise ValueError(f'Invalid count:{number}')
...         return number
```

The ._check method is considered private, only the instance should access it inside the class. In the class, the .load and .unload methods call the private method. If wanted, you could call it from outside the class. But you shouldn't, as anything with an underscore should be considered an implementation detail that might not exist in future versions of the class.

26.8 A Simple Program Modeling Flow

Let's use the class above to model the flow of skiers up a hill. You will make some basic assumptions, such as every chair has an equal probability of 0 to max_occupants riding on it. It will turn on the chairlift, load it, and run forever. Four times a second, the program prints out the current statistics:

```python
import random
import time

class CorrectChair:
    '''A Chair on a chairlift.'''
    max_occupants = 4

    def __init__(self, id):
        self.id = id
        self.count = 0

    def load(self, number):
        new_val = self._check(self.count + number)
        self.count = new_val

    def unload(self, number):
        new_val = self._check(self.count - number)
        self.count = new_val

    def _check(self, number):
        if number < 0 or number > self.max_occupants:
            raise ValueError(f'Invalid count:{number}')
        return number

NUM_CHAIRS = 100
chairs = []

for num in range(1, NUM_CHAIRS + 1):
    chairs.append(CorrectChair(num))

def avg(chairs):
    total = 0
    for c in chairs:
        total += c.count
    return total / len(chairs)

in_use = []
transported = 0
```

26. Classes

```
while True:
    # loading
    loading = chairs.pop(0)
    in_use.append(loading)
    loading.load(random.randint(0, CorrectChair.max_occupants))

    # unloading
    if len(in_use) > NUM_CHAIRS / 2:
        unloading = in_use.pop(0)
        transported += unloading.count
        unloading.unload(unloading.count)
        chairs.append(unloading)

    print(f'Loading Chair {loading.id} '
          f'Count: {loading.count} Avg: {avg(in_use):.2f} '
          f'Total: {transported}')
    time.sleep(.25)
```

The above program operates in an infinite loop, continually displaying the count of passengers on the chairlift. While the current implementation displays this data on the terminal using the `print` function, it is possible to modify this output mechanism to generate and store this information in a CSV file.

Furthermore, the behavior of this simulation is tunable. Adjustments to the global variable `NUM_CHAIRS` and the class attribute `CorrectChair.max_occupants` enable one to tailor the program to represent chairlifts of varying capacities. Additionally, the utilization of `random.randint` for passenger count determination can be substituted with a more specialized function to better mimic specific passenger distribution patterns, should the need arise.

26.9 Summary

Within this chapter, we explored classes, including the jargon associated with them. Every instance is linked to a class, which can be envisioned as a blueprint or a mold, dictating the behavior and characteristics of its instances.

The instantiation of an object is controlled by a special method called the constructor, denoted as `__init__` in Python. Beyond the constructor, a class may house multiple additional methods tailored to its needs.

When writing a class, one must deliberate on its attributes. Should an attribute maintain a consistent value or behavior across all instances, we define them as class attributes. Conversely, attributes that necessitate unique values for individual instances should be initialized within the constructor.

26.10 Exercises

1. Imagine you are designing a banking application. What would a customer look like? What attributes would she have? What methods would she have?

2. Imagine you are creating a Super Mario game. You need to define a class to represent Mario. What would it look like? If you aren't familiar with Super Mario, use your own favorite video or board game to model a player.

3. Create a class that could represent a tweet. If you aren't familiar with Twitter, Wikipedia describes it as:

    > ... an online news and social networking service where users post and interact with messages, "tweets", restricted to 140 characters.
    >
    > –https://en.wikipedia.org/wiki/Twitter

4. Create a class that could represent a household appliance (toaster, washer, refrigerator, etc.).

Chapter 27

Classes for Data Science Work

We just introduced classes. In this chapter, we will examine two real-world uses of classes. One will use the Pandas library, and the other will use Scikit-learn.

Pandas, a powerful data manipulation library in Python, leverages the power of classes to work with data. One of the most commonly used classes in pandas is the DataFrame class.

Scikit-learn is one of the most used libraries for machine learning in Python. It provides simple and efficient data modeling and prediction tools, and it's built on NumPy, SciPy, and matplotlib. It's an object-oriented library where you can create objects to leverage different algorithms.

27.1 The DataFrame Class

A DataFrame is a two-dimensional tabular data structure with labeled axes (rows and columns). Here's an example of creating an instance of the DataFrame class:

```
>>> import pandas as pd

>>> data = {
...     "Name": ["Alice", "Bob", "Charles"],
...     "Age": [24, 32, 36],
...     "Country": ["USA", "UK", "Canada"],
... }

>>> # Create an instance of the DataFrame class
>>> df = pd.DataFrame(data)
```

Let's look at the DataFrame:

```
>>> print(df)
   Name  Age Country
```

27. Classes for Data Science Work

```
0    Alice   24     USA
1      Bob   32      UK
2  Charles   36  Canada
```

In this example, we first import the pandas library. Then we define a dictionary, data, that we will use to create our DataFrame. We create an instance of the DataFrame, df, class by calling the pd.DataFrame(data) class, passing our dictionary as an argument.

27.2 Examining the DataFrame

Once we have a DataFrame, we can inspect the attributes using the dir function.

```
>>> print(dir(df))
['Age', 'Country', 'Name', 'T', '_AXIS_LEN', '_AXIS_ORDERS',
['Age', 'Country', 'Name', 'T', '_AXIS_LEN', '_AXIS_ORDERS',
['Age', 'Country', 'Name', 'T', '_AXIS_LEN', '_AXIS_ORDERS',
'_AXIS_TO_AXIS_NUMBER', '_HANDLED_TYPES', '__abs__', '__add__', '__and__',
'__annotations__', '__array__', '__array_priority__', '__array_ufunc__',
'__bool__', '__class__', '__contains__', '__copy__', '__dataframe__',
'__deepcopy__', '__delattr__', '__delitem__', '__dict__',
...
'to_feather', 'to_gbq', 'to_hdf', 'to_html', 'to_json', 'to_latex',
'to_markdown', 'to_numpy', 'to_orc', 'to_parquet', 'to_period', 'to_pickle',
'to_records', 'to_sql', 'to_stata', 'to_string', 'to_timestamp', 'to_xarray',
'to_xml', 'transform', 'transpose', 'truediv', 'truncate', 'tz_convert',
'tz_localize', 'unstack', 'update', 'value_counts', 'values', 'var', 'where',
'xs']
```

It turns out that there are over 400 different attributes on a DataFrame (I have not shown all of them). Many of these attributes are methods. Others represent state stored on the instance.

27.3 Calling a DataFrame Method

DataFrames have many built-in methods that make it easy to manipulate and analyze your data. For example, you can use the .describe method to analyze your data:

```
>>> df.describe()
            Age
count   3.000000
mean   30.666667
std     6.110101
min    24.000000
```

```
25%    28.000000
50%    32.000000
75%    34.000000
max    36.000000
```

The .describe method provides summary statistics for your data.

There are a few hundred other methods in the DataFrame class. Check out the book *Effective Pandas* to learn more about which of these methods are useful.

27.4 Using Classes with Scikit-learn

One of the classes provided by scikit-learn is the LogisticRegression class, which is used for classification tasks. Here's an example of loading a dataset dealing with iris flower shapes:

```
>>> from sklearn.linear_model import LogisticRegression
>>> from sklearn import datasets
>>> iris = datasets.load_iris()
```

Now, let's create an instance of the LogisticRegression class to predict iris varieties based on those shapes:

```
>>> # Create an instance of the LogisticRegression class
>>> model = LogisticRegression()
```

In the above example, we first import the LogisticRegression class from scikit-learn. Then we create an instance of the LogisticRegression class, model.

The Iris dataset was introduced by the British statistician and biologist Ronald Fisher in his 1936 paper[1]. The dataset consists of 50 samples from three species of Iris (setosa, virginica, and versicolor). The samples measure the petal and sepal dimensions.

We will train a predictive model to provide the type of iris based on petal and sepal dimensions.

Here is the training data:

```
>>> print(pd.DataFrame(iris.data, columns=iris.feature_names))
     sepal length (cm)  sepal width (cm)  petal length (cm)  petal width (cm)
0                  5.1               3.5                1.4               0.2
1                  4.9               3.0                1.4               0.2
2                  4.7               3.2                1.3               0.2
3                  4.6               3.1                1.5               0.2
4                  5.0               3.6                1.4               0.2
..                 ...               ...                ...               ...
145                6.7               3.0                5.2               2.3
```

---

[1] https://onlinelibrary.wiley.com/doi/10.1111/j.1469-1809.1936.tb02137.x

27. Classes for Data Science Work

```
146          6.3          2.5          5.0          1.9
147          6.5          3.0          5.2          2.0
148          6.2          3.4          5.4          2.3
149          5.9          3.0          5.1          1.8

[150 rows x 4 columns]
```

The labels are found in the .target attribute and refer to the iris variety setosa, versicolor, and virginica for 0, 1, and 2, respectively.

```
>>> pd.Series(iris.target)
0      0
1      0
2      0
3      0
4      0
      ..
145    2
146    2
147    2
148    2
149    2
Length: 150, dtype: int64
```

27.5 Calling a LogisticRegression Method

Let's train the logistic regression model. This is done by calling the .fit method and passing in our data:

```
>>> X = iris.data
>>> y = iris.target
>>> model.fit(X, y)
```

After calling the .fit method, the model will learn from the data and be ready to make predictions on new data.

Here's how to make predictions using the .predict method:

```
>>> data = [[.5, .4, .1, .05]]
>>> model.predict(data)
```

The .predict method says that the data that I passed in would be classified as a setosa (0) variety.

27.6 Summary

In this chapter, we have seen how both the pandas and scikit-learn libraries leverage the concept of classes to provide a powerful and flexible way to work with data. By creating instances of the DataFrame class and calling its methods, we can easily manipulate, analyze, and visualize our data. By creating instances of the LogisticRegression class and calling its methods, we can train a model on our data, make predictions, and analyze the performance of our model.

27.7 Exercises

1. Create a DataFrame from a CSV file, then use the .mean method to get the averages for each column.
2. Use the Logistic Regression class from scikit-learn and load the iris dataset. Use the sklearn.model_selection.train_test_split function to split the data into a training set and testing set. Call .fit on the training set. Then call .score using the testing set and evaluate the accuracy of your model on the testing data.

Chapter 28

Subclassing a Class

Besides grouping state and action coherently, classes also enable re-use. If you already have a class but want one that behaves slightly differently, one way to re-use the existing class is to *subclass* it. This chapter will introduce that concept.

28.1 Parents and Children

The class that you subclass from is called the *superclass*. (Another common term for superclass is *parent class*).

Suppose that you wanted to create a chair that can hold six people. To create a class representing a six-person chair, Chair6, which is a more specialized version of a Chair, you can create a subclass. Subclasses allow you to *inherit* methods of parent classes and *override* methods you want to change.

Here is the class Chair6, which is a subclass of CorrectChair:

```
>>> class Chair6(CorrectChair):
...     max_occupants = 6
```

Note that you put the parent class, CorrectChair, in parentheses following the class name. Notice that Chair6 doesn't define a constructor inside of the body, yet you can still create instances of the class:

```
>>> sixer = Chair6(76)
```

How does Python create an object when the class doesn't define the constructor? Here is what happens: when Python looks for the .__init__ method, it will search for it on Chair6 first. Since the Chair6 class only has a max_occupants attribute, Python will not find the .__init__ method there. But, because Chair6 is a subclass of CorrectChair, it has a __bases__ attribute that lists the base classes in a tuple:

28. Subclassing a Class

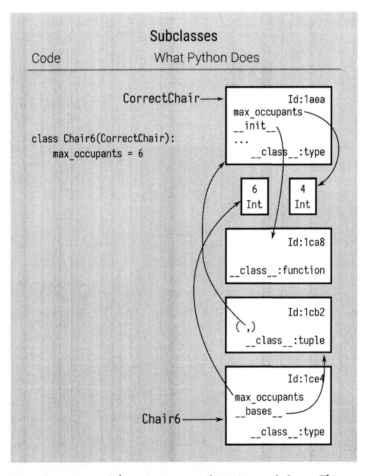

Figure 28.1: Illustration of the __bases__ attribute in a subclass. This connection between a subclass and its parent classes allows you to look up attributes in a well-defined manner. If the instance of a subclass has an attribute defined, it uses that attribute. If not, after searching the instance, the class (__class__) of the instance is searched. Failing that, parent classes (__bases__) of the class are searched.

28.1. Parents and Children

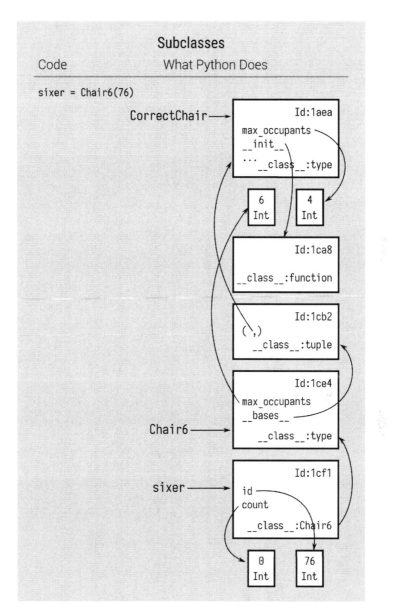

Figure 28.2: Illustration depicting the instantiation of a subclass. Note that the instance points to its class and that the class points to any parent classes using the __bases__ attribute.

28. Subclassing a Class

```
>>> Chair6.__bases__
(__main__.CorrectChair,)
```

Python will then search the base classes for the constructor. It will find the constructor in `CorrectChair` and use it to create the new class.

The same lookup happens when you call `.load` on an instance. The instance doesn't have an attribute matching the method name, so Python looks at the instance's class. `Chair6` does not have the `.load` method either, so Python looks for the attribute on the base class, `CorrectChair`. Here the `.load` method is called with a count that is too large, leading to a `ValueError`:

```
>>> sixer.load(7)
Traceback (most recent call last):
  File "/tmp/chair.py", line 30, in <module>
    sixer.load(7)
  File "/tmp/chair.py", line 13, in load
    new_val = self._check(self.count + number)
  File "/tmp/chair.py", line 23, in _check
    number))
ValueError: Invalid count:7
```

Python finds the method on the base class, but the call to the `._check` method raises a `ValueError`.

28.2 Counting Stalls

A semi-common occurrence is that a skier fails to mount the chair correctly. In that case, a chairlift operator will slow down or stop the chairlift to assist the skier. You can use Python to create a new class that can account for the number of times a stall happens.

Assume that you want to call a function every time `.load` is called, and this function will return a boolean indicating whether a stall occurred. The function takes as parameters the number of skiers and the chair object.

Below is a class that accepts an `is_stalled` function in the constructor. It will call this function every time `.load` is invoked to determine if the chairlift has stalled:

```
>>> class StallChair(CorrectChair):
...     def __init__(self, id, is_stalled):
...         super().__init__(id)
...         self.is_stalled = is_stalled
...         self.stalls = 0
...
...     def load(self, number):
...         if self.is_stalled(number, self):
...             self.stalls += 1
...         super().load(number)
```

To create an instance of this class, you must provide an is_stalled function. Here is a simple function that stalls ten percent of the time:

```
>>> import random
>>> def ten_percent(number, chair):
...     """Return True 10% of time"""
...     return random.random() < .1
```

Now you can create an instance using the ten_percent function as your is_stalled parameter:

```
>>> stall42 = StallChair(42, ten_percent)
```

28.3 super

Remember that StallChair defines its own .__init__ method, which is called when the instance is created. Note that the first line in the constructor is:

```
super().__init__(id)
```

When super is called inside of a method, it gives you access to the correct parent class. This line in the constructor allows you to invoke the CorrectChair constructor. Rather than repeat the logic of setting the id and count attributes, you can reuse the logic from the parent class. Because StallChair has additional attributes it wants to set on the instance, you can do that following the call to the parent constructor.

Note that the .load method also has a call to super:

```
def load(self, number):
    if self.is_stalled(number, self):
        self.stalls += 1
    super().load(number)
```

In the .load method, you call your is_stalled function to determine whether the chair was stalled. Then, you dispatch back to the original .load functionality found in CorrectChair by using super.

Having general code appear in one place (the base class) eliminates bugs and repeating code.

> **Note**
>
> There are two cases where super really comes in handy. One is for resolving method resolution order (*MRO*) in classes that have multiple parents. super will guarantee that this order is consistent. The other is

28. Subclassing a Class

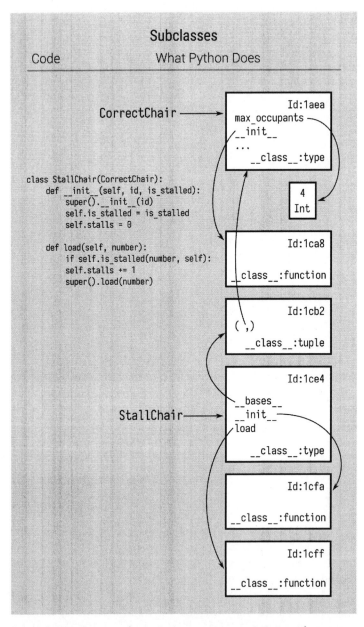

Figure 28.3: A figure showing the code for creating a subclass with custom methods. Note that you use super() to call the method on the parent class. This illustrates what objects are created when you create a class that is a subclass.

when you change the base class, super is intelligent about determining who the new base is. This aids in code maintainability.

28.4 Subclassing a Scikit-Learn Transformer

As in the previous section, you can use the same principles of inheritance and subclassing in the scikit-learn library. This becomes very useful when you want to modify or extend the functionality of an existing scikit-learn class.

Consider the case of a data preprocessing step where you want to apply a custom transformation to your data before feeding it into a machine learning model. Scikit-learn provides a base Transformer class that can be subclassed to create custom transformers.

Let's create a custom transformer that applies a logarithmic transformation to numerical features to handle skewness in the data. We'll start by subclassing the BaseEstimator and TransformerMixin classes from scikit-learn:

```
>>> from sklearn.base import BaseEstimator, TransformerMixin
>>> import numpy as np

>>> class LogTransformer(BaseEstimator, TransformerMixin):
...     def fit(self, X, y=None):
...         return self
...
...     def transform(self, X, y=None):
...         return np.log1p(X)
```

Our LogTransformer class inherits from both BaseEstimator and TransformerMixin. The fit method, in this case, does nothing and simply returns self. The transform method applies the np.log1p function to the data, X. np.log1p applies a logarithmic transformation that also adds 1 before applying the log (to account for zero values).

Now we can create an instance of our LogTransformer and apply it to some data:

```
>>> from sklearn.datasets import load_diabetes
>>> diabetes = load_diabetes()
>>> log_transformer = LogTransformer()
>>> transformed_data = log_transformer.transform(diabetes.data)
```

You can see that the original data:

```
>>> diabetes.data
array([[ 0.03807591,  0.05068012,  0.06169621, ..., -0.00259226,
         0.01990749, -0.01764613],
       [-0.00188202, -0.04464164, -0.05147406, ..., -0.03949338,
```

253

28. Subclassing a Class

```
       -0.06833155, -0.09220405],
      [ 0.08529891,  0.05068012,  0.04445121, ..., -0.00259226,
        0.00286131, -0.02593034],
      ...,
      [ 0.04170844,  0.05068012, -0.01590626, ..., -0.01107952,
       -0.04688253,  0.01549073],
      [-0.04547248, -0.04464164,  0.03906215, ...,  0.02655962,
        0.04452873, -0.02593034],
      [-0.04547248, -0.04464164, -0.0730303 , ..., -0.03949338,
       -0.00422151,  0.00306441]])
```

Has been transformed by calling the .transform method:

>>> transformed_data
```
array([[ 0.03736891,  0.04943769,  0.05986782, ..., -0.00259563,
         0.01971192, -0.01780367],
       [-0.00188379, -0.04566876, -0.05284614, ..., -0.04029441,
        -0.07077826, -0.09673565],
       [ 0.08185544,  0.04943769,  0.04349159, ..., -0.00259563,
         0.00285722, -0.02627246],
       ...,
       [ 0.0408621 ,  0.04943769, -0.01603413, ..., -0.01114135,
        -0.04801712,  0.01537197],
       [-0.0465388 , -0.04566876,  0.03831853, ...,  0.02621304,
         0.04356581, -0.02627246],
       [-0.0465388 , -0.04566876, -0.0758344 , ..., -0.04029441,
        -0.00423045,  0.00305972]])
```

Subclassing the transformer class in scikit-learn provides numerous advantages, notably compatibility and consistency. Custom transformers built this way adhere to the same interface as other scikit-learn transformers, ensuring they work seamlessly with any other scikit-learn objects.

28.5 Summary

This chapter discussed subclasses, new specialized classes that reuse code from their base class (also referred to as superclass or parent class). For any method that you don't implement in a subclass, Python will reuse the parent class' functionality. You can choose to implement a method to override completely or call out to super. When you call super, it gives you access to the parent class to reuse any functionality.

28.6 Exercises

1. Create a class to represent a cat. What can a cat do? What are the properties of a cat? Create a subclass of a cat for a tiger. How does it behave differently?

2. In the previous chapter, you created a class representing Mario from the Super Mario Brothers video game. In later editions of the game, there were different characters that you could play. They all had the same basic functionality[15] but differed in skill. Create a base class for the character, then implement four subclasses. One for Mario, Luigi, Toad, and Princess Toadstool.

Name	Mario	Luigi	Toad	Princess Toadstool
Speed	4	3	5	2
Jump	4	5	2	3
Power Special Skill	4	3	5	2 Float jump

3. Create a custom transformer class that normalizes data using the Z-score normalization.

4. Extend the LogTransformer to include an inverse transformation method that applies the exponential function to reverse the log transformation.

5. Combine multiple custom transformers and use them in a scikit-learn pipeline.

Chapter 29

DataClasses

In this chapter, we will learn about dataclasses. Dataclasses are a special shortcut in Python that allows us to create classes that store data. We will learn how to create dataclasses, how to use them, and finally, how to subclass them.

29.1 What is a Dataclass?

Python provides a special decorator when we need to make a class that stores data. I should make clear that if I need to store tabular data, I generally use the Pandas library. If I need to store matrices of numbers, I use the Numpy library. However, if I need to create Python classes that are going to store data and Pandas or Numpy are not appropriate, I could use a dataclass.

Let's assume that we want to store a class that represents a student. We could use a normal Python class and define the student's first name, last name, age, and grade.

```
class Student:
    def __init__(self, first_name, last_name, age, grade):
        self.first_name = first_name
        self.last_name = last_name
        self.age = age
        self.grade = grade
```

This class is fine, but it has a lot of boilerplate code. We have to define the __init__ method and then assign each of the parameters to the attributes. We refer to first_name three times in this code. That really bothers some folks. In fact, they went to the trouble of creating a new feature in Python to address this issue. The new feature is called a dataclass.

Another optioni would be to use a dictionary to store the data. If we use a dictionary, we would lose the inherent explanation of the class structure that comes from defining the inputs to the class. We would also lose the tab completion that comes from using a class inside of an IDE.

257

29. DataClasses

```
>>> dict_student = {'first_name': 'John', 'last_name': 'Smith',
...                 'age': 18, 'grade': 12}
```

If a unction takes a student as an input, I would have to remember the keys of the dictionary to create the input. If I use a class, I can use the tab completion to see the attributes of the class and easily create the input.

The dataclass allows us to define the class and the attributes in a simplified way. We can use the `dataclass` decorator to define the class and then mention the attributes once. Following each attribute, we insert a colon and then the type of the attribute.

In this case, the first name and last name are strings, the age is an integer, and the grade is an integer. The `dataclass` decorator tells Python to create a new constructor that accepts these four attributes as input. It then stores them as attributes on the class instance as if we had written the `__init__` method found above.

```
>>> from dataclasses import dataclass

>>> @dataclass
>>> class Student:
...     first_name: str
...     last_name: str
...     age: int
...     grade: int
```

> **Note**
>
> Decorators are an advanced Python topic. I will not cover them in detail in this book. I go over decorators in detail in my Intermediate Python book.

The `dataclass` decorator creates the `__init__` method for us. It also creates the `__repr__` method, which is the string representation of the class. When I print an instance of the class, I get the class name and the attributes.

```
>>> student = Student('John', 'Smith', 18, 12)
>>> student
Student(first_name='John', last_name='Smith', age=18, grade=12)
```

29.2 How to Create a Dataclass

To create a dataclass, we use the `dataclass` decorator. You will need to import the `dataclass` decorator from the `dataclasses` module. You must put this `@dataclass` decorator on the line before the class before the class definition. The decorator takes no arguments. You can provide a name for the class like a normal class definition. Then you define the attributes of the class. You can use type hints to specify the type of the attribute. The type hints are not enforced, but they are used by the `dataclass` decorator.

29.3 How to Use a Dataclass

You can use a dataclass like any other class. You can instantiate the class and access the attributes.

```
>>> sally = Student('Sally', 'Smith', 17, 11)
>>> sally
Student(first_name='Sally', last_name='Smith', age=17, grade=11)

>>> sally.first_name
'Sally'
```

You can even create a subclass of a dataclass. The subclass will inherit the attributes of the parent class.

```
>>> @dataclass
>>> class Person:
...     first_name: str
...     last_name: str
...     age: int

>>> @dataclass
>>> class Student(Person):
...     grade: int

>>> @dataclass
>>> class Teacher(Person):
...     subject: str

>>> mrs_jones = Teacher('Jane', 'Jones', 35, 'Math')
>>> mrs_jones
Teacher(first_name='Jane', last_name='Jones', age=35, subject='Math')
```

The subclass has all the attributes of the parent class. The subclass can define additional attributes. In the above example, the Student class has the first_name, last_name, age, and grade attributes. The first three attributes are inherited from the Person class. The Teacher class has the first_name, last_name, age, and subject attributes.

29.4 Methods in Dataclasses

Generally, folks use dataclasses as a syntactic sugar for creating classes that store data. You can provide additional functionality to your classes by defining methods. You can create methods in a dataclass like you would in a normal class.

29. DataClasses

Let's create a new subclass of the Student class that represents a CollegeStudent. We will add a method to the class that returns the student's email address.

```
>>> @dataclass
>>> class CollegeStudent(Student):
...     college: str
...     major: str
...
...     def get_email(self):
...         return f'{self.first_name}.{self.last_name}@' \
...                f'{self.college.lower()}.edu'
>>> john = CollegeStudent('John', 'Smith', 18, 12, 'Harvard',
...                       'Computer Science')
>>> john.get_email()
'John.Smith@harvard.edu'
```

29.5 Summary

Dataclasses are a convenient way to create classes that store data. You can use the dataclass decorator to create a class that stores data. Remember that if you are storing a bunch of numbers, you should use Numpy or Pandas, if you want to quickly process the data.

29.6 Excercises

1. Create a dataclass that represents a Car. The car should have the following attributes: make, model, year, color, mileage, price. Create a method that returns the car's price per mile.

2. Create a dataclass that represents a Book. The book should have the following attributes: title, author, year, pages, price. Create a method that returns the price per page.

3. Create a dataclass that represents a Movie. The movie should have the following attributes: title, director, year, length, rating. Create a method that returns the length of the movie in minutes.

Chapter 30

Exceptions

A computer may be told to perform an action it cannot do. Reading files that do not exist or dividing by zero are two examples. In these cases, Python *throws an exception* or *raises an exception*. Python allows you to deal with such *exceptions* when they occur. This chapter will discuss exceptions, both how to recover from them and raise them.

30.1 Stack Traces

Normally, when an exception occurs, Python will halt and print out a *stack trace* explaining where the problem occurred. This stack trace is useful in that it tells you the line and file of the error:

```
>>> 3/0
Traceback (most recent call last):
  File "<stdin>", line 1, in <module>
ZeroDivisionError: division by zero
```

The above states that in line 1 of the file <stdin> (this is the name of the interpreter "file"), there was a divide by zero error. When you execute a program with an exception, the stack trace will indicate the file name and line number where the problem occurred. This example from the interpreter isn't beneficial as there is only a single line of code.

But in more extensive programs, you could have deeply nested stack traces due to functions calling other functions and methods.

Here is an example of trying to read a CSV file that doesn't exist with pandas:

```
>>> import pandas as pd
>>> pd.read_csv('bad_file.csv')
Traceback (most recent call last):
  File "analyis.py", line 2, in <module>
    pd.read_csv('bad_file.csv')
```

30. Exceptions

```
File "pandas/io/parsers/readers.py", line 912, in read_csv
  return _read(filepath_or_buffer, kwds)
File "pandas/io/parsers/readers.py", line 577, in _read
  parser = TextFileReader(filepath_or_buffer, **kwds)
File "pandas/io/parsers/readers.py", line 1407, in __init__
  self._engine = self._make_engine(f, self.engine)
File "pandas/io/parsers/readers.py", line 1661, in _make_engine
  self.handles = get_handle(
File "pandas/io/common.py", line 859, in get_handle
  handle = open(
FileNotFoundError: [Errno 2] No such file or directory: 'bad_file.csv'
```

Reading a stack trace can be intimidating for beginners, but it's a valuable skill for debugging code. A stack trace provides valuable information about what went wrong in your code and where the error occurred. Let's break down the stack trace step by step:

1. *File Path and Line Numbers:* The stack trace starts with the file path and line number where the error occurred. In this example:

```
File "analysis.py[2]", line 1, in <module>
pd.read_csv('bad_file.csv')
```

The error occurred in *analysis.py* at line 2.

2. *Function Call Sequence:* The stack trace shows the sequence of function calls that led to the error. Each line represents a function call. The function calls are:

```
pd.read_csv('bad_file.csv')
_read(filepath_or_buffer, kwds)
_make_engine(f, self.engine)
get_handle
open
```

3. *File Paths and Line Numbers in Functions:* The stack trace also provides information about the file paths and line numbers within each function involved in the error.

```
File "pandas/io/parsers/readers.py", line 912, in read_csv
return _read(filepath_or_buffer, kwds)
```

The error occurred in the read_csv function within the file 'pandas/io/-parsers/readers.py' at line 912.

4. *Error Type and Message:* The last lines of the stack trace show the type of error and the error message.

```
FileNotFoundError: [Errno 2] No such file or directory: 'bad_file.csv'
```

The error type is `FileNotFoundError`, which indicates that Python couldn't find the file.

Here are some tips for understanding stack traces:

1. Look for the first line that mentions your code (usually the last line), as that indicates the direct cause of the error.
2. Read the error message carefully, as it often provides clues about what went wrong.
3. Check the file path and line numbers mentioned in the stack trace to identify the location of the error in your code.
4. Look at the function calls leading to the error to understand the sequence of events that caused the error.
5. Find a solution (Search online, ask a colleague, talk to a rubber duck, etc).

Tracebacks are easiest to read when you start from the bottom, find the error, and see where it occurred. As you move up the traceback, you look up the call chain. This can help you pinpoint what is going on in your program.

Over time, as you gain more experience with Python and debugging, reading stack traces will become easier, and you'll be better equipped to identify and fix issues in your code.

30.2 Look Before you Leap

Suppose you have a program that performs division. Depending on how it is coded, it may try to divide by zero at some point. There are two styles for dealing with exceptions that programmers commonly use. The first is *look before you leap* (LBYL). The idea is to check for exceptional cases before acting. In this case, the program would examine the denominator value and determine whether it is zero. If it is not zero, the program could perform the division. Otherwise, it could skip it.

In Python, look before you leap can be implemented with `if` statements:

```
>>> numerator = 10
>>> divisor = 0
>>> if divisor != 0:
...     result = numerator / divisor
... else:
...     result = None
```

> **Note**
>
> Look before you leap is not always a guarantee of success. If you check that a file exists before you open it (looking before leaping), that does not

mean it will still be around later. In multi-threaded environments, this is known as a *race condition*.

> **Note**
>
> None is used to represent the undefined state. This is a common idiom throughout Pythondom. Be careful, though. Try not to invoke methods on a variable assigned to None, as that will raise an exception.

30.3 Easier to Ask for Forgiveness

Another option for dealing with exceptions is known as *easier to ask for forgiveness than permission* (EAFP). The idea here is to always operate inside of a *try* block. If the operation fails, the exception will be *caught* by the *exception* block.

The try...except construct provides a mechanism for Python to catch exceptional cases:

```
>>> numerator = 10
>>> divisor = 0
>>> try:
...     result = numerator / divisor
... except ZeroDivisionError as e:
...     result = None
```

Notice that the try construct creates a block following the try statement (because there is a colon and indentation). Inside the try block are the statements that might throw exceptions. If the statements throw an exception, Python looks for an except block that *catches* that exception (or a parent class).

In the code above, the except block states that it will catch an exception that is an instance (or subclass) of the ZeroDivisionError class. When the stated exception is thrown in the try block, the except block is executed, and result is set to None.

Note that line:

```
except ZeroDivisionError as e:
```

has as e: on the end. This part is optional. If it is included, then e (or whatever you choose as a valid variable name) will point to an instance of a ZeroDivisionError exception. Inside the following block, you can inspect the exception as they often have more details. The e variable points to the *active exception*. If you leave "as e" off the end of the except statement, you will still have an active exception, but you won't be able to access the instance of it.

> **Note**
>
> Try to limit the scope of the try block. Instead of including all the code in a function inside a try block, include only the line that will possibly throw the error.

Because the "look before you leap" style of handling is not guaranteed to prevent errors, in general, most Python developers favor the "easier to ask for forgiveness" style of exception handling. Here are some rules of thumb for exception handling:

- Gracefully handle errors you know how to handle and can reasonably expect.
- Do not silence exceptions that you cannot handle or do not reasonably expect.
- Use a global exception handler to gracefully handle unexpected errors.

> **Note**
>
> If you are making a server application that needs to run without stopping, here is one way to do it. The functions process_input and log_error don't exist but serve as placeholders:
>
> ```
> while 1:
>     try:
>         result = process_input()
>     except Exception as e:
>         log_error(e)
> ```

30.4 Multiple exception cases

If there are multiple exceptions that your code needs to be aware of, you can chain a list of except statements together:

```
try:
    some_function()
except ZeroDivisionError as e:
    # handle specific
except Exception as e:
    # handle others
```

In this case, when some_function throws an exception, the interpreter checks first if it is a ZeroDivisionError (or a subclass of it). If that is not the case, it checks if the exception is a subclass of Exception. Once an except block is entered, Python no longer checks the subsequent blocks.

30. Exceptions

If an exception is not handled by the chain, code somewhere up the stack must deal with the exception. If the exception is unhandled, Python will stop running and will print the stack trace.

An example of dealing with multiple exceptions is found in the standard library. The argparse module from the standard library provides an easy way to parse command line options. It allows you to specify a type for certain options, such as integers or files (the options all come in as strings). The ._get_value method has an example of multiple except clauses. Based on the type of exception that occurs, a different error message is provided:

```python
def _get_value(self, action, arg_string):
    type_func = self._registry_get('type', action.type, action.type)
    if not callable(type_func):
        msg = _('%r is not callable')
        raise ArgumentError(action, msg % type_func)
    # convert the value to the appropriate type
    try:
        result = type_func(arg_string)
    # ArgumentTypeErrors indicate errors
    except ArgumentTypeError:
        name = getattr(action.type, '__name__', repr(action.type))
        msg = str(_sys.exc_info()[1])
        raise ArgumentError(action, msg)
    # TypeErrors or ValueErrors also indicate errors
    except (TypeError, ValueError):
        name = getattr(action.type, '__name__', repr(action.type))
        args = {'type': name, 'value': arg_string}
        msg = _('invalid %(type)s value: %(value)r')
        raise ArgumentError(action, msg % args)
    # return the converted value
    return result
```

> **Note**
>
> This code example also shows that a single except statement can catch more than one exception type if you provide a tuple of exception classes:
>
> ```python
> except (TypeError, ValueError):
> ```

30.5 Finally Clause

Another clause for error handling is the finally clause. This statement is used to place code that will always execute, regardless of whether an exception happens or not. If the try block succeeds, then the finally block will be executed.

30.5. Finally Clause

The `finally` always executes. If the exception is handled, the `finally` block will execute after the handling. If the exception is not handled, the `finally` block will execute, and then the exception will be re-raised:

```python
try:
    some_function()
except Exception as e:
    # handle errors
    ...
finally:
    # cleanup
    ...
```

Usually, the purpose of the `finally` clause is to clean up external resources, such as files, network connections, or databases. These resources should be freed regardless of whether an operation was successful.

An example from the `timeit` module found in the standard library might aid in seeing the utility of the `finally` statement. The `timeit` module allows developers to run a benchmark on their code. One of the things that it does while running the benchmark is to tell the Python garbage collector to disable itself during the run. But you want to ensure that garbage collection works after the benchmark, regardless of whether the run worked or errored out.

Here is the method, `timeit`, that dispatches to run the benchmark. It checks if the garbage collector was enabled, then turns off the garbage collector runs the timing code, and finally, re-enables garbage collection if it was previously enabled:

```python
def timeit(self, number=default_number):
    """Time 'number' executions of the main statement.
    To be precise, this executes the setup statement once, and
    then returns the time it takes to execute the main statement
    a number of times, as a float measured in seconds. The
    argument is the number of times through the loop, defaulting
    to one million. The main statement, the setup statement and
    the timer function to be used are passed to the constructor.
    """
    it = itertools.repeat(None, number)
    gcold = gc.isenabled()
    gc.disable()
    try:
        timing = self.inner(it, self.timer)
    finally:
        if gcold:
            gc.enable()
    return timing
```

30. Exceptions

It is possible that the call to self.inner will throw an exception, but because the standard library uses finally, garbage collection will always be turned back on regardless (if the gcold boolean is true).

> **Note**
>
> This book doesn't address context managers, but here is a hint to prepare you for your future as a Python expert. The try/finally combination is a code smell in Python. Seasoned Python programmers will use a *context manager* in these cases. Put this on your list of things to study after you have mastered basic Python.

30.6 Else Clause

A try statement also supports an else clause. The optional else clause in a try statement is executed when no exception is raised. It must follow any except statements and executes before the finally block. Here is a simple example:

```
>>> try:
...     print('hi')
... except Exception as e:
...     print('Error')
... else:
...     print('Success')
... finally:
...     print('at last')
hi
Success
at last
```

Here is an example from the heapq module in the standard library. According to the comments, there is a shortcut if you want to get the smallest values and you ask for more values than the size of the heap. However, if you try to get the size of the heap and get an error, the code calls pass. This ignores the error and continues with the slower way of getting the small items. If there was no error, you can follow the else statement and take the fast path if n is greater than the size of the heap:

```
def nsmallest(n, iterable, key=None):
    # Code removed here ....
    # When n>=size, it's faster to use sorted()
    try:
        size = len(iterable)
    except (TypeError, AttributeError) as e:
        pass
    else:
```

```
    if n >= size:
        return sorted(iterable, key=key)[:n]
# Code removed here .... Try slower way
```

30.7 Raising Exceptions

In addition to catching exceptions, Python also allows you to *raise* exceptions (or throw them). Remember that the Zen of Python wants you to be explicit and refuse the temptation to guess. If invalid input is passed into your function and you know you cannot handle it, you may raise an exception. Exceptions are subclasses of the `BaseException` class, and are raised using the `raise` statement:

```
raise BaseException('Program failed')
```

Normally, you will not raise the generic `BaseException` class but will raise subclasses that are predefined or defined by you.

Another common way of using the `raise` statement is to use it all by itself. Recall that when you are inside an except statement, you have an active exception. If so, you can use a *bare* `raise` statement. A bare `raise` statement allows you to deal with the exception but re-raise the original exception. If you try to use:

```
except (TypeError, AttributeError) as e:
    log('Hit an exception')
    raise e
```

You will succeed in raising the original exception, but the stack trace will state that the original exception now occurred in the line with `raise e` rather than where the exception first occurred. You have two options to deal with this. The first is a *bare "raise"* statement. The second is using exception chaining, described later.

Here is an example from the `configparser` module in the standard library. This module handles reading and creating INI files. An INI file is usually used for configuration and was popular before JSON and YAML were around. The .read_dict method will try to read the configuration from a dictionary. If the instance is in strict mode, it will raise an error if you try to add the same section more than once. If you are not in strict mode, the method allows duplicate keys; the last one wins. Here is a portion of the method showing the bare `raise` method:

```
def read_dict(self, dictionary, source='<dict>'):
    elements_added = set()
    for section, keys in dictionary.items():
        section = str(section)
        try:
```

30. Exceptions

```
            self.add_section(section)
        except (DuplicateSectionError, ValueError):
            if self._strict and section in elements_added:
                raise
        elements_added.add(section)
        # code removed from here ....
```

When a duplicate is added in strict mode, the stack trace will show the error in the .add_section method because that is where it occurred.

30.8 Wrapping Exceptions

Python 3 has introduced another feature similar to a bare raise in "3134 – Exception Chaining and Embedded Tracebacks" When handling an exception, another exception may occur in the handling code. In this case, it is useful to know about both exceptions.

Here is some basic code. The function, divide_work, might have problems dividing by zero. You can catch that error and log that it occurred. Suppose that your log function is calling out to a cloud-based service that is down (you'll simulate that by having log raise an exception):

```
>>> def log(msg):
...     raise SystemError("Logging not up")
>>> def divide_work(x, y):
...     try:
...         return x/y
...     except ZeroDivisionError as ex:
...         log("System is down")
```

When you call divide_work with 5 and 0 as input, Python will show two errors, the ZeroDivisionError, and the SystemError. It will show SystemError last because it happened last:

```
>>> divide_work(5, 0)
Traceback (most recent call last):
  File "begpy.py", line 3, in divide_work
    return x/y
ZeroDivisionError: division by zero
During handling of the above exception, another exception occurred:
Traceback (most recent call last):
  File "begpy.py", line 1, in <module>
    divide_work(5, 0)
  File "begpy.py", line 5, in divide_work
    log("System is down")
  File "begpy.py", line 2, in log
    raise SystemError("Logging not up")
SystemError: Logging not up
```

30.8. Wrapping Exceptions

Suppose your cloud logging service is now working (the log function no longer throws an error). If you want to change the type of the ZeroDivisionError in divide_work to ArithmeticError, you can use a syntax described in PEP 3134. You can use the raise ... from syntax:

```
>>> def log(msg):
...     print(msg)
>>> def divide_work(x, y):
...     try:
...         return x/y
...     except ZeroDivisionError as ex:
...         log("System is down")
...         raise ArithmeticError() from ex
```

You will see two exceptions now: the original ZeroDivisionError and the ArithmeticError which is no longer shadowed by ZeroDivisionError:

```
>>> divide_work(3, 0)
Traceback (most recent call last):
  File "begpy.py", line 3, in divide_work
    return x/y
ZeroDivisionError: division by zero
The above exception was the direct cause of the following exception:
Traceback (most recent call last):
  File "begpy.py", line 1, in <module>
    divide_work(3, 0)
  File "begpy.py", line 6, in divide_work
    raise ArithmeticError() from ex
ArithmeticError
```

If you want to suppress the original exception, the ZeroDivisionError, you can use the following code. This is described in PEP 409 – Suppressing exception context [1]:

```
>>> def divide_work(x, y):
...     try:
...         return x/y
...     except ZeroDivisionError as ex:
...         log("System is down")
...         raise ArithmeticError() from None
```

Now you only see the outermost error, ArithmeticError:

```
>>> divide_work(3, 0)
Traceback (most recent call last):
```

---

[1] PEP 409 – Suppressing exception context

30. Exceptions

```
  File "begpy.py", line 1, in <module>
    divide_work(3, 0)
  File "begpy.py", line 6, in divide_work
    raise ArithmeticError() from None
ArithmeticError
```

30.9 Defining your own Exceptions

Python has many built-in exceptions defined in the exceptions module. If your error corresponds well with the existing exceptions, you can re-use them. The following lists the class hierarchy for the built-in exceptions:

```
BaseException
     SystemExit
     KeyboardInterrupt
     GeneratorExit
     Exception
          StopIteration
          ArithmeticError
               FloatingPointError
               OverflowError
               ZeroDivisionError
          AssertionError
          AttributeError
          BufferError
          EnvironmentError
               IOError
               OSError
          EOFError
          ImportError
          LookupError
               IndexError
               KeyError
          MemoryError
          NameError
               UnboundLocalError
          ReferenceError
          RuntimeError
               NotImplementedError
          SyntaxError
               IndentationError
                    TabError
          SystemError
          TypeError
          ValueError
               UnicodeError
```

```
            UnicodeDecodeError
            UnicodeEncodeError
            UnicodeTranslateError
    Warning
        DeprecationWarning
        PendingDeprecationWarning
        RuntimeWarning
        SyntaxWarning
        UserWarning
        FutureWarning
        ImportWarning
        UnicodeWarning
        BytesWarning
```

When defining your own exception, you should subclass from Exception or below. The reason for this is that other subclasses of BaseException are not necessarily "exceptions". For example, if you caught KeyboardInterrupt, you wouldn't be able to stop the process with control-C. If you caught GeneratorExit, generators would stop working.

Here is an exception for defining that a program is missing information:

```
>>> class DataError(Exception):
...     def __init__(self, missing):
...         self.missing = missing
```

Using your custom exception is easy, use it in combination with the raise statement:

```
>>> if 'important_data' not in config:
...     raise DataError('important_data missing')
```

30.10 Summary

This chapter introduced strategies for dealing with exceptions. In Look Before You Leap, you make sure the environment will not throw an error before trying something. In Easier to Ask for Forgiveness than Permission, you wrap any code that you know might throw an error with a try/catch block. You should favor the latter style of programming in Python.

The various mechanisms for catching errors, raising them, and re-raising them were discussed. Finally, the chapter showed how you could subclass an existing exception to create your own.

30.11 Exercises

1. Write a program that serves as a basic calculator. It asks for two numbers, then it asks for an operator. Gracefully deal with input that doesn't cleanly convert to numbers. Deal with division by zero errors.

30. Exceptions

2. Write a program that inserts line numbers in front of the lines of a file. Accept a filename being passed in on the command line. Import the sys module and read the filename from the sys.argv list. Gracefully deal with a bogus file being passed in.

Chapter 31

Importing Libraries

The previous chapters have covered the basic constructs for Python. In this chapter, you'll learn about importing code. Many languages have the concept of *libraries* or reusable chunks of code. Python comes with a whole swath of libraries, which is why folks call Python a "batteries included" language. This chapter will show you how to leverage these batteries and external or third-party libraries.

31.1 Libraries

To use a library, you must load the code from that library into your *namespace* using the `import` statement. The namespace holds the functions, classes, and variables you can access. If you want to calculate the sine of an angle, you will need to define a function that does that or load a preexisting function. The built-in `math` library has a `sin` function that calculates the sine of an angle expressed in radians. It also has a variable that defines a value for pi:

```
>>> from math import sin, pi
>>> sin(pi/2)
1.0
```

The above code loads the `math` module. But it doesn't put `math` in your namespace. Instead, it creates a variable that points to the `sin` function from the `math` module. It also creates a variable that points to the `pi` variable found in the `math` module. If you inspect your current namespace using the `dir` function, you can confirm this:

```
>>> 'sin' in dir()
True
```

31.2 Multiple ways to Import

In the previous example, we imported a single function from a library. It is also possible to load the library into our namespace and reference all of its

275

31. Importing Libraries

classes, functions, and variables as attributes through the library object. To import the math module into our namespace, type:

```
>>> import math
```

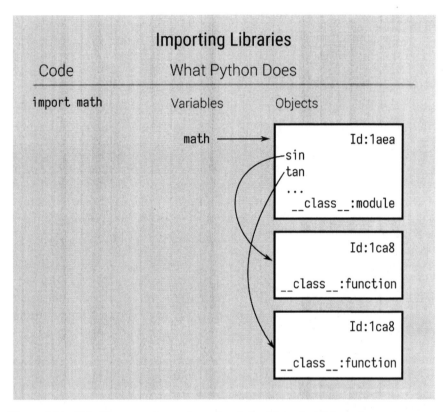

Figure 31.1: This illustrates importing a module. Note that this code creates a new variable, math, that points to a module. The module has various attributes that you can access using a period.

In the above, you imported the math library. This created a new variable, math, that points to the module.

```
>>> math
<module 'math' from '...3.10/lib-dynload/math.cpython-310-darwin.so'>
```

The module has various attributes. You can use the dir function to list the attributes:

```
>>> dir(math)
['__doc__', '__file__', '__loader__', '__name__',
```

31.2. Multiple ways to Import

```
'__package__', '__spec__', 'acos', 'acosh', 'asin',
'asinh', 'atan', 'atan2', 'atanh', 'ceil', 'copysign',
'cos', 'cosh', 'degrees', 'e', 'erf', 'erfc', 'exp',
'expm1', 'fabs', 'factorial', 'floor', 'fmod', 'frexp',
'fsum', 'gamma', 'gcd', 'hypot', 'inf', 'isclose',
'isfinite', 'isinf', 'isnan', 'ldexp', 'lgamma', 'log',
'log10', 'log1p', 'log2', 'modf', 'nan', 'pi', 'pow',
'radians', 'sin', 'sinh', 'sqrt', 'tan', 'tanh', 'trunc']
```

Most of these attributes are functions. If we want to call the tan function, we can't invoke it, because tan isn't in our namespace, only math is. But, we can do a lookup on the math variable using the period (.) operator. The period operator will look up attributes on an object. Because everything in Python is an object, we can use the period to lookup the tan attribute on the math object.

```
>>> math.tan
<built-in function tan>
```

Remember to add parentheses () to invoke the function:

```
>>> math.tan(0)
0.0
```

If we want to read the associated documentation for the tan function, we can enlist the help function for aid:

```
>>> help(math.tan)
Help on built-in function tan in module math:
tan(...)
    tan(x)
    Return the tangent of x (measured in radians).
```

> **Note**
>
> When would you import a function using from versus the import statement? If you are only using a couple of attributes from a library, you might want to use the from style import. It is possible to specify multiple comma-delimited attributes in the from construct:
>
> ```
> >>> from math import sin, cos, tan
> >>> cos(0)
> 1.0
> ```

However, if you need to access most of the library, it requires less typing to import the library using the import statement. It is also a hint

31. Importing Libraries

to anyone reading your code (including you) as to where the function (or class or variable) came from.

> **Note**
>
> If you need to import multiple attributes from a library, you might need to span multiple lines. If you continue importing functions on the next line, you will run into an error:
>
> ```
> >>> from math import sin,
> ...     cos
> Traceback (most recent call last):
>   File "<stdin>", line 1, in <module>
> SyntaxError: trailing comma not allowed
> without surrounding parentheses
> ```
>
> You can specify multiple imports with parentheses. Open parentheses (or braces, or brackets) indicate that the statement continues on the next line:
>
> ```
> >>> from math import (sin,
> ...     cos)
> ```
>
> This latter form is more idiomatic Python.

31.3 Conflicting import names

If you were working on a program that performs trigonometric operations, you might already have created a simplified function named sin.

```
>>> def factorial(n):
...     if n == 0:
...         return 1
...     else:
...         return n * factorial(n - 1)

>>> def sin(x, terms=10):
...     result = 0
...     for n in range(terms):
...         coefficient = (-1) ** n
...         numerator = x ** (2 * n + 1)
...         denominator = factorial(2 * n + 1)
...         term = coefficient * (numerator / denominator)
...         result += term
...     return result
```

31.3. Conflicting import names

What if you also want to use the `sin` function from the `math` library? One option is to `import math`, then `math.sin` would reference the library, and `sin` would reference your function.

Python has another option too. You can redefine the name of what you want to import using the as keyword:

```
>>> from math import sin as other_sin
>>> other_sin(0)
0.0

>>> sin(0)
0.0
```

Now, `other_sin` is a reference to the `sin` found in `math` and you may continue using your `sin` without having to refactor your code.

The as keyword construct also works on `import` statements. If you had a variable (or a function) that conflicted with the `math` name in your namespace, the following would be one way to get around it:

```
>>> import math as other_math
>>> other_math.sin(0)
0.0
```

> **Note**
>
> The as keyword can also be used to eliminate typing. If your favorite library has overly long and verbose names you can easily shorten them in your code. Users of the NumPy library have adopted the standard of reducing keystrokes by using a two-letter acronym:
>
> ```
> >>> import numpy as np
> ```
>
> The Pandas library has adopted a similar standard:
>
> ```
> >>> import pandas as pd
> ```
>
> One particularly nefarious use of the as keyword is to rename the NumPy module as Pandas:
>
> ```
> >>> import numpy as pd
> ```
>
> Don't do this. It is funny for internet memes and jokes, but it is terrible for code readability and maintainability. Your colleagues will hate you. Your future self will hate you. Don't do it.

31. Importing Libraries

31.4 Star Imports

Python also allows you to import everything from a library into your namespace with what are known as *star imports*:

```
>>> from math import *
>>> asin(0)
0.0
```

Notice that the above code calls the arc sine function, which was not defined. The line where asin is invoked is the first reference to asin in the code. What happened? When you say from math import *, that is a star import, and it tells Python to throw everything from the math library (class definitions, functions, and variables) into the local namespace. While this might appear handy at first glance, it is quite dangerous.

Star imports make debugging harder because it is not explicit where code comes from. Even worse are star imports from multiple libraries. Subsequent library imports might override something defined in an earlier library. As such, star imports are discouraged and frowned upon.

> **Note**
>
> Do not use star imports!

The possible exceptions to this rule are when you are writing your own testing code, or messing around in the REPL. Library authors do this as a shortcut to importing everything from the library that they want to test. And this often ends up in the documentation. Do not be tempted because you see it in other's code, to use star imports in your code.

Remember the Zen of Python:

> Explicit is better than implicit

31.5 Nested Libraries

Some Python packages have a nested namespace. For example, the XML library that comes with Python has support for minidom and etree. Both libraries live under the xml parent package:

```
>>> from xml.dom.minidom import \
...     parseString
>>> dom = parseString(
...     '<xml><foo/></xml>')
>>> from xml.etree.ElementTree import \
...     XML
>>> elem = XML('<xml><foo/></xml>')
```

Notice that the `from` construct allows importing only the functions and classes needed. Using the `import` construct (without `from`) would require more typing (but also allow access to everything from the package):

```
>>> import xml.dom.minidom
>>> dom = xml.dom.minidom.parseString(
...     '<xml><foo/></xml>')
>>> import xml.etree.ElementTree
>>> elem = xml.etree.ElementTree.XML(
...     '<xml><foo/></xml>')
```

31.6 Import Organization

According to PEP 8, import statements should be located at the top of the file following the module docstring. There should be one import per line and imports should be grouped by:

- Standard library imports
- 3rd party imports
- Local package imports

Each group should be in alphabetical order to make it easier to find modules. An example module might have the following at the start:

```
#!/usr/bin/env python3
"""
This module converts records into JSON
and shoves them into a database
"""
import json           # standard libs
import sys

import psycopg2       # 3rd party lib

import recordconverter  # local library
...
```

> **Note**
> It is useful to organize the grouped imports alphabetically.

> **Note**
> It can be useful to postpone some imports to:

281

31. Importing Libraries

- Avoid *circular imports*. A circular import is where modules mutually import one another. If you are not able (or willing) to refactor to remove the circular import, it is possible to place the import statement within the function or method containing the code that invokes it.
- Avoid importing modules that are not available on some systems.
- Avoid importing large modules that you may not use.

31.7 Summary

This chapter discussed importing libraries in Python. Python has a large standard library, and you will need to import those libraries to use them. Throughout this book, it has emphasized that everything is an object, and you often create variables that point to those objects. When you import a module, you create a variable that points to a module object. Anything within the module's namespace can be accessed using the lookup operation (.).

You can also selectively import parts out of the module's namespace, using the from statement. If you want to rename what you are importing, you can use an as statement to change what the variable name will be.

31.8 Exercises

1. Find a package in the Python standard library for dealing with JSON. Import the library module and inspect the attributes of the module. Use the help function to learn more about how to use the module. Serialize a dictionary mapping 'name' to your name and 'age' to your age, to a JSON string. Deserialize the JSON back into Python.
2. Find a package in the Python standard library for listing directory contents. Using that package, write a function that accepts a directory name. The function should get all the files in that directory and print out a report of the count of files by extension type.

Chapter 32

Packages and Modules

The previous chapter discussed how to import libraries. This chapter will dive a little deeper into what constitutes a library.

32.1 Modules and Packages

Modules are Python files that end in .py, and have an importable name. PEP 8 states that module filenames should be short and in lowercase. Underscores may be used for readability.

A *package* in Python is a directory that contains a file named __init__.py. The file named __init__.py can have any implementation it pleases or be empty. In addition, the directory may contain an arbitrary number of modules and sub-packages.

When writing code, should you prefer a module or a package? I usually start out simple and use a module. When I need to break coherent parts into their own modules, I refactor them into modules in a package.

Here is an example from the directory layout of the popular SQLAlchemy project (an Object Relational Mapper for databases).

```
sqlalchemy/
  __init__.py
  engine/
    __init__.py
    base.py
  schema.py
```

PEP 8 also states that directory names for packages should be short and lowercase. Underscores should not be used.

32.2 Importing Packages

There are two requirements for importing a library:

32. Packages and Modules

1. The library must be a *module* or a *package*
2. The library must exist in the PYTHONPATH environment variable or sys.path Python variable.

To import a package, use the import statement with the package name (the directory name):

```
>>> import sqlalchemy
```

This will import the sqlalchemy/__init__.py file into the current namespace if the package is found in PYTHONPATH or sys.path.

If you wanted to use the Column and ForeignKey classes found in the schema.py module, either of the code snippets below would work. The first puts sqlalchemy.schema in your namespace, while the latter only puts schema in your namespace:

```
>>> import sqlalchemy.schema
>>> col = sqlalchemy.schema.Column()
>>> fk = sqlalchemy.schema.ForeignKey()
```

or:

```
>>> from sqlalchemy import schema
>>> col = schema.Column()
>>> fk = schema.ForeignKey()
```

Alternatively, to access only the Column class, import that class in one of the following two ways:

```
>>> import sqlalchemy.schema.Column
>>> col = sqlalchemy.schema.Column()
```

or:

```
>>> from sqlalchemy.schema import Column
>>> col = Column()
```

32.3 PYTHONPATH

PYTHONPATH is an environment variable listing the directories that Python searches to find modules or packages to load. This variable is usually empty. It is not necessary to change PYTHONPATH unless you are developing code and want to use libraries that have not been installed and are located in locations that Python doesn't normally use to load libraries from.

> **Note**
>
> Leave PYTHONPATH empty unless you have a good reason to change it. This section illustrates what can happen if you change it. This can be confusing to others trying to debug your code who forget that PYTHONPATH has been changed.

> **Note**
>
> Python packages can be installed via package managers, Windows executables, or Python-specific tools such as pip. My recommendation is to use pip in combination with a virtual environment.

32.4 sys.path

The sys module has an attribute, path, that lists the directories that Python searches for libraries. If you inspect sys.path, you will see all the locations that are scanned:

```
>>> import sys
>>> sys.path
['',
'/usr/lib/python35.zip',
'/usr/lib/python3.6',
'/usr/lib/python3.6/plat-darwin',
'/usr/lib/python3.6/lib-dynload',
'/usr/local/lib/python3.6/site-packages']
```

> **Note**
>
> If you see errors like:
>
> ```
> ImportError: No module named plot
> ```
>
> Look at the sys.path variable to see if it has the directory holding foo.py (if it is a module). If plot is a package, then the plot/ directory should be located in one of the paths in sys.path:
>
> ```
> >>> import plot
> Traceback (most recent call last):
>   File "<stdin>", line 1, in <module>
> ImportError: No module named plot
> >>> sys.path.append('/home/test/a')
> >>> import plot
> >>> plot.histogram()
> ```

32. Packages and Modules

> Again, typically you don't manually set sys.path or PYTHONPATH, normally you install libraries, and the installer puts them in the correct location.

Note

If you want to know the location of the library on the filesystem, you can inspect the __file__ attribute:

```
>>> import json
>>> json.__file__
'/usr/lib/python3.6/json/__init__.py'
```

This only works with libraries implemented in Python. The sys module is implemented in C, not Python, so this fails:

```
>>> import sys
>>> sys.__file__
Traceback (most recent call last):
  ...
AttributeError: module 'sys' has no attribute '__file__'
```

32.5 Summary

This chapter discussed modules and packages. A module is a Python file. A package is a directory with a file named __init__.py. A package may also contain other modules and packages.

A list of paths determines where Python looks to import libraries. This list is stored in sys.path. You can inspect it to see where Python looks. You can also update its value via the PYTHONPATH environment variable, or mutate the list directly. But typically, you don't set this variable to install packages, you use something like pip .

32.6 Exercises

1. Create a module, begin.py, that has a function named prime in it. The prime function should take a number and return a boolean indicating whether the number is a prime number (divisible only by 1 and itself). Go to another directory, launch Python, and run:

   ```
   from begin import prime
   ```

   It should fail. Update the sys.path variable, so that you can import the function from the module. Then, set PYTHONPATH to get it to load.

32.6. Exercises

2. Create a package, utils. In the __init__.py file, place the prime code from the previous exercise. Go to a different directory in the terminal, launch Python, and run:

   ```
   from utils import prime
   ```

   It should fail. Update the sys.path variable, so that you can import the function from the package. Then, set PYTHONPATH to get it to load.

Chapter 33

Regression with XGBoost

In this chapter, we're going to look at a real-world data science example using regression.

Regression is a type of machine learning where we try to predict a numeric value. In this case, we will try to predict the flow of the Dirty Devil River.

The Dirty Devil River is a river located in Utah. At some point, I was interested in floating down this river. The issue is that this river is not always floatable. There are only certain times of the year when the flow is high enough to float it. So, I downloaded various data sets to make a model to determine if I could predict a week out whether I could float the river or not.

33.1 Data for Regression

This next section will show how to download and prepare the data for machine learning. You can see in this code that I'm importing the libraries we will use.

```
import matplotlib.pyplot as plt
import numpy as np
import pandas as pd
from sklearn import linear_model, metrics, model_selection, pipeline, tree
import xgboost as xgb
from yellowbrick import regressor
```

In this code, I will access the Dirty Devil River flow data from the US government. I'm using the pandas library to convert the *datetime* column into the Denver timezone, rename some columns, and pull out some selected columns.

I'll put that code in a function called tweak_river. After you've created a function, it is a good idea to try it out and make sure it works.

```
url = 'https://github.com/mattharrison/datasets/raw/master'\
    '/data/dirtydevil.txt'
```

33. Regression with XGBoost

```
raw = pd.read_csv(url, skiprows=lambda num: num <34 or num == 35,
                  sep='\t', dtype_backend='pyarrow')
def to_denver_time(df_, time_col, tz_col):
    return (df_
     .assign(**{tz_col: df_[tz_col].replace('MDT', 'MST7MDT')})
     .groupby(tz_col)
     [time_col]
     .transform(lambda s: pd.to_datetime(s)
         .dt.tz_localize(s.name, ambiguous=True)
         .dt.tz_convert('America/Denver'))
    )

def tweak_river(df_):
    return (df_
     .assign(datetime=to_denver_time(df_, 'datetime', 'tz_cd'))
     .rename(columns={'144166_00060': 'cfs',
                      '144167_00065': 'gage_height'})
     .loc[:, ['datetime', 'tz_cd', 'cfs', 'gage_height']]
    )

river_df = tweak_river(raw)
```

Let's inspect `river_df` to get warm fuzzies that our loading and cleaning logic works:

```
>>> print(river_df)
                       datetime tz_cd    cfs  gage_height
0      2001-05-07 01:00:00-06:00   MDT  71.00          NaN
1      2001-05-07 01:15:00-06:00   MDT  71.00          NaN
2      2001-05-07 01:30:00-06:00   MDT  71.00          NaN
3      2001-05-07 01:45:00-06:00   MDT  70.00          NaN
4      2001-05-07 02:00:00-06:00   MDT  70.00          NaN
...                         ...   ...    ...          ...
539300 2020-09-28 08:30:00-06:00   MDT   9.53         6.16
539301 2020-09-28 08:45:00-06:00   MDT   9.20         6.15
539302 2020-09-28 09:00:00-06:00   MDT   9.20         6.15
539303 2020-09-28 09:15:00-06:00   MDT   9.20         6.15
539304 2020-09-28 09:30:00-06:00   MDT   9.20         6.15

[539305 rows x 4 columns]
```

We also want temperature data. Let's load a data set of meteorological data from Hanksville, Utah. The previous river data set did not have temperature data, and I wanted to see if I could get some predictive power from temperature data.

33.1. Data for Regression

This data has daily temperature data and precipitation data as well. It might be useful to know that if it rained in the past week, that might impact the river's flow.

I'm also using pandas to clean that data. You can see that I am converting the *DATE* column into the America Denver time zone, and then I'm pulling off the other columns I want. In this case, the date column, the precipitation column, the temperature, the minimum column, the temperature max column, and the observation temperature. The temperature of observation is the temperature in Fahrenheit when precipitation was reported.

```
url = 'https://github.com/mattharrison/datasets/raw/master/data/'\
    'hanksville.csv'

temp_df = pd.read_csv(url, dtype_backend='pyarrow', engine='pyarrow')

def tweak_temp(df_):
    return (df_
        .assign(DATE=pd.to_datetime(df_.DATE)
            .dt.tz_localize('America/Denver', ambiguous=False))
        .loc[:,['DATE', 'PRCP', 'TMIN', 'TMAX', 'TOBS']]
    )

temp_df = tweak_temp(temp_df)
```

Let's run `tweak_temp` and make sure that it works.

```
>>> print(temp_df)
                          DATE  PRCP  TMIN  TMAX  TOBS
0     2000-01-01 00:00:00-07:00  0.02  21.0  43.0  28.0
1     2000-01-02 00:00:00-07:00  0.03  24.0  39.0  24.0
2     2000-01-03 00:00:00-07:00  0.00   7.0  39.0  18.0
3     2000-01-04 00:00:00-07:00  0.00   5.0  39.0  25.0
4     2000-01-05 00:00:00-07:00  0.00  10.0  44.0  22.0
...                         ...   ...   ...   ...   ...
6843  2020-09-20 00:00:00-06:00  0.00  46.0  92.0  83.0
6844  2020-09-21 00:00:00-06:00  0.00  47.0  92.0  84.0
6845  2020-09-22 00:00:00-06:00  0.00  54.0  84.0  77.0
6846  2020-09-23 00:00:00-06:00  0.00  47.0  91.0  87.0
6847  2020-09-24 00:00:00-06:00  0.00  43.0  94.0  88.0

[6848 rows x 5 columns]
```

Let's combine these two datasets. Before I merge these together, I need to make sure both have the same date frequency. Right now, the river data is at the 15-minute frequency, and the temperature data is at the day frequency.

To merge them, we'll use group-by functionality to get the river data at the day frequency. We'll take the median value of each column for the

33. Regression with XGBoost

aggregation. Then, we'll use the .merge method to merge the temperature data. You can also see that I'm using the validate='1:1' parameter. This is a handy parameter to ensure that the result of the merge is a one-to-one mapping.

```
dd2 = (river_df
 .groupby(pd.Grouper(key='datetime', freq='D'))
 .median(numeric_only=True)
 .merge(temp_df, left_index=True, right_on='DATE', how='inner',
        validate='1:1')
)
```

Let's inspect the result. It looks good.

```
>>> print(dd2)
       cfs  gage_height                      DATE  PRCP  TMIN  TMAX  TOBS
492   71.50         NaN  2001-05-07 00:00:00-06:00   0.0  41.0  82.0  55.0
493   69.00         NaN  2001-05-08 00:00:00-06:00   0.0  43.0  85.0  58.0
494   63.50         NaN  2001-05-09 00:00:00-06:00   0.0  36.0  92.0  64.0
495   55.00         NaN  2001-05-10 00:00:00-06:00   0.0  50.0  92.0  67.0
496   55.00         NaN  2001-05-11 00:00:00-06:00   0.0  46.0  87.0  60.0
...    ...         ...                       ...    ...   ...   ...   ...
6843   6.83        6.07  2020-09-20 00:00:00-06:00   0.0  46.0  92.0  83.0
6844   6.83        6.07  2020-09-21 00:00:00-06:00   0.0  47.0  92.0  84.0
6845   7.39        6.09  2020-09-22 00:00:00-06:00   0.0  54.0  84.0  77.0
6846   7.97        6.11  2020-09-23 00:00:00-06:00   0.0  47.0  91.0  87.0
6847   9.53        6.16  2020-09-24 00:00:00-06:00   0.0  43.0  94.0  88.0

[6356 rows x 7 columns]
```

33.2 EDA

In this section, we will perform exploratory data analysis or EDA. We will examine, summarize, and visualize the river data.

EDA is a common step in machine learning before we start modeling, and it's something that you want to make sure that you do to understand the data. The more time you spend with your data, the better your understanding of the model will be. You can understand what features might be missing and create them if necessary. This should lead to better-performing models.

33.3 Line Plots

I will start by looking at line plots of the cubic feet per second over time. We'll use pandas to create this plot.

This first plot is not particularly remarkable. It's a little bit hard to see what is going on. This is because a few entries for CFS are above 25,000, and those outliers make it hard to see what's going on otherwise. I'm not an expert on this river data set, but my understanding would be that if that is indeed the case that the CFS was above 25,000 during that time, that would be a flash flood-type event, and I probably want to remove those.

```
fig, ax = plt.subplots(figsize=(8,4))

(dd2
 .set_index('DATE')
 .cfs
 .plot(ax=ax, title='Flow (cfs) for Dirty Devil'))
```

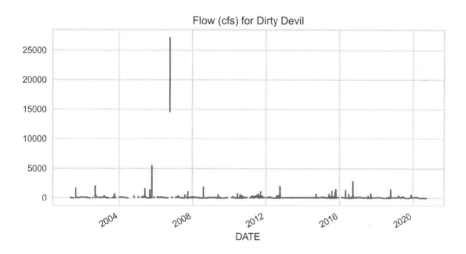

Figure 33.1: Time series plot of *cfs* over time

I'll use some pandas code to limit the CFS so it's below 2,000.

```
fig, ax = plt.subplots(figsize=(8,4))
(dd2
 .set_index('DATE')
 .query('cfs < 2000')
 .cfs
 .plot(ax=ax, title='Flow (cfs) for Dirty Devil'))
```

33.4 Predict cfs in a week

Let's start to make some predictions. Out goal is to be able to predict the value of the flow in the future. First, we will make a class, TweakDirtyTransformer.

33. Regression with XGBoost

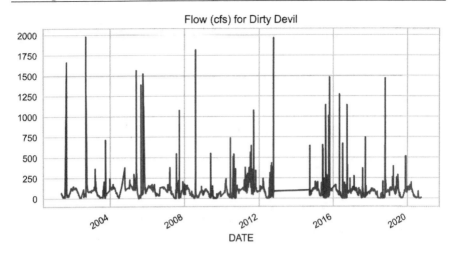

Figure 33.2: Time series plot of *cfs* over time filtered to remove outliers

```
from sklearn import base

class TweakDirtyTransformer(base.BaseEstimator,
    base.TransformerMixin):
    def __init__(self, ycol=None):
        self.ycol = ycol
        self.y_val = None

    def transform(self, X):
        return tweak_dirty(X)

    def fit(self, X, y=None):
        return self
```

TweakDirtyTransformer is a child of two classes, the base.BaseEstimator and the base.TransformerMixin class from Scikit-learn's base module. Subclassing allows us to use this transformer in a Scikit-learn pipeline.

The TweakDirtyTransformer class has the following methods:

- .__init__: This constructor initializes the transformer object. It takes one optional parameter, ycol, which is the column of the target variable. It also initializes a self.y_val attribute to None.

- .transform: This method is where the actual transformation of the data occurs. It calls the function tweak_dirty on the input data X.

33.4. Predict cfs in a week

- .fit: This method is necessary for compatibility with Scikit-learn's Transformer interface, but it doesn't actually do anything in this class. It just returns self.

Next, we have a bunch of functions.

```
def cyclic_encode(adf, col, x_suffix='_x', y_suffix='_y'):
    return (adf
            .assign(**{f'{col}{x_suffix}':
                np.sin((2*np.pi*adf[col])/(adf[col].nunique())),
                    f'{col}{y_suffix}':
                np.cos((2*np.pi*adf[col])/(adf[col].nunique())),
            })
    )

def tweak_dirty(adf):
    return (adf
            .assign(dow=adf.DATE.dt.day_of_week,
                    day=adf.DATE.dt.day,
                    month=adf.DATE.dt.month,
                    doy=adf.DATE.dt.day_of_year
                )
            .query('month <= 5')   # limit to spring
            .pipe(cyclic_encode, col='dow')
            .pipe(cyclic_encode, col='day')
            .pipe(cyclic_encode, col='month')
            .pipe(cyclic_encode, col='doy')
            .loc[:, ['cfs', 'gage_height', 'PRCP', 'TMIN', 'TMAX',
                    'TOBS', 'dow', 'day', 'month', 'doy', 'dow_x',
                    'dow_y', 'day_x', 'day_y', 'month_x',
                    'month_y', 'doy_x', 'doy_y']]
            .astype({'PRCP': float,
                    'TMIN': float,
                    'TMAX': float,
                    'TOBS': float,
                    'cfs': float,
                    'gage_height': float})
    )
```

The cyclic_encode function creates cyclical features from a column in the dataframe. This is particularly useful when dealing with periodic data, like the day of the week, month, or any other cyclical data. It encodes these cyclical features into two dimensions using sine and cosine transformations.

The tweak_dirty function is used to preprocess a pandas dataframe. It first adds new features to the dataframe based on the DATE column, such as day of the week (dow), day of the month (day), month, and week. Then it

33. Regression with XGBoost

filters the dataframe to only include records in the spring (where *month* is less than or equal to 5). It then applies cyclic encoding to the newly created time-based features using the cyclic_encode function. It finally drops the *DATE* and *site_no* columns. This is the code that the transformer class will use to transform the data.

33.5 Creating a Dataset for Modelling

Now that we have data, we will put it in a pipeline to create a model.

```
pl = pipeline.Pipeline([('tweak', TweakDirtyTransformer())])

X = dd2
y = dd2.cfs.shift(-7)

# drop missing y values
y = y[~y.isna()]
X = X.loc[y.index]

X_train, X_test, y_train, y_test = model_selection.train_test_split(
    X, y, random_state=42)
X_train = pl.fit_transform(X_train)
X_test = pl.transform(X_test)

# refilter y
y_train = y_train.loc[X_train.index]
y_test = y_test.loc[X_test.index]

X = pd.concat([X_train, X_test], axis='index')
y = pd.concat([y_train, y_test], axis='index')
```

In the provided code snippet, a data processing pipeline, the variable pl, is initialized using the pipeline.Pipeline class. This pipeline comprises a single step labeled 'tweak', which employs the TweakDirtyTransformer() as its transformation logic. Then, the data matrices X and y are defined, with y being a shifted version of the dd2.cfs column by seven units. We shift the values of y by seven units to predict the CFS value in a week.

Following this, any instances with missing values in y are purged, and the corresponding rows in X are likewise adjusted. The data is then partitioned into training and testing sets using the train_test_split function. We set the random_state parameter to 42 to ensure reproducibility.

We split the data into training and testing sets to avoid overfitting. We will train the model on the training set and then test it on the testing set. Evaluating the model on the testing set will give us a better idea of how the model will perform on unseen data.

33.5. Creating a Dataset for Modelling

This data is then processed through the pipeline by calling `pl.fit_transform` on the training set. This calls two methods under the hood: `pl.fit` and `pl.transform`. The *fit* portion fits the data to the pipeline and then transforms it. The fitting step is where the transformer learns the parameters of the transformation. In this example calling `fit` does nothing but return self. Other machine learning algorithms, like linear regression, would learn the parameters of the model during the fitting step.

The second step is the *transform* step. In this case, the transform step cleans the data. Note that we only call `pl.fit_transform` on the training set. We only want to fit the training set to the pipeline. We don't want to fit the testing set. We only want to transform it.

Next, we transform the testing set using `pl.transform`. This only transforms the data and does not fit it. The `pl.transform` method is used to transform the testing set because we don't want to fit the testing set. This allows us to simulate how the model will perform on unseen data. We only want to transform the testing set. We don't want to fit it.

Next, we will use the `loc` operator in Pandas to ensure that the indices of the y sets are synchronized with their corresponding X sets.

Finally, we consolidate the processed training and testing datasets for X and y respectively, utilizing the `pd.concat` function. This allows us to view all of the cleaned data in one place.

After running the code we have data to feed to our model.

```
>>> print(X_train)
        cfs   gage_height  ...      doy_x          doy_y
3307   97.8          3.92  ...   0.915773  -4.016954e-01
2595  140.0           NaN  ...   0.363508  -9.315911e-01
5937   78.4          6.73  ...  -0.475947  -8.794738e-01
3034   30.8          3.17  ...  -0.439197   8.983910e-01
2586  114.0           NaN  ...   0.677282  -7.357239e-01
...     ...           ...  ...        ...            ...
4466   69.6          3.56  ...  -1.000000  -1.836970e-16
2232    NaN           NaN  ...   0.285336  -9.584275e-01
6624  101.0          6.76  ...   0.958427  -2.853362e-01
1481  128.0           NaN  ...   0.763084   6.462992e-01
5970   38.1          6.41  ...  -0.958427   2.853362e-01

[1558 rows x 18 columns]

>>> print(y_train)
3307    107.0
2595    186.0
5937     56.1
3034     61.9
2586    114.0
         ...
```

33. Regression with XGBoost

```
4466     80.9
2232    127.0
6624    131.0
1481    112.0
5970     38.4
Name: cfs, Length: 1558, dtype: double[pyarrow]
```

33.6 Creating some Models

Let's create three different models and compare their performance. Building multiple models for a single problem can be beneficial for several reasons:

- Performance: Different models have different strengths and can perform differently on various datasets. By training several models, you can choose the one that performs best on your specific data.

- Robustness: If the models make different types of errors, an ensemble of these models can often perform better than any individual model because the errors of one model might be compensated by the others.

- Insights: Different models can provide different insights into the data. For example, decision trees are good at showing feature interactions, while linear models can provide clear coefficients for interpretation.

This code fits a Linear Regression model to the training data and evaluates it on the test data. The .fillna(0) method is used to fill any missing values in the datasets with zeros.

```
lr = linear_model.LinearRegression()
lr.fit(X_train.fillna(0), y_train)
lr.score(X_test.fillna(0), y_test)
```

This code fits a Decision Tree Regressor with a maximum depth of 3 to the training data and evaluates it on the test data. The maximum depth is a hyperparameter limiting the depth of the tree, which can help to avoid overfitting.

```
dt = tree.DecisionTreeRegressor(max_depth=3)
dt.fit(X_train.fillna(0), y_train)
dt.score(X_test.fillna(0), y_test)
```

This code fits an XGBoost (eXtreme Gradient Boosting) Regressor to the training data and evaluates it on the test data. The early_stopping_rounds=10 parameter means that the training process will stop if the performance on a validation set doesn't improve for 10 rounds to avoid overfitting. The eval_set parameter is used to provide a validation set for this purpose.

```
xg = xgb.XGBRegressor(early_stopping_rounds=10)
evaluation = [(X_train, y_train),
              (X_test, y_test)]
xg.fit(X_train, y_train, eval_set=evaluation)
xg.score(X_test, y_test)
```

33.7 Visualization

Let's use some visualization to understand our model performance. We are going to use the Yellow Brick library to create a *residual plot*. A residual plot is a graphical representation used to assess the performance and validity of a regression model. It displays the differences (*residuals*) between the observed and predicted values of the dependent variable in a regression analysis.

By examining the pattern of the residuals in the plot, we can identify potential issues with the regression model. Ideally, a residuals plot should exhibit a random scatter of points around the horizontal line at zero, indicating that the model's predictions are unbiased and accurate. However, if the residuals exhibit a distinct pattern or trend, such as a curve or funnel shape, it suggests that the model may not be capturing all the underlying relationships in the data or may violate some assumptions of linear regression.

In such cases, further investigation may be required, and model improvements may be needed, like considering a different functional form, including additional predictors, or addressing heteroscedasticity. In summary, a residuals plot is a valuable diagnostic tool that helps us interpret a regression model's performance and guides us in making necessary adjustments to ensure the model's reliability and accuracy in capturing the relationships between variables.

```
fig, ax = plt.subplots(figsize=(8,4))
viz = regressor.residuals_plot(lr, X_train.fillna(0), y_train,
                               X_test.fillna(0), y_test,
                               qqplot=True, hist=False)
fig.savefig('img/resids-lr.png', dpi=600)


fig, ax = plt.subplots(figsize=(8,4))
viz = regressor.residuals_plot(dt, X_train.fillna(0), y_train,
                               X_test.fillna(0), y_test,
                               qqplot=True, hist=False)
fig.savefig('img/resids-dt.png', dpi=600)


fig, ax = plt.subplots(figsize=(8,4))
viz = regressor.residuals_plot(xg, X_train.fillna(0), y_train,
                               X_test.fillna(0), y_test,
```

33. Regression with XGBoost

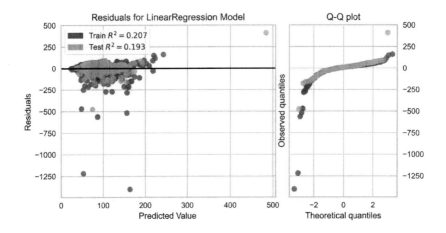

Figure 33.3: Residuals plot for linear regression model

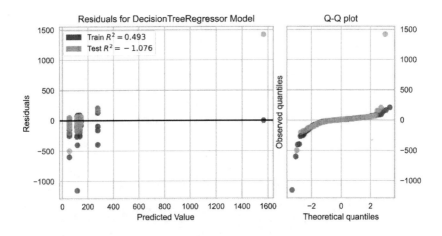

Figure 33.4: Residuals plot for decision tree model

33.8. Summary

```
                        qqplot=True, hist=False)
fig.savefig('img/resids-xg.png', dpi=600)
```

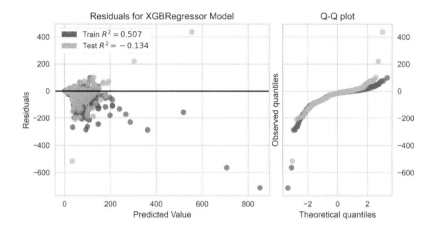

Figure 33.5: Residuals plot for XGBoost model

Remember, a negative residual means that the observed value is smaller than the predicted value. So the model is overpredicting. A positive residual means that the observed value is greater than the predicted value. The model would be underpredicting.

It looks like all of these models have more variability on the negative side. The model tends to have more error when it overpredicts.

To help deal with this

33.8 Summary

The chapter introduces regression with XGBoost by setting up a practical example: predicting the flow of the Dirty Devil River in Utah to determine its floatability. The process starts with downloading and preparing the necessary datasets. Data from the Dirty Devil River, which indicates the flow in cubic feet per second (cfs), is merged with the temperature dataset from Hanksville, Utah. This temperature data provides daily temperature values along with precipitation data. Through Exploratory Data Analysis (EDA), patterns, outliers, and general trends in the data are visually inspected. The chapter concludes by using scikit-learn and XGBoost to create regression models.

33. Regression with XGBoost

Exercises:

1. Load the `river_df` and `temp_df` datasets. What are the main features? Are there any missing values?

2. Create a histogram of the `cfs` values from the `river_df` dataset. What do you notice about the distribution?

3. Plot the precipitation data (`PRCP`) from `temp_df` against time. Can you see any correlation between precipitation and increased river flow?

4. Create a model to predict `TOBS` from the non-temperature columns. How does it perform?

Chapter 34

A Complete Example

This chapter provides an overview of how to implement a tool to remove content from a file. I write a lot of content that often includes doctests and associated doctest directives. However, I often want to remove those directives and keep everything else. This cleanup script showcases the development of a utility function, cleanup, designed to process and refine text lines based on specific markers.

The cleanup function can identify and handle multiple text markers, such as # doctest, <BLANKLINE>, and several others. The main objective of this utility is to simplify and sanitize input text or code by removing or adjusting lines containing these markers.

34.1 cleanup.py

Below is a brief outline of our Python cleanup utility:

I've predefined several markers that our cleanup function is programmed to recognize. These markers serve as flags indicating how each line should be processed.

- # doctest: Any line containing this marker will be truncated at its position.
- <BLANKLINE>: This marker will be replaced with an empty space.
- # REMOVELINE: Lines containing this marker will be entirely omitted from the output.
- # REMOVESTART and # REMOVEEND: Any lines between these markers will be removed from the output.

The cleanup function processes a list of strings (lines) and returns a new list of cleaned-up lines.

This is an example incorporating a lot of what we have discussed in this book to make a real-world utility. You can incorporate this cleanup utility into various applications where text or code sanitation is required. Save this

34. A Complete Example

utility in a file named `cleanup.py` and use it as part of larger projects or as a standalone script.

Here is the contents of `cleanup.py`:

```python
#!/bin/env python
"""Text Cleanup Utility
-------------------


This module provides utilities for cleaning text from files or lists of
strings based on specific markers like '# doctest', '<BLANKLINE>', etc.
It allows for selective removal of content from the input source and
produces cleaned output.

"""

import argparse
import os
import sys

DOC = '# doctest'
BLANK = '<BLANKLINE>'
REMOVE = '# REMOVELINE'
START = '# REMOVESTART'
END = '# REMOVEEND'

def cleanup(lines):
    r"""
    Remove unwanted markers and content from a list of lines.

    Parameters
    ----------
    lines : list of str
        List of strings to be cleaned.

    Returns
    -------
    output_lines : list of str
        Cleaned list of strings.


    >>> lines = '''# Start
    ... >>> import time
    ... >>> time.sleep(10) # doctest: +SKIP'''

    >>> cleanup(lines.split('\n'))
    ['# Start', '>>> import time', '>>> time.sleep(10) \n']
```

34.1. cleanup.py

```
    """
    in_delete = False
    output_lines = []

    for line in lines:
        if DOC in line:
            line = line.split(DOC)[0] + '\n'
        if REMOVE in line:
            continue
        if line.startswith(START):
            in_delete = True
        elif line.startswith(END):
            in_delete = False
        elif not in_delete:
            line = line.replace(BLANK, '')
            output_lines.append(line)

    return output_lines


def get_files_with_extension(directory, extension='rst'):
    """
    Retrieve all files with a given extension from a directory.

    Parameters
    ----------
    directory : str
        Path of the directory to search.
    extension : str, optional
        File extension to filter by. Default is 'rst'.

    Returns
    -------
    list of str
        List of filenames with the specified extension.

    """
    files = []
    for f in os.listdir(directory):
        if f.endswith(f'.{extension}'):
            files.append(f)
    return files


def main():
```

34. A Complete Example

```python
    """Main function to clean content from provided source.

    Returns
    -------
    list of str, optional
        Cleaned list of strings if `input_lines` is provided, otherwise None.

    """
    parser = argparse.ArgumentParser(
        description="Cleanup utility for text files.")
    parser.add_argument("-i", "--input-lines",
        help="Read from standard input for cleanup", action="store_true")
    parser.add_argument("-d", "--directory",
        help="Directory containing files for cleanup")
    parser.add_argument("-o", "--out-directory",
        help="Output directory for cleaned files")
    parser.add_argument("-e", "--extension",
        help="File extension to filter by (default: 'md')", default='md')
    parser.add_argument('--run-tests',
        action='store_true',
        help='Run module tests')

    args = parser.parse_args(sys.argv[1:])
    if args.run_tests:
        import doctest
        doctest.testmod()

    # If -i flag is set, read lines from stdin
    input_lines = None
    if args.input_lines:
        input_lines = sys.stdin.readlines()

    if args.directory and args.out_directory:
        for name in get_files_with_extension(args.directory, args.extension):
            print(f'{name=}')
            full_path = os.path.join(args.directory, name)
            with open(full_path) as fin:
                content = fin.readlines()
            cleaned_content = cleanup(content)
            out_path = os.path.join(args.out_directory, name)
            with open(out_path, 'w') as fout:
                fout.writelines(cleaned_content)
    elif input_lines:
        return cleanup(input_lines)
```

```
if __name__ == '__main__':
    main()
```

34.2 What Does this Code Do?

This code will process a directory of Markdown files and place cleaned-up files in a directory (removing lines according to the rules above).
One might execute it like this:

```
$ python3 cleanup.py -d . -o /tmp
```

This will process all files ending with *md* in the current directory and place the results in the /tmp directory.
If you run this code with -h it will print out the help documentation for the command line arguments:

```
$ python3 cleanup.py -
Usage: cleanup.py [-h] [-i] [-d DIRECTORY] [-o OUT_DIRECTORY]
                  [-e EXTENSION] [--run-tests]

Cleanup utility for text files.

options:
  -h, --help            show this help message and exit
  -i, --input-lines     Read from standard input for cleanup
  -d DIRECTORY, --directory DIRECTORY
                        Directory containing files for cleanup
  -o OUT_DIRECTORY, --out-directory OUT_DIRECTORY
                        Output directory for cleaned files
  -e EXTENSION, --extension EXTENSION
                        File extension to filter by (default: 'md')
  --run-tests           run module tests
```

The command line parsing functionality is implemented in the main function and provided by the argparse module found in the standard library. The argparse module handles command line argument parsing.
If you want to know what the argparse module does, you can look up the documentation on the web or you can use the help function. The basic idea of the module is that you create an instance of the ArgumentParser class and call .add_argument for each command line option. You provide the command line switches, tell it what kind of action to do (the default stores the value following the switch), and provide help documentation. After you have added arguments, you call the .parse_args method on the command line arguments (we get that from sys.argv). The result of .parse_args is an object that has attributes attached to it based on the option names. In this case, there will be a .files attribute and a .number attribute.

34. A Complete Example

> **Note**
>
> You can also use the REPL to inspect this module and any documentation it ships with. Remember the `help` function? You can pass a module to it, and it will print out the module level docstring.
>
> If you want to look at the source code for this module, you can do that too. Remember the `dir` function? It lists the attributes of an object. If you inspect the `argparse` module, you see that it has a `__file__` attribute. This points to the location on your computer where the file is:
>
> ```
> >>> import argparse
> >>> argparse.__file__
> '/usr/local/Cellar/python3/3.6.0/Frameworks/
> Python.framework/Versions/3.6/lib/python3.6/argparse.py'
> ```

Because it is written in Python (some modules are written in C), you can inspect the source. At this point, you should be able to read the module and understand what it is trying to do.

This example might seem a little overwhelming, but you have covered all of the syntax it illustrates throughout the book. The rest of this chapter will discuss this code's layout and other aspects.

34.3 Common Layout

Here are the common components found in a Python module and the order in which they are found:

- `#!/usr/bin/env python3` (shebang) (used if module also serves as a script.)
- module docstring
- imports
- metadata/globals
- logging
- implementation
- `if __name__ == '__main__':` (used if module also serves as a script.)
- argparse

> **Note**
>
> The above list is a recommendation. Most of those items can be in an arbitrary order. And not every file will have all these items. For instance, not every file must be executable as a shell script.

You can organize files however you please, but you do so at your own peril. Users of your code will likely complain (or submit patches). As a reader of code, you will appreciate code that follows the recommendation since it will be quickly discoverable.

34.4 Shebang

The first line in a file (that is also used as a script) is the *shebang* line (`#!/usr/bin/env python3`). On Unix operating systems, this line is parsed to determine how to execute the script. Thus, this line is only included in files meant to be executable as scripts.

It should say `python3`, as `python` refers to Python version 2 on most systems.

> **Note**
>
> The Windows platform ignores the shebang line. So this is safe to include. Indeed you will find it in libraries that are also popular on Windows.

Rather than hardcoding a specific path to a Python executable, `/usr/bin/env` selects the first `python3` executable found on the user's `PATH`. Tools such as `venv` will modify your `PATH` to use a custom `python3` executable and will work with this convention.

> **Note**
>
> On Unix systems, if the directory containing the file is present in the user's `PATH` environment variable and the file is executable, then the file name alone is sufficient for execution from a shell.
>
> Type:
>
> ```
> $ chmod +x <path/to/file.py>
> ```
>
> to make it executable.

34.5 Docstring

A module may have a module-level docstring at the top of the file. It should follow the shebang line but precede any other Python code. A docstring serves as an overview of the module and should contain a basic summary of the code. Also, it may contain examples of using the module.

> **Note**
>
> Python includes a library, `doctest` that can verify examples from an interactive interpreter. Using docstrings that contain REPL code snippets can serve both as documentation and simple sanity tests for your library.
>
> `cleanup.py` includes doctest code at the end of its docstring. When `cleanup.py` runs with `--run-tests`, the `doctest` library will check any docstrings and validate the code found in them. This was included for illustration purposes only. Normally a non-developer end user would not see options for running tests in a script, though you could include

doctests in the docstrings. In this case, the --run-tests option is included as an example of using the doctest module.

34.6 Imports

Imports are usually included at the top of Python modules. The import lines are normally grouped by the location of the library. First, list any libraries found in the Python standard library. Next list third-party libraries. Finally, list the libraries that are local to the current code. Such an organization allows end users of your code to quickly see imports, requirements, and where the code comes from.

34.7 Metadata and Globals

If you have legitimate module-level global variables, define them after the imports. This makes it easy to scan a module and quickly determine what the globals are.

Global variables are defined at the module level and are accessible throughout that module. Because Python allows any variable to be modified, global variables are potential sources of bugs. In addition, it is easier to understand code when variables are defined and modified only within the function scope. Then you can be sure of your data and who is changing it. If you have multiple places where a global variable is being modified (especially if it is in a different module) you are setting yourself up for a long debugging session.

One legitimate use for globals is to emulate *constants* found in other programming languages. A constant variable is a variable whose value does not change. Python doesn't support variables that don't change, but you can use a convention to indicate to the user that they should treat a variable as read-only. 8 states that global constants should have names that are the same as variables, except they should be capitalized. For example, if you wanted to use the golden ratio, you could define it like this:

```
>>> GOLDEN_RATIO = 1.618
```

If this code was defined in a module, the capitalization serves as a hint that you should not rebind this variable.

> **Note**
>
> By defining constants as globals and using well thought out variable names, you can avoid a problem found in programming—*magic numbers*. A magic number is a number sitting in code or a formula that is not stored in a variable. That in itself is bad enough, especially when someone else starts reading your code.

Another problem with magic numbers is that the same value tends to propagate through the code over time. This isn't a problem until you want to change that value. Do you do a search and replace? What if the magic number actually represents two different values, i.e. the number of sides of a triangle and the number of dimensions? In that case, a global search and replace will introduce bugs.

The solution to both these problems (context and repetition) is to put the value in a named variable. Having them in a variable gives context and naming around the number. It also allows you to easily change the value in one place.

In addition to global variables, there are also *metadata* variables found at that level. Metadata variables hold information about the module, such as author and version. Normally metadata variables are specified using "dunder" variables such as __author__.

For example, PEP 396 recommends that the module version should be specified in a string, __version__, at the global module level.

> **Note**
>
> It is a good idea to define a version for your library if you intend on releasing it to the wild. PEP 396 suggests best practices for how to declare version strings.

Other common metadata variables include author, license, date, and contact. If these were specified in the code, they might look like this:

```
__author__  = 'Matt Harrison'
__date__    = 'Jan 1, 2017'
__contact__ = 'matt_harrison <at> someplace.com'
__version__ = '0.1.1'
```

34.8   Logging

One more variable that is often declared at the global level is the logger for a module. The Python standard library includes the `logging` library that allows you to report different levels of information in well-defined formats.

Multiple classes or functions in the same module will likely need to log information. It is common to perform logger initialization once at the global level and then reuse the logger handle you get back throughout the module.

34.9   Other Globals

You should not use a global variable when a local variable will suffice. The common globals found in Python code are metadata, constants, and logging.

It is not uncommon to see globals scattered about in sample code. Do not fall to the temptation to copy this code. Place it into a function or a class. This will pay dividends in the future when you are refactoring or debugging your code.

34.10 Implementation

Following any global and logging setup comes the actual meat of the code—the implementation. Functions and classes will be a substantial portion of this code. The Catter class would be considered the core logic of the module.

34.11 Testing

Normally, the bonafide test code is separated from the implementation code. Python allows a small exception to this. Python docstrings can be defined at module, function, class, and method levels. Within docstrings, you can place Python REPL snippets illustrating how to use the function, class, or module. These snippets, if well crafted and thought-out, can be effective in documenting common usage of the module.

Another nice feature of doctest is validation of documentation. If your snippets once worked, but now they fail, either your code has changed or your snippets are wrong. You can easily find this out before end users start complaining to you.

> **Note**
>
> doctest code can be in a stand-alone text file. To execute arbitrary files using doctest, use the testfile function:
>
> ```
> import doctest
> doctest.testfile('module_docs.txt')
> ```

In addition to doctest, the Python standard library includes the unittest module that implements the common xUnit style methodology—setup, assert and teardown. There are pro's and con's to both doctest and unittest styles of testing. doctest tends to be more difficult to debug, while unittest contains boilerplate code that is regarded as too Java-esque. It is possible to combine both to achieve well documented and well tested code.

34.12 if name == `main`:

If your file is meant to be run as a script, you will find this snippet at the bottom of your script:

```
if __name__ == '__main__':
    sys.exit(main(sys.argv[1:]) or 0)
```

To understand the statement, you should understand the __name__ variable.

34.12. if name == 'main':

Python defines the module level variable __name__ for any module you *import*, or any file you execute. Normally __name__'s value is the name of the module:

```
>>> import sys
>>> sys.__name__
'sys'
>>> import xml.sax
>>> xml.sax.__name__
'xml.sax'
```

There is an exception to this rule. When a module is *executed* (i.e. python3 some_module.py), then the value of __name__ is the string "__main__".

In effect, the value of __name__ indicates whether a file is being loaded as a library, or run as a script.

> **Note**
>
> It is easy to illustrate __name__. Create a file, some_module.py, with the following contents:
>
> ```
> print(f"The __name__ is: {__name__}")
> ```
>
> Now run a REPL and *import* this module:
>
> ```
> >>> import some_module
> The __name__ is: some_module
> ```
>
> Now *execute* the module:
>
> ```
> $ python3 some_module.py
> The __name__ is: __main__
> ```

It is a common idiom throughout Pythondom to place a check similar to the following at the bottom of a module that could also serve as a script. This check will determine whether the file is being executed or imported:

```
if __name__ == '__main__':
    # execute
    sys.exit(main(sys.argv[1:]) or 0)
```

This simple statement will run the main function when the file is executed. Conversely, if the file is used as a module, main will not be run automatically. It calls sys.exit with the return value of main (or 0 if main does not return an exit code) to behave as a good citizen in the Unix world.

The main function takes the command line options as parameters. sys.argv holds the command line options. It also contains python3 at the front, so you need to slice sys.argv to ignore that, before you pass the options into main.

313

34. A Complete Example

> **Note**
>
> Some people place the execution logic (the code inside the `main` function) directly under the `if __name__ == '__main__':` test. Reasons to keep the logic inside a function include:
>
> - The `main` function can be called by others
> - The `main` function can be tested easily with different arguments
> - Reduce the amount of code executing at the global level

34.13 Summary

In this chapter, you dissected Python code in a script. The chapter discussed best practices and common coding conventions.

By laying out your code as described in this chapter, you will be following best practices for Python code. This layout will also aid others needing to read your code.

34.14 Exercises

1. Copy the `cleanup.py` code. Get it working on your computer. This isn't just busy work. Much of the time when you are programming, you aren't creating something from scratch, but rather are reusing code that others have written.
2. Write a script, `convert.py`, that will convert a file from one encoding to another. Accept the following command line options:
    - An input filename
    - An input encoding (default to utf-8)
    - An output encoding
    - An option for handling errors (ignore/raise)

Chapter 35

Conclusion

Congratulations! You are at the end of this book. You should have a strong grasp of Python fundamentals. You should be able to read and write Python code, and have a solid understanding of the Python standard library. You also have been exposed to a number of third-party libraries that are commonly used in Python projects.

Along the way I showed you many warnings and pitfalls. I hope you have internalized these warnings and will avoid these pitfalls in your own code.

What's next? I strongly encourage you to continue your Python journey. Here are some ideas:

- Practice, practice, practice. The best way to learn is to write code.
- Do the exercises at the end of each chapter.
- Find a project that interests you and write it in Python.
- Use Python at work.
- Reach out and connect with other Pythonistas. The Python community is very welcoming and supportive.
- Share your knowledge. Write a blog post, give a talk, or post on social media.

I would love to hear your plans. Please share them on social media and tag me. I'm @__mharrison__ on Twitter. I'm also on LinkedIn.

Best of luck on your Python journey!

Index

=, 111
() (invocation)', 182
() (tuple literal), 127
**, 60, 65
** (dict unpacking), 172
** (exponentiation), 136
** (power), 61
*, 57
* (multiplication), 58, 61, 136
+=, 152
+, 56
+ (addition), 61, 136
-np.inf, 68
-, 131
- (subtraction), 57, 61, 136
..., 15
.append, 121
.assign, 176
.assign with functions, 189
.astype, 175
.close, 206
.decode, 217
.describe, 242
.endswith, 77, 82
.fillna (Series method), 146
.find, 84
.flush, 205
.format, 84
.get, 167
.iloc, 197
.insert, 121
.items, 171
.join, 85
.keys, 170
.lower, 85
.lstrip, 86
.pipe with functions, 190
.pop, 121
.readlines, 204
.readline, 202
.removeprefix, 77
.removesuffix, 77
.remove, 121
.rename with functions, 190
.reshape, 136
.rstrip, 86
.setdefault, 167
.shape, 136
.sort_values, 145
.startswith, 86
.strip, 86
.upper, 87
.values, 170
.write, 205
//, 58
// (floor), 61
/, 58
/ (division), 61, 136
:=, 161
: (indenting), 116
: (slices), 194
;, 97
==, 111
= (f-string debug specifier), 77
??, 96
?, 96
Counter, 168
False, 102
LogisticRegression, 243

317

Index

NoneType, 107
None, 107
PATH, 309
PATH variable, 9
PYTHONPATH, 283, 284
True, 102
UnicodeDecodeError, 217
#
    (shebang), 26, 309
(comment), 101
%, 57, 65
% (modulo), 59, 61
% (string operator), 75
&, 131
^, 131
__bases__, 247
__bool__, 105
__builtin__, 42
__builtins__, 43, 184
__dict__, 235
__file__, 286
__init__, 228
__iter__, 204
__main__, 312
__name__, 312
\ (escape sequences), 72
\ (line continuation), 278
|, 131
| (dict union), 172
>=, 111
>>>, 15
>, 111
<=, 111
<, 111
{} (dictionary literal), 163
{} (format placeholder), 74
{} (set literal), 130
{ and }, 116
add, 139
and, 112
assign, 176
as, 278
break, 152
brew, 10
chmod, 27
class, 227

close, 206
collections.Counter, 168
collections.defaultdict, 169
continue, 153
decode, 214, 217
defaultdict, 169
def, 179, 180, 228
del, 121, 169, 184
describe, 242
dict, 163, 164
dir() function, 43
dir, 93, 235
divide, 139
elif, 114
else, 114, 115, 155
else (exception handling), 268
encode, 214
enumerate, 151
except, 264
exp, 139
fillna, 146
finally, 266
flip(), 138
float, 55
flush, 205
format, 74
for, 149
from, 277
functools.total_ordering, 112
get, 167
globals, 184
hello.py, 25
help, 75, 96
id() function, 45
if, 114
iloc, 197
import, 275
input, 30
int, 55
in, 131, 153, 166
is not, 111
is, 46, 107, 111
items, 171
juptyer notebook, 20
keys, 170
keyword module, 41

318

Index

key, 122
lambda functions, 187
len, 151
list (constructor), 119
locals, 184
log, 139
max, 137
mean, 137
median, 137
min, 137
multiply, 139
not, 112
np.add(), 139
np.array() (array creation), 135
np.divide(), 139
np.exp(), 139
np.flip(), 138
np.inf, 68
np.log(), 139
np.max(), 137
np.mean(), 137
np.median(), 137
np.min(), 137
np.mod, 65
np.multiply(), 139
np.nan, 68
np.power, 65
np.ravel(), 138
np.reshape(), 138
np.sqrt(), 139
np.std(), 137
np.subtract(), 139
np.sum(), 137
np.transpose(), 138
np.var(), 137
object, 227
open, 201
or, 112
pass, 268
pd.concat, 144
pdb.set_trace, 98
pdb, 97
pip, 20
print, 29
python3, 25
python, 15

raise, 269
range, 126, 151
ravel(), 138
read_csv function, 208
readlines, 204
readline, 202
reshape(), 138
reshape, 136
return, 181
set_trace, 98
setdefault, 167
set (constructor), 130
shape, 136
sort_values (Series method), 145
sorted, 122, 171
sort, 122
sqlite3, 219
sqrt, 139
stdin, 30
std, 137
subtract, 139
sum, 137
super(), 250
super, 251
sys.path, 283, 285
transpose(), 138
try, 264
tuple (constructor), 127
type() function, 47
values, 170
var, 137
while, 158
with, 206
write, 205
[] (Series indexing), 144
[] (Series literal), 143
[] (index operation), 164, 193
[] (list literal), 119
[] (slices), 194
8 bit integers, 175

active exception, 264
active learning, 159
addition, 56
anonymous functions, 187
append, 121

319

Index

appending to a list, 156
applying a function to each item in a list, 156
arguments, 184
assign with functions, 189
assignment expressions, 161
attributes, 93
augmented assignment, 152

binary files, 204
boolean, 102
boolean logic, 112
breakpoint, 98
built-in function, 96
built-in scope, 182
builtins, 42
byte strings, 204

calculations, 56
calling a function, 182
calling a method, 234
calling methods, 79
camel case, 227
cattle tags, 33
child, 247
class, 223
class attribute, 228
class docstring, 228
closing files, 206
coercion, 57
combining conditionals, 112
command mode, 21
comments, 101
compiler, 13
complete variable names, 94
concatenation, 85
conditional statements, 114
constructor, 228
contains, 153
context managers, 206
CPU, 13
CSV files in pandas, 208
curly braces, 116

debugger, 97

debugging with print statements, 98
decode, 217
decode a byte string to a Unicode string, 217
default parameters, 185
delete key, 169
designing around files, 207
dict comprehensions, 175
dict merging, 172
dict unpacking, 172
dictionary, 163
dictionary deletion, 169
dictionary iteration, 170
dictionary retrieval, 166
difference (-), 131
division, 58
docstring, 96, 228, 309
documentation string in Jupyter, 96
double quotes, 71
dtype, 64
duck typing, 48
dunder methods, 95
duplicates (removing), 130

EAFP, 264
Easier to ask for forgiveness than permission, 264
edit mode, 21
else (try statement), 268
end, 127
endswith, 77, 82
equal to, 111
exception chaining, 270
exception hierarchy, 272
exception raised when decoding fails, 217
exceptions, 261
exceptions, defining, 272
executing methods, 79

f-strings, 74
file input, 201
File modes, 202
filtering, 156

Index

filtering with comprehensions, 157
finally clause, 266
find, 84
float, floating point, 55
for loop, 149
format, 84
function, 179, 180
function naming conventions, 191
functions with pandas, 189

garbage collection, 37
global scope, 182
greater than, 111
greater than or equal to, 111
Guido van Rossum, 193

half-open interval, 127, 194
hash-bang, 26
help, 61
Homebrew, 10

identical object, 111
identity, 45, 48, 107
immutable, 48
index operation, 164
index sequence, 120
indexing, 193
indexing in pandas, 197
infinity, 68
inheritance, 247
inline functions, 187
insert, 121
install numpy, 63
install pandas, 89
installing Python, 9
instance, 223, 231
integer, 55
interactive interpreter, 15
interpreter, 13
intersection (&), 131
invocation, 182
invoking a method, 234
invoking methods, 79
iteration, 149
iteration, dictionary, 170

Japanese word for character mutation (mojibake), 217
join, 85
Jupyter, 19
Jupyter documentation, 96
jupyter modes, 21
Jupyter Notebook, 49, 94

keywords, 41

lab, 19
lambda functions, 187
LBYL, 263
less than, 111
less than or equal to, 111
library, 275, 283
lines in a file, 202, 204
list, 119
list comprehensions, 156
list deletion, 121
list insertion, 121
list object attributes, 93
list vs tuple, 129
loading CSV files in pandas, 208
local scope, 182
logistic regression, 243
long, 60
Look before you leap, 263
looping over files, 204
lower, 85

magic methods, 95
mapping, 156
membership, 131, 153
memory, 60
merging dictionaries, 172
method, 228, 234
method chaining, 116
methods, 79
missing values, 107
mode (Jupyter), 21
modeling flow, 237
module, 283
modulus, 57
mojibake, 217
multiplication, 57

Index

multiplyhs, 58
mutability, 48
mutable, 48, 119
mutation, 36

namespace, 275
namespaces, 182
naming conventions, 41
naming conventions for functions, 191
naming variables, 41
negative indexing, 193
negative infinity, 68
nil, 107
non-ASCII data, 220
not a number, 68, 108
not equal to, 111
not identical object, 111
Note, 105
notebook, 19
np.nan, 108
NULL, 107
numbers, 55
numpy, 63
numpy addition, 64
numpy array, 135, 136
numpy arrays, 63
numpy division, 65
numpy exponentiation, 65
numpy inf, 68
numpy infinity, 68
numpy installation, 63
numpy matrix operations, 66
numpy mod, 65
numpy modulo, 65
numpy multiplication, 65
numpy nan, 68, 108
numpy not a number, 68
numpy overflow, 64
numpy power, 65
numpy subtraction, 65
numpy.dtypeq, 64
numpy.float64, 63
numpy.int_, 63

object, 223

objects, 33
opening files, 201
operator precedence, 61
order of operations, 61
output, 29
overflow, 60, 64

package, 283
Pandas chains, 116
pandas installation, 89
pandas Series, 89
pandas, slicing, 197
parameters, 184
parent, 247
parentheses, 61
pemdas, 61
PEP 8 function naming conventions, 191
pip, 63, 89
pipe with functions, 190
position, 120
precedence, 61
print debugging, 98
programs, 25
prompt, 15

range comparison, 113
raw string, 72
raw strings, 201
Raymond Hettinger, 172
read, evaluate, print loop, 15
rebinding variables, 39
reference count, 37
removal during iteration, 154
remove whitespace, 86
removeprefix, 77
removesuffix, 77
removing items from a list, 121
rename with functions, 190
REPL, 15
reserved words, 41
retrieving values from a dictionary, 166
running a method, 234

scikit learn, 243

Index

scope, 182, 184
self-documenting f-string, 77
semicolon, 97
sequence index, 120
Series, 89, 143
Series Indices, 144
Series Insertion and Deletion, 144
series truthiness, 106
set, 130
set operations, 131
shadow, 183
shadowing, 43
shebang, 26, 309
single quotes, 71
singleton, 107
ski resort model, 237
skip items, 153
slices, :, 194
slicing in pandas, 197
Sorting Series, 145
spaces, 116
SQLite, 219
stack trace, 261
standard in, 30
standard out, 29
start, 127
startswith, 86
state, 36
statements, 114, 115
stepping through code, 97
stride, 196
string concatenation, 85
string formatting, 74
string literals, 71
String methods, 87
string methods (pandas), 89
STRINGMETHODS, 87
strings, 71
strip, 86
subclass, 247
subtract, 57

tab completion, 94
tabs, 116
tags, 36
traceback, 261

triple quotes, 71
truthiness in pandas, 106
tuple, 127
tuple vs list, 129
type, 47

undefined, 107
unicode, 211
UnicodeDecodeError, 217
union (|), 131
Unix, 26
upper, 87

variable naming, 41
variables, 33, 36
views, 170

Walrus Operator, 161
while example, 159
while loops, 158
whitespace, 116
whitespace removal, 86
Windows paths, 201

xgboost, 159
xor (^), 131

zero-based indexing, 120, 127

About the Author

Matt Harrison, a seasoned Python expert since 2000, is the driving force behind MetaSnake, a renowned Python and Data Science consultancy and corporate training enterprise. With a diverse professional background, Matt has made significant contributions in areas including search, build management, testing, business intelligence, and storage.

He is a recognized voice in the Python community, having imparted knowledge at esteemed conferences like ODSC, SciPy, SCALE, PyCON, and PyData, as well as various local user events. Drawing from his extensive experience in teaching Python, this book encapsulates the insights and strategies he has found most effective in his instructional journey.

He blogs at hairysun.com and occasionally tweets useful Python related information at @__mharrison__.

About the Author

Also Available

If you are interested in learning Python or Data Science in a corporate training, please reach out to MetaSnake. MetaSnake has conducted live and virtual trainings for teams all over the world. See https://metasnake.com for details.

If you are interested in on-demand training, please visit the website at https://store.metasnake.com for on-demand course offerings.

One More Thing...

Thank you for buying and reading this book.

If you have found this book helpful, I have a big favor to ask. As a self-published author, I don't have a big Publishing House with lots of marketing power pushing my book. I also try to price my books so that they are much more affordable.

If you enjoyed this book, I hope that you would take a moment to leave an honest review on Amazon or social media. A short comment on how the book helped you and what your learned makes a huge difference. A quick review is useful to others who might be interested in the book.

Thanks again!